101
Business
Ratios

101 Business Ratios

A manager's handbook of definitions, equations, and computer algorithms.

How to select, compute, present, and understand measures of sales, profit, debt, capital, efficiency, marketing, and investment.

Sheldon Gates

MP | McLane Publications
Scottsdale, Arizona

Publisher's Cataloging in Publication
(Prepared by Quality Books Inc.)

Gates, Sheldon Wilbur, 1927-
    101 business ratios : a manager's handbook of definitions, equations, and computer algorithms / Sheldon Gates.
    p. cm.
    Includes bibliographical references, glossaries and index.
    ISBN 1-881502-00-7 (alk. paper)

    1. Ratio analysis. 2. Managerial accounting. I. Title. II. Title: One hundred and one business ratios.

    HF5681.R25G38 1993   658.151'1   92-90816
                                                    QBI92-961

Address editorial and general inquiries to:
    McLane Publications, P.O. Box 9-C, Scottsdale, AZ 85252.

To purchase books, contact:
    McLane BookSales, P.O. Box 25556, Tempe, AZ 85285.

Casebound International Standard Book Number: 1-881502-00-7

Library of Congress Catalog Card Number: 92-90816

Printed in the United States of America on acid-free paper.

First edition 1 2 3 4 5 6 7 8 9 10

Trademark Credits

Dedicated

to the memory of Mindy, Joe, Mom and Dad, and others gone before.

Contents

Figures

Tables

About the Book

When I started Jensen Tools in the 1960's, little thought was given to number comparing. Sales and costs were all that mattered. But as the enterprise grew and day-to-day decisions became more difficult, I found myself intuitively using ratios to measure progress. How many sales dollars were realized for each catalog mailed? How much were we spending on wages and other expenses relative to sales?

Significant relationships like this weren't formally documented. They were just written down on scraps of paper or carried in my head. But I knew they were important, and believe today that success in that enterprise resulted largely from a conscious and continuous effort to maintain many business ratios at levels consistent with preconceived plans for growth and profitability.

Many years later, after the tool business was sold, my involvement with business ratios took on new dimensions. I was working then as treasurer and member of the board of directors of an electrical supply company. Fellow board members asked me to provide a set of business ratio graphs to show how well we were managing the company. Many questions needed answering. The board wanted to know if certain expenses were too high, if inventory was getting out of control, and whether or not we were collecting our debts satisfactorily. Within a short time the necessary numbers were located, ratios calculated, and the graphs prepared. That was the first step. A colleague then provided a copy of Dun & Bradstreet's *Selected Key Business Ratios in 125 Lines of Business*. This periodical, reporting on thousands of individual firms, listed average values for 14 important financial ratios. Now we had an opportunity to compare our company's performance to others.

The comparative reports showed we were doing just fine — better, in fact, than most of our contemporaries. The story might have ended there had it not been for a lingering feeling that something was wrong. The original business plan called for rapid sales growth. We were achieving that. But it also called for much higher levels of profit to finance our expansion, and for comparable growth in the acquisition of repeat customers. These goals remained elusive. It was apparent that we had not found a repeatable marketing formula that would economically turn these expectations into realities. In addition, we were troubled by high employee turnover and difficulty meeting our budget plans. None of the 14 financial ratios dealt with such issues.

Could ratio analysis still help in some way? I began collecting entirely new numbers — about expenses, employees, customers, transactions, mailings. New graphs were prepared which helped us to recognize many of our mistakes, and to focus managerial effort (and the board's attention) on the issues that we believed were most important.

Armed with the confidence that came from discovering so many new and important relationships between financial and non-financial numbers, my interest in and respect for ratio analysis grew rapidly. I read what was available on the subject, and began compiling a personal anthology of well-known, little-known, and entirely new ratios. This book is the result of that effort.

The work is directed primarily to managers of small and medium-sized businesses. In the smaller firms, the manager is most often an owner-entrepreneur. In larger firms, the financial officer, controller, or treasurer is the individual most likely to use the book. Lenders may discover in the text some new ways to evaluate firms to which funds have been entrusted. Management consultants, also, will find among the ratios presented not just the ones with which they are already familiar, but some new ones that might reveal a previously overlooked condition in a client's company. Business brokers and investors may also discover, among the 101 ratios described, many that will help them to assess a firm's financial health and relative value.

It is my hope that practicing accountants will increase their reporting to clients of significant business ratios, some of which they might select from formulas presented in this book. Accountants have at times been scurrilously labeled "bean counters" because (through tradition, law, and in the interest of consistency) they tend to look at things statically. But this should not preclude them from providing, as adjuncts to traditional statements, managerial accounting reports in the form of business ratios. Particularly for small-business customers, where the management may be less familiar with the meaning of raw financial information, presentation of relevant ratios by an outside accountant or tax preparer could be valuable.

The work is organized into two parts. The first (chapters 1 through 7) introduces the reader to ratio analysis and then describes 101 specific measures, as well as formulas for their computation. The second part (chapters 8 through 11) is a "how to" section dealing with practical matters associated with the use of ratios. There are also appendixes which provide a list of ratios, list of input statistics, usage table, suggestions for acronymic naming of variables, stock market ratios, and other information intended to be useful to readers. A glossary defines many of the technical terms that appear in the text.

The book can be used in many ways. For some, it will be a handbook of business ratios — a reference to needed explanations and equations. Others may use it as a textbook to open their worlds to an important part of managerial accounting. Readers possessing ability to create their own computer programs will find a few suggestions and examples that may be helpful.

The titles chosen for the 101 ratios in the text are inconsistent in style. This results not from carelessness, but from recognition that many of the titles have been around a long time. Changing *QUICK RATIO* to another form (just for the sake of consistency) would confuse many readers. Therefore, familiar titles have been preserved wherever possible. The same thinking applies to how well-known ratios are measured. Some are traditionally calculated in dollars, some as percentages, some as "times", and some as straight ratios (3:1). Familiarity has intentionally been put ahead of consistency. Why 101 ratios? The exact number is unimportant. 101 suggests that there are more ratios out there if one cares to look for them. That is exactly the point.

Technical books are written to communicate facts. An author's subjective views are considered by some to be unwelcome content. But because the study of business ratios has as a primary purpose the finding of roads to success, I have intentionally departed from this policy. Business management is an art, and for that reason the text includes expressions of my own philosophy. It comes from many years of experience and observation, and hopefully enhances the otherwise objective content.

Some of the editorial positions taken are these: Growth is healthy for an enterprise — perhaps necessary if the destructive consequences of inflation are to be avoided. Profits are *good*, and also necessary. They come not at the expense of others, but as rewards for wise and efficient management. In the modern world, they benefit not just individual companies and owners, but society at large. Debt is a tool. Used skillfully by a mature management, it enables startup and enhances growth. But gearing as a fundamental strategy for success is best avoided by all but the most skillful. As to marketing, the better methods are those that build cadres of loyal customers. And businesses should be run primarily for the benefit of owners — not managers. Lastly, there are no "right" ratio numbers. It always depends — on the industry, on the particular company and its business plan, on choices made by customers, and on global economic realities.

My goal in writing this book is to help managers run their companies more efficiently. Aided by information that comes from ratio analysis, they will be able to track their own progress and self-diagnose many problems. Each time a ratio is computed and understood, thinking takes place. Thinking leads to action and change, and that is the process intended.

If, with the help of this book, an occasional business failure is avoided, or a struggling mundane operation is turned around, my effort is rewarded.

Business ratios, like cooking recipes, evolve from a limited number of ingredients that may reasonably be combined to produce the final product. Over time, most every possible combination is likely to be tried or tested by someone. Those found useful survive and are passed along to future generations. But the circumstances of their beginnings are quickly forgotten. For this reason, few if any ratios are named after their originators. About half of the ratios in this book are like that — described in scores of textbooks and business publications. Although I am unable to identify and credit their creators, I have done the next best thing — listed in the bibliography many sources of ratio information. These books (some decades old) shed a bit of light on the evolution of the so-called common or anecdotal financial ratios.

Expanding the book's content to 101 ratios became possible only when input numbers not found in financial statements were utilized — things like number of employees, customers, orders, floor space, interest rates and price indexes. Although I believe myself to be the discoverer of and first to publish many of the ratios in this category, it would not surprise me to learn otherwise. With so few input numbers to start with, the laws of probability suggest that others may have made the same comparisons.

I acknowledge with appreciation and respect, the invaluable influence of a cadre of partners and business friends with whom I have been associated over the years. When problems in our dealings arose, they did not hesitate to ask questions, raise issues, and offer contrary points of view. Differences were expressed with deep conviction — often with emotion. Sometimes we could agree — sometimes not. Invariably, this led me to a search for facts and figures, and in many instances a new ratio or measure was utilized or discovered to aid in resolution. Each individual and each shared experience added significantly to my understanding of business and the content of this work. Thank you (naming just a few alphabetically) Uma Aggarwal, Robert Barton, Kenneth Holden, Sherman Jensen, Charles Mitchell, John Sanborne, Richard Schultz, and Charles Wotton.

Although the text for this work could have been written out by hand or produced on a typewriter, it was created and typeset on a computer. Despite many years of programming experience, keeping up with all the software changes and challenges was a formidable task. I acknowledge the generous and invaluable assistance of three Richards (brilliant computer gurus all): Richard Laverty, Richard Schultz, and Richard Valenti. How could I be so lucky?

Thank you also Kristine Laverty and Helmut Stich. You know how you helped. Thank you Lori (my daughter) for your repeated expressions of interest. And (surely most important) thank you Betsy (my wife) for your encouragement, unflagging support, and half a century of remarkable friendship.

S.G.

Chapter 1
Introduction to Business Ratios

Half of all new businesses fail or are discontinued within two years. After five years, according to the Small Business Administration, two-thirds of them are gone.[1] These failures are more than personal setbacks for entrepreneurs. They also mean lost jobs, unpaid lenders, and disillusioned customers. If the failed company is small and closely held, shutting down may be a real-life tragedy for its owners. Under the best of circumstances, years are required to recover from the severe financial losses that accompany most business closures.

Why do so many businesses fail? Richard Sanzo, writing for the SBA, says that failures result from either the inability of the principals to manage their affairs, or mistakes in the way funds are handled.[2] He adds that most business failures, large and small, stem from management's inability to adapt to change, or to control finances properly. Kenneth J. Albert, a recognized business consultant, reaches about the same conclusion when he says that (in addition to marketing) the apparent cause of most small business failures is "internal operating difficulties."[3]

Managerial control, then, is essential to success in business. Control can be difficult — particularly of finances. Without good information it may be impossible. No amount of managerial talent or effort will suffice if vital information is lacking. And because businesses are run by numbers, it follows that successful management requires familiarity with all the significant numerical facts bearing on the company's progress and current problems. But isolated numbers are not enough. Just as a good physician performs many tests and reviews a patient's history before making a diagnosis, a good manager looks beyond isolated numerical facts to find out what is *really* happening in the business. Raw information presented by an accountant about sales, margins, expenses, profits and taxes tells only part of the story. The trick is to know what the numbers mean — to relate them to each other, to plans and goals, to past experience, and to industry norms. This process of *relating* business numbers is called ratio analysis, and is the subject of this book.

What's Missing in Financial Statements

American businesses rely primarily on two accounting reports to express their financial status and progress. One is the *balance sheet* and the other the *profit and loss statement*. In accounting terms, the former tells where things stand now, and the latter what happened in the recent period. Most managers find the scope and content of these financial statements satisfactory because (1) they are more interested in developing products and markets than in analyzing financial information, (2) the reports fully meet their tax needs, and (3) their accountants have not offered them anything else.

The traditional statements provide a great deal of useful information. The balance sheet, for example, assigns values to equipment and other assets, describes amounts owed on both a current and long-term basis, lists funds available for continued operation of the business, and determines the value of the stockholders' equity as of the day of the report. The profit and loss statement tells what dollar value of goods or services was sold in the period, how much gross profit or markup was made in the turnover of product, what funds were expended to make all of this happen, and (finally) how much profit or loss resulted. Some modern formats also provide comparative figures for preceding periods, year-to-date summaries, and percentage numbers which relate costs and profits to sales as a base. "What more do I need?" a manager might ask.

Before answering that question, it should be pointed out that the form and content of traditional statements are dictated by the needs of outsiders — banks and other lenders, taxing authorities, employment commissions, regulators, insurers, and investors. The requirements of these organizations and groups are always complicated, sometimes bewildering, and occasionally even contradictory and intimidating. When change or creativity come into play, it is usually to accommodate the preparation of yet another report — not to provide managers with tools to improve decision making. What is needed is information to help in problem solving and the development of intelligent strategies. Traditional financial statements are lacking in this respect because (1) they report only financial information, (2) they report only the "now" or recent past, (3) they omit even rudimentary ratio comparisons, and (4) they ignore the effects of inflation on historic costs and prices.

Most financial-statement numbers are presented out of context to the physical world they represent. Example: a profit and loss statement shows rent of $8,600. This isolated number prompts more questions than it answers: For how many square feet? To process what dollar volume of production? Representing how much of an increase or decrease over last year? Questions like these can only be answered by comparing the number *to something* — to another number, to a plan, to a different time, to another manager or another company.

Compare is the all-important word. It is when sterile financial-statement numbers are compared to one another and to non-financial information that they come alive. That is when they talk, reveal, instruct, warn, and satisfy. Ratio analysis *means* comparing.

What Ratios Are

No matter how important a stand-alone number appears when first encountered, it is meaningless until it is compared to something. This is true not just in business and science, but in everyday living. Recall, if you will, your first visit to a foreign country and the frustration felt in adapting to an unfamiliar money system. Like most of us, you probably found it difficult to comprehend the true cost of everything from taxi fares to goods displayed in shop windows. How did you solve this problem? Chances are, you learned to *convert* the foreign prices to home-currency prices. You did this by multiplying those foreign prices by an exchange rate. Armed with equivalent home-currency prices, you were then able to make intelligent buying decisions. It is only through comparison that isolated numbers acquire meaning.

There are many ways to compare numbers. One simple way (if they are unequal) is to observe that one is larger than the other. That might solve an occasional problem. A much better way is to determine their *relative* magnitudes. Consider the two statements, "I am *taller* than my granddaughter," and, "I am *twice* as tall as my granddaughter." Both are enlightening, but the second is clearly more informative.

This type of relative comparing is accomplished by dividing one number into the other. In the example of height, if I am 72" tall and my granddaughter is 36" tall, then 72 divided by 36 equals two. Our heights thus differ in magnitude by a factor of two (sometimes expressed as 2:1). Still another way to communicate the same idea is to use the word *times*. "My height is two times my granddaughter's height."

We also compare numbers by measuring one thing against another. When driving an automobile, we note its speed to be 55 miles per hour. This is not a sterile number — it is a comparison. The number tells us we are moving at a *rate* that allows us to traverse 55 road miles in one hour of time. The speedometer continuously makes the computation and conveniently presents the result on the dash. Think about similar rates — MPG (miles per gallon), RPM (revolutions per minute), FPS (feet per second), dollars per hour, and so forth.

In commerce and science it is customary to express certain relationships not in terms of a single unit, but of 100 units. We call these *percentages*. Using the height example, we make the statement, "My height is 200% of my granddaughter's height." Regardless of the form in which the relationship is expressed (two, twice, 2, 2:1, 200%, two times), the result is a comparison of the two numbers.

A ratio is expressed when one number is divided by another. Some sources *define* ratios this way. Others even require that the divided numbers be of like kind (as in the height example — inches divided by inches).[4] But these very narrow definitions miss the true meaning of the word. *Ratio* from the Latin means *reason*. Scholarly dictionaries mention "the real ground or nature of things," and "the capacity to think and make abstractions." *Webster's Third International Dictionary* defines a ratio as, "The fixed or approximate relationship of one thing to another or between two or more things (as in number, quantity, or degree)." *Barron's Dictionary of Accounting Terms*, in a similar vein, explains a ratio as simply the "relationship of one amount to another."[5] None of these sources *requires* dividing the numbers, or that the compared items be of like kind. A relationship is all that is needed. An old saw says you can't compare apples and oranges, but you really can. A fruit broker does it every day when looking at revenues and costs associated with the two different products.

Thus a great many possibilities exist for comparing numbers and legitimately describing the comparisons as ratios. For example: We can observe that one number is larger or smaller than another. We can differentiate between numbers according to their signs (plus or minus). We can measure the extent of the difference between two numbers ("I am three feet taller than my granddaughter"). We can divide like numbers to determine their relative magnitudes ($48 / $40 = 1.2 = 120%). We can divide unlike numbers to determine rates (16 miles / 0.5 hours = 32 MPH). Numbers are also operated upon mathematically to find averages and to analyze trends. They may be combined and studied as indices, indicators, or comparators. A ratio may be inverted into its reciprocal to express the same idea in a different form. One or more ratios may be added to or subtracted from one or more others to create a model. The purpose of all of these comparisons is to find worldly meaning in abstract information. Defining ratios liberally, greatly broadens possibilities for number comparing. This is especially important in business where the goal is to reveal underlying truths and solve problems.

Brief History of Business Ratios

It's difficult to say when business ratios were first used. In simple form, some have undoubtedly been around as long as humans have engaged in commerce. Sister Isadore Brown discusses the use of banking ratios in the annual report to Congress in 1872 by then Controller of the Currency, John J. Knox.[6] R. A. Foulke talks about the *current ratio* being used in the late 1800's.[7] Sanzo discusses a study of shoe store expenses done at Harvard University in 1913.[8] Early *managerial* use of ratios by department stores is mentioned by James O. Horrigan.[9] C. A. Westwick describes the use of a simple integrated set of ratios by the DuPont Company in 1919, and he talks about the important work of H. Ingham and L. Taylor Harrington in the 1950's.[10] Whatever the exact history, the use of financial ratios has grown dramatically in the twentieth century, particularly by lenders and credit analysts.

Among the other early pioneers in the field were the principals and employees of Robert Morris Associates, a national association of bank loan and credit officers. Two individuals associated with this organization, Alexander Wall and Raymond Duning, summarized much of their knowledge and published it in 1928 under the title, *Ratio Analysis of Financial Statements.*[11] It's possible that their text is one of the first to present and explain a broad series of ratios useful in measuring a firm's financial strength. Wall and Duning classified ratios as being either static or dynamic, and they placed great importance on measuring the activity of invested capital.

Figure 1-1. Wall and Duning's *Ratio Analysis of Financial Statements* — preserved at the New York Public Library Annex.

Scholars traditionally group financial ratios into four broad categories: *Liquidity ratios* (which measure ability to meet short-term obligations), *leverage or solvency ratios* (which measure the relationships between debt and equity), *activity ratios* (which measure how the firm uses its resources), and *profitability or overall ratios* (which measure bottom-line management performance and returns on investment). Accountants usually classify ratios according to the source of the underlying numbers, such as *balance sheet ratios, income statement ratios*, and *interstatement ratios.*[12] The difficulty with such classifications is that they have their origins in the traditions of banking and accounting rather than management. Important ratios that might be derived from non-financial data are ignored. For these reasons, a different set of categories (based on managerial interest) organizes the chapters of this book.

As the number of known ratios has grown, complaints have been heard that a manager's time is too valuable to be spent calculating yet another ratio. This was a valid criticism when computers were unknown in most offices. But today, the calculation of more than a hundred ratios can be accomplished in a few minutes. Computers have changed the way we do things, including ratio analysis.

How Ratios are Used in Business

Although business ratios have been around a long time, that does not mean they are universally used and respected by all managers. The contrary may be true. Entrepreneurs, for example, are likely to focus their energies primarily on sales and production. A common belief is that if expectations are met in these two areas, everything else somehow takes care of itself. Even managers of large and seasoned companies (who should know better), sometimes make the mistake of concentrating their efforts disproportionately in one or two areas or on the wrong problems. But sooner or later, even if a business is succeeding, the inevitability of change forces the examination of aspects of the enterprise previously ignored or misunderstood.

Change comes at unexpected times and in many disguises. Most managers understand technological change and competition. But how often is growth itself recognized as a change capable of bringing down a successful enterprise? Each morning when a business opens its doors, it needs to deal with changes that have occurred overnight — changes in costs, competition, customer preference, and global economics. However imperceptible these changes may be, they are cumulative and inescapable. Maintaining a pattern of success requires continuous rethinking about the unique and complex business parameters that have provided that success. Ratio analysis is one of the best tools available to managers willing to engage in that rethinking process.

The usefulness of ratio information is limited not by the availability of underlying numbers needed for their computation, but by the willingness of managers to put those numbers to work. Consider the list below (presented in no special order) of important uses for business ratios.

- ❏ Monitor growth
- ❏ Monitor costs
- ❏ Measure profitability and return on investment
- ❏ Identify trends
- ❏ Define business plans
- ❏ Compare one operating period to another
- ❏ Compare actual results to plans
- ❏ Compare current costs to historical costs
- ❏ Measure adequacy of cash and working capital
- ❏ Monitor asset allocation
- ❏ Monitor collections
- ❏ Diagnose problems
- ❏ Compare performance of company to a competitor
- ❏ Compare performance of one manager to another
- ❏ Adjust performance to different interest rate environments
- ❏ Convert ratios and statistics to constant dollars
- ❏ Compare financial to non-financial information

- ☐ Monitor employee productivity
- ☐ Measure managerial efficiency
- ☐ Communicate with lenders, investors, partners, owners
- ☐ Track budget performance
- ☐ Determine break-even levels
- ☐ Warn of impending bankruptcy
- ☐ Monitor employee turnover
- ☐ Monitor back orders
- ☐ Measure average order size
- ☐ Measure tax rates
- ☐ Measure return on marketing expenditures
- ☐ Interpret financial statements
- ☐ Help prepare budgets and plans
- ☐ Clarify relationships between statement items
- ☐ Instruct trainees in business principles
- ☐ Estimate business valuations
- ☐ Estimate share prices for unlisted stocks
- ☐ Measure returns to shareholders

Readers already working with ratios should have little difficulty adding to the list.

Business ratios are well known for their ability to answer questions like, "Can our company pay its bills if things tighten up temporarily?" *(current ratio)*. "Is the money we have invested in our business bringing as much return as we could obtain from alternate investments?" *(return on net worth)*. "Are our inventories working hard enough?" *(inventory turnover)*. Not so well known is their ability to evaluate non-financial information, effects of changes in the worth of the currency, marketing statistics, and areas of performance that may be uniquely important to a particular firm or line of business. Scores of useful ratios can be derived from the many numerical facts available to most managers, and many of these facts are non-financial.

Understanding the Formulas

A consistent protocol is used to describe the ratios presented in this book. First, each ratio appears in one of six chapters depending on its type (sales ratio, profit ratio, debt or capital ratio, investment ratio, and so forth). Second, it is assigned a number from 1 to 101. This ratio identification number is shown in bold type and is used consistently in formulas, charts, and tables. Following the ratio number and the title by which the ratio is best known, a definition (telling how it is calculated) appears in italics. Next comes a short essay explaining the ratio — what it measures, who uses it, and what the numbers mean.

If only a few ratios are to be studied, formulas are not required. The written definitions are sufficient to make the calculations. The ratio *debt to equity*, for example, is equal to *total liabilities divided by tangible stockholders' equity*. The words tell all. When there is interest in many ratios, however, it is advantageous to express them as equations which identify the variables and show precisely in what order the steps of calculation are made.

Business ratio equations are written in many ways, depending on personal preference and intended usage. One form may be best for teaching, for example, and another for computerization. In order to accommodate a wide range of applications, three forms of equation follow the text for each ratio described in the forthcoming chapters. These formula types are called *verbal, acronymic* and *symbolic*.

Verbal equations impart maximum understanding of how the ratio is derived. They are in algebraic form. But instead of designating variables by single letters such as X or A, entire words or phrases are used. Thus the verbal equation for a common expense ratio is:

$$\textbf{INSURANCE EXPENSE RATIO} = 100 \text{ X } \frac{\text{Insurance Expense}}{\text{Net Sales}}$$

Ratio names are shown bold in all capital letters. The names of input numbers are shown in upper-lower case as above. The *operators* are those of traditional algebra. The equal sign = separates the ratio name from the components used in its derivation. The capital letter X means multiply. A horizontal line means divide what is above the line by what is below it. The signs + and − signify addition or subtraction. More complicated (logical) operations are indicated by additional explanatory words or symbols. Brackets sort out the order in which complex calculations are made. In order to keep the presentations as short as possible in the verbal equations, input number names are sometimes shown that are the result of previous calculations. Working Capital, for example, is used in place of Current Assets − Current Liabilities.

Acronymic equations use variable names created by tagging together the first letters or abbreviations of relatively longer business terms and phrases.[13] Variables named this way are short enough to allow (in most cases) immediate recognition of the words they represent (**RENTSPACE** means *rent to space*). In these equations, input statistic names are also shown in capital letters (but not in bold). Acronymic names fit nicely on ledgers and are legal in many computer languages. For example,

RENTSPACE=RENTEXP / SPACE

RENTEXP means rent expense. SPACE means floor space.

Symbolic equations, intended primarily for computer algorithms (including spreadsheets), are the most concise.[14]

$$R63 = S21 / S48$$

Here, letter-number combinations identify the variables. Each variable symbol begins with an R (meaning a ratio) or an S (meaning an input number). Immediately following either of these letters is a number signifying *which* ratio or input statistic is intended. Thus **R63** means the same as **RENTSPACE**. S21 means rent expense and S48 floor space. More information on variable names is found in the Appendix.

The operators used in acronymic and symbolic equations are those familiar to computer programmers. The equal sign = separates the ratio name from its components of derivation. An asterisk * means multiply what comes before by what comes after. A slash / means divide what comes before by what comes after. As before, the signs + and − mean add or subtract. Parentheses are used to sort out nested calculations. The greater-than > and less-than < comparators are used in a few equations along with the logical operators IF, THEN, and ELSE to provide instructions not readily communicated by ordinary algebra. When the absolute value of an expression is required, it is preceded by ABS.

Associated with every ratio and input number is a measurement unit. If not specified, it is implied. Most ratio equations are measured as percentages (%). Others are measured in dollars ($). Some are expressed as real numbers (N) or integer numbers (#). Out of tradition, certain ratios that could be measured as percentages are instead expressed as times relationships (X). The choice of measurement unit is sometimes made to solve complex problems associated with setting up computer program report fields and handling the wide range of values likely to be encountered.

Most ratios are computed from input statistics of the current year. A few ratio formulas, however, use input statistics from the prior year and sometimes *ratios* computed for the prior year. In verbal equations, the words "Last Year" are included in the appropriate phrase. In equations using acronymic variable names, the additional word LASTYEAR is tagged on to the appropriate name. Thus NETSALESLASTYEAR signifies net sales for the year prior to the year for which the particular ratio is computed. In equations where symbolic variable names are used, the letters LY are added to the appropriate variable name. Thus S16LY signifies last year's net sales. (If the ratio is computed for 1993, for example, the variables NETSALESLASTYEAR and S16LY both mean net sales for 1992.)

Order of execution is evident in the case of the verbal equations. But for the acronymic and symbolic equations, the rules of computer programming must be followed. Calculations within parentheses are made first. Within or without parentheses, the order of execution is exponentiation, multiplication, division, addition, subtraction. Failure to follow this order results in severe errors. Example: $X = 5 * 3 - 1$. The correct value for X is 14. Subtracting before multiplying gives an erroneous result of 10. Of course, the equation could be written:

$$X = (5 * 3) - 1$$

Parentheses clarify what needs to be done and thus reduce the likelihood of error. But they also add to the amount of computer code, and so are used only when the rules of execution order do not suffice.

Following the equations for some of the ratios, long-term graphs are provided to illustrate how values varied for one particular company over a 13-year period. The DEMO COMPANY ratios are derived from the records of a real business. The specific numbers presented by these graphs are unimportant. What *is* important is their ability to demonstrate that much more information is communicated by a chart than a column of figures. Hopefully, managers will be stimulated to analyze their own situations and, where appropriate, utilize similar graphs.

Because it is not always clear whether higher values or lower values for any ratio are desirable, arrows on the graphs signify which direction is generally considered favorable. *Generally* is an important word here, because for some of the ratios *either* high values or low values might be best *depending on the circumstances*. This illustrates an important fact about ratio analysis: Ratios are tools — not substitutes for enlightened human judgment. It always depends.

The ratios are grouped into six areas of managerial interest: sales ratios (Chapter 2), profit ratios (Chapter 3), debt and capital ratios (Chapter 4), efficiency ratios (Chapter 5), marketing ratios (Chapter 6), and investment ratios (Chapter 7). When reviewing the equations, keep in mind that the ratios they define may be known to you and others by different names. *CURRENT RATIO (30)*, for example, has the familiar alias *liquidity ratio*. Where two or more names for a ratio exist, the one believed most popular was selected for the descriptions.

Welcome now, to 101 business ratios!

Notes — Chapter 1

1.   Wendel O. Metcalf, *Starting and Managing a Small Business of Your Own*, Small Business Starting and Management Series Volume 1 (Washington, DC: Small Business Administration, 1973), p. 9.

2.   Richard Sanzo, *Ratio Analysis for Small Business*, Small Business Management Series No. 20 (Washington, DC: Small Business Administration, 1977), p. 3.

3.   Kenneth J. Albert, *Straight Talk About Small Business* (New York: McGraw-Hill, 1981), p. 26.

4.   *The World Book Encyclopedia* (Chicago: World Book, Inc., 1987), Volume 16, p. 143.

5.   Joel G. Siegel and Jae K. Shim, *Dictionary of Accounting Terms* (Hauppauge, NY: Barron's Educational Series, 1987), p. 566.

6.   Sister Isadore Brown, *The Historical Development of the Use of Ratios in Financial Statement Analysis to 1933*, Studies in Economics, Abstract Studies (Washington, DC: The Catholic University of America Press, 1955), p. 9.

7.   R. A. Foulke, *Practical Financial Statement Analysis* (New York: McGraw-Hill, 1968), p. 176.

8.   Sanzo, p. 20

9.   James O. Horrigan, "A Short History of Financial Ratio Analysis," *The Accounting Review*," Vol. XLIII, No. 2 (April, 1968), p. 286.

10   C. A. Westwick, *How to Use Management Ratios* (New York: Wiley, 1973), p. xiv. *See also*, 1987 edition (Epping, Essex [U.K.]: Gower Press, Ltd.).

11.   Alexander Wall and Raymond Duning, *Ratio Analysis of Financial Statements* (New York: Harper, 1928), p. 107-140.

12.   Kenneth W. Perry, *Accounting An Introduction* (New York: McGraw-Hill, 1971), p. 566.

13.   In creating the acronymic variable names shown in this book, use of the first few letters of words occasionally resulted in duplication or a lack of clarity. When this occurred, non-acronymic abbreviations were substituted. *See*, Appendix D.

14.   For use in spreadsheets, the symbolic equations require adaptation to the location method of naming variables.

Chapter 2
Sales Ratios

"How's business?" It's a question frequently asked over coffee. The query is about sales, of course — the lifeblood of free enterprise. However serious a problem may be that relates to costs, interest rates, solvency or taxes — chances are good that a healthy increase in sales will solve it. It's no wonder that sales are in the foreground of most business thinking.

The answer to the question might be, "Good." Or it might be, "Not so good." And even if specific sales numbers are mentioned ("We did $97,000 last month"), *comparisons* are thought about — comparisons to expectations, plans, or needs for survival. "Good" probably means "Good compared to last year," or "Good compared to the business plan." "Not so good" may mean "Not as good as I had expected," or "Not good enough to pay off the bank loan." This kind of comparative thinking is automatic, with conclusions coming to mind almost as quickly as the "How's business?" question can be asked. The person answering is (consciously or not) computing and evaluating sales ratios.

Sales do not exist in a vacuum. In one way or another, they result from marketing programs or a history of satisfying customer needs. Sales vary greatly in quality. That is, each of the company's individual transactions (which add up to total net sales) comes with its own cost of acquirement, credit risk, and contribution to gross and net profit. Sales come easy or hard depending on many diverse factors such as the company's reputation in the marketplace, competition, cost of product, and general economic conditions. Therefore, sales should be studied in conjunction with other statistics which relate to their creation and impact on the bottom line.

This chapter describes eight different ways to think about sales. Managers now performing the ritual of totting up and posting monthly revenues should find among them a number of more meaningful alternatives. Sales ratios have the ability to reveal aspects of company performance which sterile accounting numbers cannot.

1 SALES GROWTH

Definition: The difference between this year's net sales and last year's net sales, divided by last year's net sales, multiplied by 100 to provide a percentage.

"Grow or die" is familiar advice. Most managers recognize the importance of staying in the race by staying ahead. Even if the owners of a firm and its management are satisfied with no growth in real terms, keeping up with inflation requires an annual increase in sales. This ratio measures just how well the company is doing in keeping its sales curve pointed upward.

Inadequate growth can originate from within the company (not enough attention paid to marketing or to needs and preferences of customers), or from without (inroads of competitors, technological change, or a slump in the economy). Whatever the cause, a failure to grow usually sows seeds of future difficulty.

Managers like to think about growth relative to the prior year. ("Sales are up 12%.") That is what this ratio measures. For some businesses, however, significant annual sales fluctuations (having nothing to do with growth) may be unavoidable. When this is the case, growth is better measured over a number of years using average sales values or by a mathematical technique called regression. This procedure fits a line (usually straight) to a set of coordinates using the method of least squares.[1] It smooths out the year-to-year fluctuations and is useful in identifying trends.

The long-term graph of this ratio reveals *how* a company grows. If the pattern is essentially horizontal and the average rate of growth is satisfactory, an efficient and reliable expansion of the business is suggested. Uncontrolled or erratic growth, on the other hand, appears as an up-down pattern on the chart.

(verbal equation)

$$\text{SALES GROWTH} = 100 \times \frac{\text{Net Sales} - \text{Net Sales Last Year}}{\text{Net Sales Last Year}}$$

(acronymic equation)

$$\text{SALESGROW} = 100 * (\text{NETSALES} - \text{NETSALESLASTYEAR}) / \text{NETSALESLASTYEAR}$$

(symbolic equation)

$$\text{R1} = 100 * (\text{S16} - \text{S16LY}) / \text{S16LY}.$$

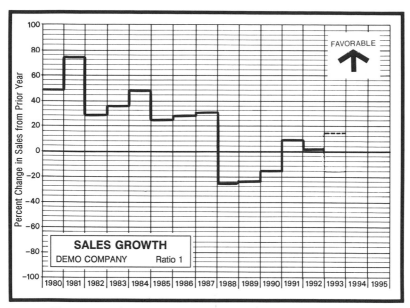

Figure 2-1. One company's 14-year chart of *Sales Growth*.

2 AFFORDABLE GROWTH RATE

Definition: Net retained profit after taxes divided by last year's tangible net worth, multiplied by 100 to provide a percentage.

Although growth is probably essential to long-term business success and survival, there is such a thing as growing too fast. Growth needs to be financed, either by borrowing, increasing the equity base, or from profits. When growth is not financed by profits, management is forced to seek help from outsiders. This can be an unpleasant (and sometimes unsuccessful) process.

AGR is the strategy for growth adopted by Hewlett-Packard Company in the 1950's.[2] Two assumptions are made. First, that sales are allowed to grow no faster than assets (inventory, receivables and fixed assets). Second, that lenders will extend credit for sales growth if equity increases at the same rate (debt-to-equity ratio more or less constant). Thus a company's growth is affordable only to the extent that profits are available to provide the funds.

Although the concept is simple, many underlying factors determine retained return on equity. Profit margin, rate of turnover of assets, amount of leverage in the balance sheet, and dividend policy are all important. Growth in sales at a rate faster than the AGR is a normal event for many companies. But over time, it may prove difficult (even impossible) to sustain. This formula defines a useful strategy for efficient growth.

The numerator in the equation is found by subtracting dividends from net profit after taxes. This adjustment recognizes the fact that profits paid out to stockholders are not available to finance growth. That is why so-called growth companies typically pay small dividends. Intangible assets are subtracted from net worth in the denominator because they are difficult to value and are usually not recognized by lenders in evaluating the capital mix.

The strategy is not applicable to companies that are losing money, and the ratio is undefined in that case. Unprofitable companies will need to find another strategy.

(verbal equation)

$$\text{AFFORDABLE GROWTH RATE} = 100 \times \frac{\text{Net Retained Profit After Taxes}}{\text{Tangible Stockholders' Equity Last Year}}$$

(acronymic equation)

$$\text{AFFGROWRATE} = 100 * (\text{NETPROFAFTTAX} - \text{DIV}) / (\text{STKHOLDEQLASTYEAR} - \text{INTANLASTYEAR})$$

(symbolic equation)

$$R2 = 100 * (S30 - S31) / (S14LY - S7LY)$$

3 SALES GROWTH CONSISTENCY

Definition: Number of consecutive years sales revenues have exceeded those of the prior year.

This frequently-overlooked statistic becomes significant when the time comes to sell a small business or a stockholder's shares. It is an important measure, because businesses perceived as steadily growing command higher prices in the marketplace. How far back a buyer might wish to look for evidence of consistent growth depends on the circumstances. But if the pattern has continued for five to seven years, the likely result is a higher value placed on the company's shares.

The business-value premium awarded to a growth company comes not just from the implication that the trend will continue, but from the evidence that the company is controlling its economic destiny. Management serves its stockholders admirably when it provides consistent growth represented by a flawless stairway pattern on the long-term graph.

Note that this ratio uses last year's value for the same ratio as an input number. If there is no value for last year, it is assumed to be zero.

(verbal equation if net sales exceed last year's net sales)
SALES GROWTH CONSISTENCY = 1 + **SALES GROWTH CONSISTENCY LAST YEAR**

(verbal equation if net sales do <u>not</u> exceed last year's net sales)
SALES GROWTH CONSISTENCY = 0

(acronymic equation)
IF NETSALES>NETSALESLASTYEAR THEN **SALESGROWCON**=1+**SALESGROWCONLASTYEAR**
ELSE **SALESGROWCON**=0

(symbolic equation)
IF S16>S16LY THEN **R3**=1+**R3LY** ELSE **R3**=0

Figure 2-2. Example graph of *Sales Growth Consistency* shows eight years of steady progress and then a fallback.

4 BUDGET COMPLIANCE (SALES)

Definition: Actual net sales divided by budgeted net sales, multiplied by 100 to provide a percentage.

Business budgets are financial plans. Budget *compliance* measures success in realizing those plans. Budgets sometimes go awry when confused with goals. In most companies, optimistic targets are set to motivate employees and please shareholders. Good budgeting, however, is objective and defendable. Whatever technique is used, the process should be open, unemotional, and free of political influence.

Budgets are typically structured around a projected level of sales — the sales forecast. If sales will be up, more money can be allocated to create and service those sales. If sales will be down, expenses may need to be curtailed. This first of three budget compliance ratios compares the reality of actual sales to the fiction of planned sales. But good forecasting is a difficult art. Some managers build their forecasts by carefully summing all components of the company's sales — each product, each price, each customer, each salesperson, each territory. Others rely on projection of trends, using simple or sophisticated regression formulas. Larger firms may hire consultants or economists to provide the needed numbers. Whatever the nature of the forecast (even if it is just a guess), the resulting number is important. Expenditure plans and possibly risky expansion will be based on it.

One way to improve forecasting is to assign the task independently to several individuals or groups. The differences can be surprising. Review and resolution of differences usually results in a better final forecast. Once results are in, feedback to those who prepared the original numbers is important — if only to help them do a better job next time.

Written down, circulated budgets are more likely to be met than informal or secretive ones. Putting the numbers down on paper and making them known brings team spirit into play. It also inspires caution and tempers emotion in most situations. No manager wants to develop a reputation of being overly optimistic, overly pessimistic, or just plain inept when it comes to understanding customers and markets.

(verbal equation)

$$\textbf{BUDGET COMPLIANCE (SALES)} \ = \ 100 \ \text{X} \ \frac{\text{Net Sales}}{\text{Budgeted Net Sales}}$$

(acronymic equation)

$$\textbf{BUDGCMPLSALES} = 100 * \text{NETSALES} / \text{BUDGNETSALES}$$

(symbolic equation)

$$\textbf{R4} = 100 * \text{S16} / \text{S41}$$

5 DEFLATED SALES GROWTH

Definition: The difference between this year's deflated net sales and last year's net sales, divided by last year's net sales, multiplied by 100 to provide a percentage.

A problem with the traditional sales growth measure is that it does not take into account changes in the value of the currency. A growth rate that might be envious in normal times could represent backsliding during periods of high inflation. This measurement problem is overcome by substituting a constant-dollar value for net sales in the growth equation.

The deflator is derived from the Consumer Price Index (CPI), the Producer Price Index (PPI), or any other suitable index that's available.[3] For purposes of this year-to-year growth ratio, the deflator is defined as last year's value for the price index divided by this year's value. For example, if the CPI is 133.8 at the end of 1990 and 137.9 at the end of 1991, the 1991 deflator is equal to the quotient of the two numbers, or .97. *Deflated* net sales for 1991 are thus equal to reported net sales multiplied by the deflator.

While there is no standard or rule requiring that a certain value of constant dollar sales growth be achieved by a company each year, common sense dictates that the result of the calculation be a positive number. Otherwise, in an environment of rising costs, negative real growth results in lower profits and an inability to maintain dividends.

If sales fluctuate significantly from year to year, the rate of growth is better measured by averaging, or more sophisticated techniques such as linear or exponential regression. This is true whether or not constant dollars are used to make the measurements.

(verbal equation)

$$\text{DEFLATED SALES GROWTH} = 100 \times \frac{\left[\text{Net Sales} \times \dfrac{\text{Price Index Last Year}}{\text{Price Index}} \right] - \text{Net Sales Last Year}}{\text{Net Sales Last Year}}$$

(acronymic equation)

DEFLSALESGROW=
100∗(NETSALES∗(PRICEINDEXLASTYEAR/PRICEINDEX)−NETSALESLASTYEAR)/
NETSALESLASTYEAR

(symbolic equation)

R5=100∗(S16∗(S50LY/S50)−S16LY)/S16LY

6 BREAK-EVEN SALES FACTOR

Definition: Gross profit divided by total expenses, multiplied by 100 to provide a percentage.

Because profits for most businesses represent a small percentage of sales, they are described as highly leveraged.   This means that a relatively minor percentage reduction in sales can result in a major (perhaps catastrophic) decline in profits. Conversely, a small percentage increase in sales has potential for giving profits a disproportionately significant boost.

This ratio (in which the break-even level of sales is represented by 100%) reveals to the manager just how much cushion is available. Assuming that gross-margin factors and total expenses remain constant, it shows simply how far down or up sales have to go for the break-even point to be reached. A value of 110, therefore, means that sales are 10% higher than needed to break even. A value of 90, on the other hand, means that the company is operating at a loss with sales at 90% of what is required to break even.

Profit-minded managers can benefit from monitoring this ratio on a regular basis.   Doing so helps develop a sense of importance for maintaining sales at or above planned levels, or where this is not possible, at or above the break-even point. Many business ratios are undefined or inappropriate if applied to companies losing money. This measure is an exception, as it shows clearly what improvement in sales is needed to bring results into the black.

Although sales are not mentioned in the definition or the equations, this is nevertheless a sales ratio. The explanation is that gross profit (the numerator) is equal to net sales less cost of goods sold. Changes in net sales are therefore passed through proportionately to gross profit.

(verbal equation)

$$\text{BREAK-EVEN SALES FACTOR } = 100 \text{ X } \frac{\text{Gross Profit}}{\text{Total Expenses}}$$

(acronymic equation)

$$\text{BRKEVENSALESFACT} = 100 * \text{GROSSPROF}/\text{TOTEXP}$$

(symbolic equation)

$$R6 = 100 * S18/S28$$

7 REVENUE TO SPACE

Definition: Net sales divided by number of square feet of plant space.

This analysis compares sales to the total amount of floor space required to create and process those sales. When real estate was relatively cheaper than it is now, this ratio may have been less important. But in today's difficult business climate, management is under pressure to achieve maximum efficiency in the use of physical facilities. Efficient use of space ultimately translates to lower rent expense and increased profit.

The ratio is particularly important when the nature of the business requires the leasing of very-expensive or uniquely zoned land or buildings. Retail shops in fashionable locations, for example, *must* pay special attention to the level of sales relative to space, or risk being overcome by the inordinately high cost of using premium property. In 1989, the average yield on Tiffany & Company's U.S. stores was reported to be about $2,079 per square foot.[4] This suggests correspondingly high rents, which are appropriate to the sale of luxury goods. But when sales volume or average ticket price are low, such locations cannot be economically justified.

Another use for this measure (in any business) is planning. It can provide answers to questions asked about the amount of new space needed to accommodate anticipated expansion of sales.

This ratio (which reports dollar sales per square foot) does not look directly at the *cost* of space. Rather, it measures architectural efficiency and assumes that cost follows. Whenever this ratio is reviewed, *RETURN ON SPACE (29)* and *RENT EXPENSE RATIO (53)* should be looked at concurrently.

Significantly different amounts of space are required by different industries and lines of business. For that reason, comparisons are best restricted to similar activities. And because changes in the price level (inflation) affect the numerator but not the denominator, comparisons between distant years may be misleading.

(verbal equation)

$$\textbf{REVENUE TO SPACE} \ = \ \frac{\text{Net Sales}}{\text{Floor Space}}$$

(acronymic equation)
REVSPACE = NETSALES / SPACE

(symbolic equation)
R7 = S16 / S48

8 SALES PER EMPLOYEE

Definition: Net sales divided by average number of employees.

This measurement of sales looks at the firm's bank of human resources. It answers the question, "Are we maintaining a level of revenues proportionate to the size of our staff?"

In very small companies, it is not uncommon for one person to do many different jobs. The founding entrepreneur may do the selling, the company's bookkeeper may double as secretary, and the warehouse manager may do the purchasing. But as companies grow, they hire trained specialists. Economists call this *division of labor* and say that it improves efficiency. In practice, however, labor costs sometimes increase faster than revenues as companies transfer what were once part-time jobs to specialists who make them into full-time jobs. Risk of expanding too fast is real for small and medium-size companies.

An increase in this ratio (more dollar sales per employee) is usually a sign of improving efficiency. A decreasing ratio may mean that too many people have been assigned to do the available work, or that anticipated sales have not been realized. The ratio can be an indication of how much labor-saving equipment a firm uses. High-technology companies (such as computer software) usually have a higher ratio, as do companies with a so-called competitive edge.

Management's long term objective is to make division of labor a reality by bringing this ratio down over time. Because changes in the general price level affect the numerator and not the denominator, very long-term comparisons can be misleading.

In many businesses, the number of employees varies significantly during the year because of seasonal factors, growth, or a large number of part-time workers. For this reason, an average value is used in the denominator.

(verbal equation)

$$\textbf{SALES PER EMPLOYEE} \ = \ \frac{\text{Net Sales}}{\text{Employees}}$$

(acronymic equation)

$$\textbf{SALESEMP} = \text{NETSALES} / \text{EMP}$$

(symbolic equation)

$$\textbf{R8} = \text{S16} / \text{S46}$$

Notes — Chapter 2

1. William Mendenhall and Robert J. Beaver, *Introduction to Probability and Statistics* (Boston, MA: PWS-Kent Publishing Co., 1991), p. 398-401.

2. Charles W. Kyd, "How Fast is Too Fast?", *INC.* (December, 1986), p. 123-126.

3. Bureau of Labor Statistics, *The Consumer Price Index* and *The Producer Price Index* (Washington, DC: U.S. Department of Labor).

4. Tatiana Pouschine, "Tiffany: Act II," *Forbes* (November 11, 1991), p. 70-77.

Chapter 3
Profit Ratios

It should not be necessary in a book about business ratios to explain profits, or to point out why they are important. Most managers understand that profits are essential to a firm's survival and success. Unfortunately, some of the activities that lead to profit enhancement (budgeting, cost cutting, downsizing, layoffs) are not satisfying to managers. It is human nature to prefer to spend one's time thinking about positive things like new products, sales growth, expansion of market share, and the corporate image. But that is exactly why an understanding of profits is so important. They do not come easily.

A simple definition of profit is that it is what remains from all money taken In after all expenses are paid. It is, in effect, a reward bestowed on the enterprise for success in the marketplace. Therefore, it is also a measure of the ability and efficiency of management. The profit concept is closely linked to ideas of capitalism. Indeed, advocates of capitalistic systems believe that the benefits provided come not in spite of profits but because of them. Writers have made the point that *all* living organisms, because they inevitably encounter difficult situations in the environment that interrupt the reproductive cycle, must produce more than they consume in order to survive. Even Lenin is said to have insisted that socialistic, state-owned enterprises operate without loss (ergo, with a profit).

Why are profits so important? First, unless the company has unlimited resources, operating unprofitably over a period of time inevitably depletes capital until nothing is left to pay wages or buy raw materials. Continuous break-even operations are not acceptable because they provide no cushion for contingencies. Second, without profit or expectation of profit, investors do not invest. Profit is the return, the reward, the "interest" paid to those institutions and individuals willing to temporarily turn over their capital to the enterprise. Third, profits help pay for growth and expansion. Lenders rarely supply funds to companies that are chronically unable to earn a return.

Twenty-one profit ratios are described in this chapter. They are useful tools for measuring the adequacy of profits on an overall basis, controlling profits, and monitoring the return received by the company on various components of its operation.

9 GROSS MARGIN FACTOR

Definition: Gross profit divided by net sales, multiplied by 100 to provide a percentage.

This ratio (also known as gross profit on sales or gross profit percentage) shows the average spread between sales and cost of goods sold. It changes whenever prices change (whether in buying or selling). In a going business, gross margin must be maintained sufficiently high to cover expenses *and* to provide a satisfactory profit.   That is why managers watch this ratio carefully, as there is often more flexibility in buying and selling than in controlling expenses.

An unacceptably low margin means than on an overall basis too much is being paid for merchandise, or selling prices are too low, or both. Changes in *what* is sold can also affect overall margin if the mix of high-margin and low-margin products shifts unfavorably. The upper limit to this ratio is 100%, which occurs when the cost of goods sold is nil (seawater, or stolen property?). A value of zero means that the goods are sold for the same price paid for them. Negative values are theoretically possible if selling prices are below cost on an overall basis.

Gross profit varies widely between industries and lines of business. It is typically low in grocery retailing, for example, and high in the manufacture of proprietary products. Margin is lower where the customer can choose between many suppliers, and higher where choices are limited. The margin maintained by an electrical supplies distributor might average 25%.   At the same time, the margin of the popcorn-candy concession at the movie theater down the street might exceed 90%. Business risk increases as margins decline.

Margin is closely related to pricing. In some small businesses, if the owners do not wish to optimize their pricing, margin is maintained by consistently setting selling prices at a fixed multiple of the cost of goods. Retailers sometimes rely on simplistic pricing policies such as "doubling up" their cost. Small manufacturers may *keystone* — that is, sell to the public at one price and to retailers at one-half that price. These policies work best when competition is minimal and customer loyalty high.

(verbal equation)

$$\text{GROSS MARGIN FACTOR} = 100 \text{ X } \frac{\text{Gross Profit}}{\text{Net Sales}}$$

(acronymic equation)

$$\text{GROSSMARGFACT} = 100 * \text{GROSSPROF} / \text{NETSALES}$$

(symbolic equation)

$$R9 = 100 * S18 / S16$$

Figure 3-1. Sample chart of *Gross Margin Factor* shows the portion of sales available to pay expenses and provide a profit.

10 BREAK-EVEN MARGIN

Definition: Total expenses divided by net sales, the result multiplied by 100 to provide a percentage.

Whereas the *BREAK-EVEN SALES FACTOR (6)* shows by what percentage sales must change for break-even operation to occur, this ratio provides the gross-margin factor for a break-even condition. It is a number that even the unsophisticated business manager should keep in mind, as it signals the lower limit of profitable operation when setting margins.

The ratio is useful in pricing, when making close-to-cost competitive bids, and when negotiating contracts with customers or suppliers. Decisions are best made that result in a gross-margin factor sufficiently higher than the value of this ratio to insure the desired profit.

Some managerial control over margins is available in both buying and selling. In buying, costs can usually be reduced by purchasing in larger quantities, improving relationships with suppliers, negotiating better prices and terms, or finding alternate sources of supply. In selling, higher prices are sometimes realized by an upgrade in packaging, increased personal selling, certain types of advertising, a switch to proprietary products, or the offering of non-price concessions appropriate to the business.

Attempts to increase profits by increasing margins (through price increases) may fail because of the dynamic relationship between prices and sales. Higher prices may or may not work through to increased gross profit. The customers decide.

If the graphs of ratios 9 and 10 are superimposed, profitable operation is seen to occur whenever the value for 9 exceeds that of 10.

(verbal equation)

$$\text{BREAK-EVEN MARGIN} = 100 \text{ X } \frac{\text{Total Expenses}}{\text{Net Sales}}$$

(acronymic equation)

$$\text{BRKEVENMARG} = 100 * \text{TOTEXP} / \text{NETSALES}$$

(symbolic equation)

$$R10 = 100 * S28 / S16$$

Figure 3-2. *Break-Even Gross Margin* example graph reveals the lower limit of profitable operation.

11 OPERATING MARGIN

Definition: Net profit before taxes plus interest expense and depreciation, the result divided by net sales and multiplied by 100 to provide a percentage.

Gross profit describes the spread between a company's net sales and cost of goods sold, and net profit tells what is left after all costs of doing business are subtracted. A third measurement, operating profit, shows how the company is doing irrespective of leverage, income taxes, and the accounting variations of depreciation.[1] When compared to sales, operating profit is known as operating margin. It is considered a better indicator of management skill and operating efficiency than net profit margin. In fact, it has been described as probably the most important measure one can use to assess a company's competitive position in its industry.[2]

The ratio is important to investors, acquirers, and others interested in the underlying profitability of the business without regard to how it is capitalized, how it is taxed, or what it paid for its inventory of depreciable assets. For example, a highly-leveraged manufacturer using accelerated depreciation might report losses from year to year. But its product may be a good one, its customer base sound, and its management efficient. With different capitalization (no change in operating methods) the company could be showing a profit, and this will interest an acquirer.

Even firms in bankruptcy, where net worth is negative and debt excessive, may have underlying operating margins that are healthy. This ratio, therefore, provides insight into a company's potential value to new owners.

Don't try to compare the operating margins of firms in different industries. Average margins vary widely for dissimilar lines of business.

(verbal equation)

$$\text{OPERATING MARGIN} = 100 \times \frac{\substack{\text{Net Profit} \\ \text{Before} \\ \text{Taxes}} + \substack{\text{Interest} \\ \text{Expense}} + \substack{\text{Depreciation} \\ \text{Expense}}}{\text{Net Sales}}$$

(acronymic equation)

$$\text{OPERMARG} = 100 * (\text{NETPROFBEFTAX} + \text{INTEREXP} + \text{DEPREXP}) / \text{NETSALES}$$

(symbolic equation)

$$\text{R11} = 100 * (\text{S29} + \text{S22} + \text{S24}) / \text{S16}$$

12 PROFIT GROWTH

Definition: The difference between this year's net profit after taxes and last year's net profit after taxes, divided by last year's net profit after taxes, multiplied by 100 to provide a percentage.

In the words of a venerable commodity trader, "We never stand still. The world does not and we cannot. Unless we progress, we go backwards."[3] This philosophy is apropos to successful business strategies just as it is to speculation. Where *SALES GROWTH (1)* monitors the company's ability to build its customer base and markets, this ratio measures success in the greater challenge of transferring revenue growth to bottom-line profit growth.

When profit growth fails to match sales growth, the most likely causes are erosion of gross profit (perhaps the buying of sales with attractive pricing), or a managerial inability to adequately control expenses.

The ratio is undefined if the company operated at a loss in the prior year. Another warning — do not rely on this ratio when profits are a small percentage of revenues or when they fluctuate significantly from year to year. Example: On sales of $100-Million, a firm earns just $10,000. The next year it earns $20,000. Profit growth is 100%. Presented out of context, the figure suggests important progress for the company. In reality, profits are essentially nil (0.02% of sales) and should be so reported. If profits fluctuate significantly from year to year, their rate of growth is better measured by averaging or trendline analysis. Statistical services having investors as clients, for example, typically report profit growth averaged over five or seven years.

The long-term graph of this ratio approximates a horizontal straight line if the rate of profit growth is consistent. When the average value for the ratio is at a satisfactory level, this straight-line pattern identifies a company with tight control of its market and internal operations.

(verbal equation)

$$\text{PROFIT GROWTH} = 100 \times \frac{\begin{array}{c}\text{Net Profit}\\\text{After Taxes}\end{array} - \begin{array}{c}\text{Net Profit}\\\text{After Taxes}\\\text{Last Year}\end{array}}{\begin{array}{c}\text{Net Profit}\\\text{After Taxes}\\\text{Last Year}\end{array}}$$

(acronymic equation)

PROFGROW=
100＊(NETPROFAFTTAX−NETPROFAFTTAXLASTYEAR)/NETPROFAFTTAXLASTYEAR

(symbolic equation)
R12=100＊(S30−S30LY))/S30LY

13 PROFIT GROWTH CONSISTENCY

Definition: Number of consecutive years net profits after taxes have exceeded those of the prior year.

Consistency of profit growth is harder to achieve than consistency of sales growth. It is also more significant in showing that a company's management is truly in control of bottom-line results. Where sales can almost always be increased by spending more money on selling and advertising, profit growth requires that those same expenditures be marginally economical (that is, profitable in the short run). The time lag between marketing action and marketing results often renders this strategy unsuccessful.

The fact that such a measure is difficult to manipulate directly (for short-run results) does not lessen its value. It is one of the best indicators of long-term managerial success and an envied characteristic of many of the world's superior enterprises.

Corporate stock is frequently valued on the basis of a multiple of earnings (P/E ratio). If profits have grown consistently for five or more years, the multiple a buyer pays for the stock is usually higher — perhaps double or more. Thus a management working to enhance its stockholders' long-term interests pays as much attention to this ratio as it does to measures of current performance.

Whereas most ratios are computed entirely from raw input statistics taken from accounting records or other sources, some measures are best expressed in terms of previously computed ratios. That is the case with this calculation, which builds on the consistency number from the prior year.

(verbal equation if net profit after taxes exceeds last year's net profit after taxes)

PROFIT GROWTH CONSISTENCY = 1 + PROFIT GROWTH CONSISTENCY LAST YEAR

(verbal equation if net profit after taxes does <u>not</u> exceed last year's net profit after taxes)

PROFIT GROWTH CONSISTENCY = 0

(acronymic equation)

IF NETPROFAFTTAX>NETPROFAFTTAXLASTYEAR THEN **PROFGROWCON=**
1+PROFGROWCONLASTYEAR ELSE **PROFGROWCON=0**

(symbolic equation)

IF S30>S30LY THEN **R13=1+R13LY** ELSE **R13=0**

14 BUDGET COMPLIANCE (PROFITS)

Definition: Actual net profit after taxes divided by budgeted net profit after taxes, multiplied by 100 to provide a percentage.

Of the three budget compliance ratios (sales, profits, expenses), this one is surely the most important — and probably most challenging. The challenge comes from the dynamic nature of profits. There can never be certainty that an action *intended* to increase profits *will* increase profits.

So how does a manager budget for profits? The first step is recognizing the difficulty of the task, and understanding all factors that affect the bottom line. The next step is collection of available factual information. A sales budget or forecast may exist. An expense budget may have been prepared. Last year's gross margin factor is probably known. If any of these starting numbers are missing, they need to be found. Superficially, this is all that is needed.

Experienced managers know, however, that profits are illusive. Many uncertainties need to be taken into account. Suppliers may unexpectedly increase prices, resulting in lower margins. Income tax rates may change. The economy may take a nose-dive, or a major customer may switch to a competitor. Many things can happen that are beyond company control. Profit forecasting is clearly an art. To be successful, it must be undertaken objectively and with humility.

For this ratio, a result exceeding 100% means that management has met its profit objective. If the ratio is consistently below 100%, likely causes are unrealistic sales forecasting or failure to control expenses.

Living up to profit budgets can be difficult. Even if revised plan numbers are collected every few months and the exercise repeated, rapid changes in costs and markets can throw things off. It's an important gauge of managerial performance anyway, because success in entrepreneurship requires including market risk in the list of uncertainties to be encountered and overcome. That is what management is about.

Both the budget and the measurement can be based on before-tax numbers if desired. An after-tax version is used here.

(verbal equation)

$$\text{BUDGET COMPLIANCE (PROFITS)} = 100 \text{ X } \frac{\text{Net Profit After Taxes}}{\text{Budgeted Net Profit}}$$

(acronymic equation)
BUDGCMPLPROFAFTTAX = 100 * NETPROFAFTTAX / BUDGNETPROFAFTTAX

(symbolic equation)
R14 = 100 * S30 / S43

15 DEFLATED PROFIT GROWTH

Definition: The difference between this year's deflated net profit after taxes and last year's net profit after taxes, divided by last year's net profit after taxes, multiplied by 100 to provide a percentage.

An erosion in the value of the monetary unit can distort the significance of accounting numbers to such a degree that what looks like up might in fact be down. Since profits represent the final measure of achievement or lack of it for an enterprise, it is important that year-to-year measurements of change take prevailing price levels into account.[4]

The same technique is used to calculate this ratio as *DEFLATED SALES GROWTH (5)*. That is, a constant dollar value for net profit is substituted in the year-to-year growth equation. The deflator is defined as last year's value for a suitable price index divided by this year's value. The Consumer Price Index (CPI) and Producer Price Index (PPI) are commonly used for these purposes, as are indexes based on commodity prices.

Whenever year-to-year growth measurements are made, there is a risk that market or industry anomalies will impact more on the result than underlying expansion or contraction of the business. Also, if profits are a small percentage of sales, year-to-year improvement measured as a percentage may have little meaning. When either of these conditions apply, growth is better examined over a time frame longer than one year using averages or the regression techniques previously mentioned.

(verbal equation)

$$\text{DEFLATED PROFIT GROWTH} = 100 \times \frac{\left[\begin{array}{c}\text{Net Profit} \\ \text{After} \\ \text{Taxes}\end{array} \times \dfrac{\begin{array}{c}\text{Price Index} \\ \text{Last Year}\end{array}}{\text{Price Index}}\right] - \begin{array}{c}\text{Net Profit} \\ \text{After Taxes} \\ \text{Last Year}\end{array}}{\text{Net Profit After Taxes Last Year}}$$

(acronymic equation)

DEFLPROFGROW=
100 ∗ (NETPROFAFTTAX ∗ (PRICEINDEXLASTYEAR / PRICEINDEX) − NETPROFAFTTAXLASTYEAR) / NETPROFAFTTAXLASTYEAR

(symbolic equation)
R15 = 100 ∗ (S30 ∗ (S50LY / S50) − S30LY) / S30LY

16 ADEQUACY OF PROFITS

Definition: Net retained profit after taxes divided by last year's total assets, divided again by the year's sales growth (expressed as a decimal), then multiplied by 100 to provide a percentage.

Although business growth is usually measured in terms of sales, asset growth deserves equal attention. The reason for this is that for most companies, sales increases are accompanied by fairly predictable increases in major assets such as receivables and inventory. These asset increases must be financed by supplier credit, borrowing, increasing the equity base, or profits.[5]

This ratio compares the company's realized retained profits to its theoretical requirement for asset growth, and shows what portion of the period's needed growth capital was provided by these profits. A value of 100% means that profits are just sufficient to finance the company's growth. If the ratio is below 100%, it means that although the company may be growing, its retained profits are not keeping up. Ultimately, this puts pressure on management to find outside sources of new capital or to retard growth. Values above 100% are extremely favorable. The company is growing and retained earnings exceed needed asset increases.

The ratio is useful in predicting future needs for new capital (from borrowing or stock sales), and in showing whether or not funds are likely to be available to pay dividends. The ratio is undefined when sales growth is zero or negative, and when the company operates at a loss.

Note that the previously computed ratio *SALES GROWTH (1)* serves as an input number in the equations below.

(verbal equation)

$$\text{ADEQUACY OF PROFITS} = 100 \times \frac{\dfrac{\text{Net Profit After Taxes} - \text{Dividends}}{\text{Total Assets Last Year}}}{\text{SALES GROWTH} \times .01}$$

(acronymic equation)

ADEQPROF = 100 * (NETPROFAFTTAX − DIV) / TOTASSETLASTYEAR / (**SALESGROW** * .01)

(symbolic equation)

R16 = 100 * (S30 − S31) / S8LY / (**R1** * .01)

17 RETURN ON SALES

Definition: Net profit after taxes divided by net sales, multiplied by 100 to provide a percentage.

This key profitability ratio (also known as net profit margin) measures, relative to sales, the difference between what a company takes in and what it spends in conducting its business.

A high value usually goes hand-in-hand with long-term business success. High returns provide capital for growth as well as protection against unexpected economic downturns. Low returns, on the other hand, reward suppliers, employees, and customers, but not shareholders. (A contrary and questionable viewpoint is that a low return on sales makes it possible to capture an otherwise elusive market, and results will be satisfactory if turnover and volume are high enough.)

How does a company obtain higher returns? The Strategic Planning Institute identifies a number of characteristics of more-profitable firms. Among them are: A high-quality product or service. High value added per employee. Less need for large amounts of capital. A larger share of market relative to competitors. Their reports suggest that being in the right business may be more important than doing things well.[6]

The most likely cause for an unsatisfactorily low return is insufficient gross margin (perhaps resulting from too-low pricing). Another possibility is that expenses are too high relative to sales. Low returns are also predictable when many rival companies court the same customers. Conversely, high returns are common for firms offering proprietary products, or possessing some form of competitive edge.

Year-to-year trends in this ratio are significant because they demonstrate how well a company's overall business strategy is working. A more-or-less constant return on sales at a satisfactory level is an excellent proof that management has things under control.

(verbal equation)

$$\text{RETURN ON SALES} = 100 \times \frac{\text{Net Profit After Taxes}}{\text{Net Sales}}$$

(acronymic equation)

$$\text{RETSALES} = 100 * \text{NETPROFAFTTAX} / \text{NETSALES}$$

(symbolic equation)

$$\text{R17} = 100 * \text{S30} / \text{S16}$$

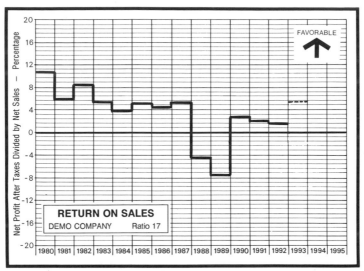

Figure 3-3. Sample graph of *Return on Sales* shows portion of total revenues retained to the bottom line.

18 RETURN ON SALES BEFORE TAXES

Definition: Net profit before taxes divided by net sales, multiplied by 100 to provide a percentage.

Why measure return on a before-tax basis? The answer is that income taxes depend on things other than operating results — size of firm, carryovers from prior years or acquired subsidiaries, and special credits. When comparisons are made between companies, before-tax numbers are usually more meaningful.

Many of the ratios in this chapter use after-tax net profit in numerator or denominator. Keep in mind that in most instances the calculations can also be made using before-tax profit.

(verbal equation)

$$\text{RETURN ON SALES BEFORE TAXES} = 100 \times \frac{\text{Net Profit Before Taxes}}{\text{Net Sales}}$$

(acronymic equation)

$$\text{RETSALESBEFTAX} = 100 * \text{NETPROFBEFTAX} / \text{NETSALES}$$

(symbolic equation)

$$R18 = 100 * S29 / S16$$

19 RETURN ON GROSS PROFIT

Definition: Net profit after taxes divided by gross profit, multiplied by 100 to provide a percentage.

Firms with high returns exhibit common characteristics. They are in good lines of business. Their products or services are usually of high quality — sometimes unique. They enjoy the solid support of satisfied customers. Competition is not too severe.

RETURN ON SALES (17) is one of the traditional tests for overall profitability. When the ratio is high it suggests the things mentioned above, but it also suggests an efficient operation with expenses under tight control. But what if expenses are not under control at all, and the high value for the ratio originates in a high gross margin and the structural qualities described? Despite satisfactory overall profitability, the suggestion of high efficiency may be incorrect. The point is that the traditional measure can come up short when one is searching for the reason for a high or low return on sales. This ratio overcomes the problem by comparing net profit to gross profit instead of to sales.

The ratio is useful to lenders, brokers, investors and others who may need to compare the efficiency of two firms in totally different lines of business. A wholesale company selling in a competitive market where margins are extremely thin can be looked at alongside a high-margin retail operation. The reviewer using this ratio understands that two different markets dictate two different margins, and *really* wants to know how successful was each company in converting gross into net profit for its owners.

Those new to business often fail to fully understand the important differences between high-margin and low-margin businesses. Many ratio comparisons (between companies) are all but impossible if the measures are made relative to sales.

(verbal equation)

$$\begin{matrix} \textbf{RETURN} \\ \textbf{ON} \\ \textbf{GROSS PROFIT} \end{matrix} = 100 \times \frac{\text{Net Profit After Taxes}}{\text{Gross Profit}}$$

(acronymic equation)

RETGROSSPROF = 100 * NETPROFAFTTAX / GROSSPROF

(symbolic equation)

R19 = 100 * S30 / S18

20 RETURN ON ASSETS

Definition: Net profit after taxes divided by last year's tangible total assets, multiplied by 100 to provide a percentage.

This ratio indicates how successful a management is in putting its assets to work in making profits. Stated another way, it measures the *earning power* of the firm's investment in assets. It should be noted that in this ratio it does not matter whether the assets represent creditor equity or owner equity.

National averages for the ratio vary greatly by line of business, the extent to which products or services are competitive, and the degree of employee value added in the enterprise. High-technology companies offering proprietary products have excellent potential to achieve enviable returns relative to assets.

Some reviewers use this ratio to measure overall efficiency. Their reasoning is that the company's assets are all that the management has to work with, and that should be the base of measurement.

The calculation is usually based on assets in place at the start of the year. If a substantial increase in assets takes place during the year, it is common practice to use an average of opening and closing figures in the denominator.

Intangibles (such as goodwill) are typically subtracted from assets because of the belief that they do not contribute to the earning of profits, and also because they are difficult to value. Of course, some intangibles *do* contribute to profits (high profile trademarks, for example). When that is the case, they can be left in the equation.

Variations of the ratio look only at fixed assets. Also, when net profit includes extraordinary items (such as the gain on a sale of assets or a subsidiary), appropriate adjustments are made.

(verbal equation)

$$\text{RETURN ON ASSETS} = 100 \times \frac{\text{Net Profit After Taxes}}{\text{Tangible Total Assets Last Year}}$$

(acronymic equation)

$$\text{RETASSET} = 100 * \text{NETPROFAFTTAX} / (\text{TOTASSETLASTYEAR} - \text{INTANLASTYEAR})$$

(symbolic equation)

$$\text{R20} = 100 * \text{S30} / (\text{S8LY} - \text{S7LY})$$

21 RETURN ON WORKING CAPITAL

Definition: Net profit after taxes divided by last year's working capital, multiplied by 100 to provide a percentage.

This profitability ratio measures return against the firm's working capital on hand at the start of the year — that is, the excess of current assets (cash, inventory, notes and accounts receivable) over current liabilities (notes and accounts payable, accrued expenses and taxes). On a day-to-day basis, working capital is (realistically) the only thing the business manager can manipulate to earn profits.

Ratios that measure profitability against total assets or against equity may hide how well management is really doing with the tools immediately available. For that reason, this measure might be described as a manager's ratio. Particularly in smaller companies, a hired CEO may not enjoy freedom to do things like change the line of business, acquire other companies, or dispose of fixed assets. Ownership and control may rest in the hands of founders or board members unwilling to allow major structural change. In reviewing the performance of a company president or general manager in situations like this, a board of directors might give this ratio special attention.

Because the denominator in this comparison is usually smaller than is the case for the other profitability ratios, the result may be a relatively large number. There is no reason, for highly profitable businesses with rapid turnover, why the ratio can't exceed 100%.

The result may be meaningless for companies experiencing wide swings in working capital during the year. When that is true, average figures are used in the denominator.

(verbal equation)

$$\text{RETURN ON WORKING CAPITAL} = 100 \times \frac{\text{Net Profit After Taxes}}{\text{Working Capital Last Year}}$$

(acronymic equation)

RETWORKCAP=
100 * NETPROFAFTTAX / (CURRASSETLASTYEAR − CURRLIABLASTYEAR)

(symbolic equation)

$$R21 = 100 * S30 / (S5LY − S10LY)$$

22 RETURN ON NET WORTH

Definition: Net profit after taxes divided by last year's tangible stockholders' equity, multiplied by 100 to provide a percentage.

Sometimes called return on equity, this is the best known of the ROI (return on investment) ratios. Many believe it is the final criterion of profitability. Venture capitalists and investors pay particular attention to this ratio because it tells them how much the company is making from money invested. They see it as a key indicator of overall operating efficiency and the quality of management.

National averages for the ratio vary from 5 to 25%, depending on the line of business. 10% is considered a desirable objective. Lower returns may restrict growth and dividend-paying ability.[7]

When comparing ROI ratios, terms must be carefully defined. Many variations exist, and the resulting numbers differ. Some use operating profit in the numerator. Others take dividends into account. There are also versions based on market value of the company's stock, and still others that calculate compounded return from the time the company was first capitalized. For all of these reasons, the general term ROI should be avoided. It is meaningful only when the content of numerator and denominator are clearly stated.

If significant additions to paid-in capital have been made during the year, an average of the year's opening and closing figures is used in the denominator to provide more accuracy. This is true not just for this equation, but for all of the return ratios based on capital structure in place at the beginning of the year.

As with similar ratios, intangibles are excluded from the denominator unless they clearly contribute to earnings and have measurable values.

(verbal equation)

$$\text{RETURN ON NET WORTH} = 100 \text{ X } \frac{\text{Net Profit After Taxes}}{\text{Tangible Stockholders' Equity Last Year}}$$

(acronymic equation)
RETNETWORTH=
$100*NETPROFAFTTAX/(STOCKHOLDEQLASTYEAR-INTANLASTYEAR)$

(symbolic equation)
$R22=100*S30/(S14LY-S7LY)$

23 RETURN ON INVESTED CAPITAL

Definition: The sum of net profit after taxes and interest expense on long-term debt, divided by the sum of last year's tangible stockholders' equity and last year's long-term liabilities, the result multiplied by 100 to provide a percentage.

The previously-described ratio *RETURN ON NET WORTH (22)* is a good indicator of profitability and managerial skill. Sometimes overlooked, however, is the influence of balance-sheet leverage on the calculated return. If a company's capital, for example, consists entirely of stockholder equity it will report a higher return than an otherwise identical company with long-term debt in its capital structure. Why? Because the interest cost of the borrowed money reduces net profit.

Investors and acquirers, in particular, are interested in knowing what return the company makes on *all* of its invested capital (equity plus debt). They reason that this is a better indicator of management's skill in effectively using its resources.[8]

The numerator in this modified equation is after-tax earnings before interest expense on long-term debt. The denominator is net worth plus long-term debt. A problem sometimes arises when a company reports only a single figure for interest expense (no way to know how much is short-term and how much long-term). One solution is to allocate the interest expense in proportion to the amount of long-term debt shown on the balance sheet relative to total debt on which interest is paid. Another very practical solution (particularly for small companies) includes total interest expense in the numerator and total debt (less accounts payable on which interest is not normally paid) in the denominator. After all, for many businesses continuously rolling over short-term debt, there may be little practical difference between the two forms of borrowing from a capital allocation point of view. An equation for computing the ratio this way is included in the chapter endnotes.[9] The revised equation is valid only if year-end figures are representative of the year as a whole. For a company with no debt, ratios 22 and 23 yield the same result.

A refinement to the computation of this ratio subtracts from interest expense (in the numerator) the income-tax benefits of the appropriate interest deductions. This varies from company to company, of course, depending on its tax rate.[10]

In the equations that follow, interest expense is assumed to arise from long-term debt. If this is not the case, one of the previously-described adjustments should be made. In using prior-year capital figures in the denominator, it is assumed that profit generated in the current year is a return on the capital structure in place at the start of the year. The ratio is undefined if the company is unprofitable.

(verbal equation)

RETURN ON INVESTED CAPITAL $= 100 \times \dfrac{\text{Net Profit After Taxes} + \text{Interest Expense}}{\substack{\text{Tangible} \\ \text{Stockholders' Equity}} + \substack{\text{Long-Term} \\ \text{Liabilities}}}$

Tangible Stockholders' Equity Last Year + Long-Term Liabilities Last Year

(acronymic equation)
RETINVESCAP=100∗(NETPROFAFTTAX+INTEREXP)/
(STOCKHOLDEQLASTYEAR−INTANLASTYEAR+LONGTERMLIABLASTYEAR)

(symbolic equation)
R23=100∗(S30+S22)/(S14LY−S7LY+S11LY)

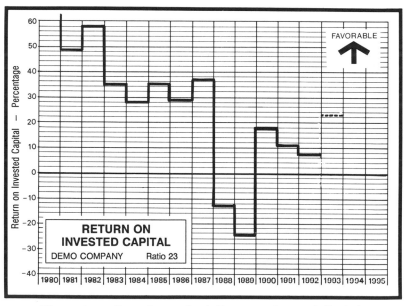

Figure 3-4. Example graph of *Return on Invested Capital* compares profits to total of equity *and* debt.

24 RETURN ON RISK

Definition: Net profit after taxes divided by last year's tangible stockholders' equity, multiplied by 100 to provide a percentage, the result reduced by the interest rate prevailing for long-term corporate bonds.[11]

It is said that most new businesses close their doors voluntarily or file for bankruptcy within a few years.[12] For this reason, venture capitalists expect profits from their equity investments to be two to three times greater than yields obtainable from conservative, fixed-income securities. What this means is that businesses must earn returns that are substantially higher than bond yields if new investors are to be attracted and present stockholders satisfied. It follows that when interest rates are high, pressures on management to increase profits are also high. Unfortunately for management, higher interest rates usually have a deleterious impact on profits.

This ratio measures risk reward by subtracting a safe, fixed-income return from total return.

Because businesses and the demands of their stockholders vary so much, there is no exact number representing a lower limit for this ratio. Whenever it falls into negative territory, however, stockholders are likely to protest. Why shouldn't they, when their money invested in high-quality securities would be safe, liquid, and provide current income?

Bond yields are used in the equations because of their time comparability to long-term equity investments. There is nothing wrong, however, in using some other appropriate interest rate. The point is simply to recognize that all forms of capital compete in the marketplace.

If tangible net worth or interest rates have changed significantly during the year, averages may be used for these numbers. A variation of the ratio uses before-tax profit in the numerator instead of after-tax.

(verbal equation)

$$\text{RETURN ON RISK} = 100 \times \frac{\text{Net Profit After Taxes}}{\text{Tangible Stockholders' Equity Last Year}} - \text{Interest Rate}$$

(acronymic equation)

RETRISK=
100*NETPROFAFTTAX/(STOCKHOLDEQLASTYEAR−INTANLASTYEAR)−INTERRATE

(symbolic equation)

R24=100*S30/(S14LY−S7LY)−S49

25 RETURN ON EMPLOYEE COMPENSATION

Definition: Net profit after taxes divided by employee compensation, multiplied by 100 to provide a percentage.

"Return" is another (and softer) way to describe profit. It's also a better way, as it suggests a relationship to something else. We talk about returns on sales, gross profit, assets, working capital, net worth, invested capital and risk (to name just a few). This return ratio compares the bottom line to the cost of human resources.

The ratio relates what the stockholders earn to what the employees earn. Comparisons between different businesses are difficult, as some are more labor intensive than others. But for one business over a period of time, the ratio provides answers about the stockholders' return relative to wages. Are profits holding their own, or are rising labor costs squeezing profits? Conversely, is the company reasonably sharing its success with employees when times are good?

In terms of managerial action, critics of this ratio argue that for most businesses, profits cannot be successfully manipulated by arbitrary changes in wage rates. They reason that the marketplace for labor functions as effectively as the marketplace for a company's goods or services. This suggests that management's options are limited only to changing what and how things are done — not the wages paid to get them done. This may or may not be correct, but even if it is, it does not negate the usefulness of the ratio in showing trends and in providing management with an early warning of potential discontent on the part of owners or workers.

The ratio is higher in industries where fewer numbers of workers are required to perform the business function, where high technology is involved, or where the company's product or service is relatively unique.

Variations of the ratio are used to look at different employee categories — production, administration, officers, and so forth.

(verbal equation)

RETURN ON EMPLOYEE COMPENSATION $= 100 \times \dfrac{\text{Net Profit After Taxes}}{\text{Wages Expense}}$

(acronymic equation)

RETEMPCOMP = 100 * NETPROFAFTTAX / WAGEEXP

(symbolic equation)

R25 = 100 * S30 / S19

26 PROFIT PER EMPLOYEE

Definition: *Net profit after taxes divided by average number of employees.*

This profitability ratio measures earnings against the number of workers required to produce those earnings. For a company operating in a stable market environment, it is an indicator of efficiency. That is, it tells management how much profit (on average) is produced by each employee. When different companies are compared, the ratio reveals the degree to which labor is involved in the business function.

Companies selling proprietary products, dealing in high technology, or having largely automated operations tend to report higher ratios. Conversely, firms participating in markets that require large amounts of hand labor have lower ratios.

This measure can be usefully employed in negotiating wage rates with workers, and in calculating contributions to bonus and profit-sharing plans. During periods of inflation, the long-term trend in this ratio has an upward bias. This does not necessarily mean that productivity is rising. It simply reflects the measurement of increasingly-cheapened dollars in the numerator.

An important number used in the equation for this ratio (average number of employees) is not likely to be found in a financial statement. Because business ratios have their origins in banking and credit, reviewers traditionally compute only those ratios that can be derived from available data. But managers are not so limited. Many valuable comparisons can be made to the size of a company's labor force.

Because the number of workers often varies seasonally, an average value is used in the denominator. Similarly, if part-time workers are employed, the denominator is adjusted to full-time equivalents. Note that this ratio is expressed in dollars and not as a percentage.

(verbal equation)

$$\text{PROFIT PER EMPLOYEE} = \frac{\text{Net Profit After Taxes}}{\text{Employees}}$$

(acronymic equation)
$$\text{PROFEMP} = \text{NETPROFAFTTAX} / \text{EMP}$$

(symbolic equation)
$$\text{R26} = \text{S30} / \text{S46}$$

27 RETURN ON PRESIDENT'S COMPENSATION

Definition: Net profit after taxes divided by president's compensation.

On theory that the buck stops at the president's desk, this profitability ratio measures return to stockholders on compensation paid to the company's chief operating officer. Reduced to very simple terms, it tells how well the president is performing. For that reason the ratio is likely to be of greater interest to owners and investors than to company management. It's a tough measure, because it assigns the results of market vagaries to the company's leader (this in addition to traditional responsibilities for nurturing sales and controlling costs).

The ratio can be a useful tool for structuring executive compensation, for comparing wages paid to presidents of similar firms, and for determining when a leader has outgrown the company or vice-versa. Another use (for closely held corporations) is to review (and perhaps justify to authorities) the reasonableness of executive salaries. Tax auditors look for evidence that very high wages (taxed once) are dividends (taxed twice).

A general manager's compensation may be substituted in the denominator for situations where the president does not actually run the company on a day-to-day basis. A variation of the ratio uses total executive compensation in the denominator, thus measuring the effectiveness of an entire management.

If a significant part of the president's compensation is in the form of perquisites not available to most of the other employees (stock options, bonuses, automobile, generous insurance, etc.) then if only for reasons of accuracy, the market value of these items should be included.

Because the calculation often produces a very large number, it is best expressed as a times ratio — not a percentage. That is, it tells how many dollars of profit are earned for each dollar paid to the key individual running the company.

(verbal equation)

$$\text{RETURN ON PRESIDENT'S COMPENSATION} = \frac{\text{Net Profit After Taxes}}{\text{President's Compensation}}$$

(acronymic equation)

$$\text{RETPRESCOMP} = \text{NETPROFAFTTAX} / \text{PRESCOMP}$$

(symbolic equation)

$$\text{R27} = \text{S30} / \text{S34}$$

28 RETURN ON OWNERS' COMPENSATION

Definition: Net profit after taxes divided by the sum of dividends and any other compensation paid to owners.

Corporate stockholders receive their ownership rewards in the form of dividends and/or appreciation in the value of stock. In cases where the owners are closely involved, they may also receive an added or alternate return in the form of expensed compensation — salaries (earned or unearned), consulting fees, director fees, stock options, travel, vehicles, vacation homes, insurance, and other perquisites. Such owner-executive compensation packages are found in companies of all sizes.

This times ratio measures the return on *total* remuneration paid to owners — dividends *plus* income that may be buried in company expense accounts. The purpose for calculating the ratio is not to judge the appropriateness of the form of compensation. It is to gain insight into the extent to which *total* compensation paid to owners earns a return.

In discussing a previous ratio, the point was made that growth is affordable only to the extent that capital is available to support it. Borrowing, stock sales, and profits are sources of growth capital. Reliance on profits, however, may be incompatible with overly generous payout to owners. A high value for this ratio, therefore, is a healthy sign that distributions to shareholders are not restricting long-term growth.

The ratio becomes controversial when questions about taxation are asked. Some business owners *do* skirt the law by writing off lifestyle expenditures on their company's books. Another problem is that one owner may contribute a substantial amount of time to company activities and another none at all, with both receiving the same compensation. Calculating and writing down the ratio is, therefore, a potential cause for rancor. Managers may not want to report the number. That does not negate its value in special situations.

Be consistent when determining the number to be entered into the denominator as owners' compensation. Leaving out the wages of an executive holding only a small amount of stock is reasonable. Include the market value of perquisites if it can be determined.

(verbal equation)

$$\text{RETURN ON OWNERS' COMPENSATION} = \frac{\text{Net Profit After Taxes}}{\text{Owners' Compensation} + \text{Dividends}}$$

(acronymic equation)

$$\text{RETOWNCOMP} = \text{NETPROFAFTTAX} / (\text{OWNCOMP} + \text{DIV})$$

(symbolic equation)

$$R28 = S30 / (S35 + S31)$$

29 RETURN ON SPACE

Definition: Net profit after taxes divided by number of square feet of floor space.

This profitability ratio makes the comparison to the amount of physical space used to perform the business function. Real estate costs are almost always significant in business, and it makes sense to insure that every square foot of plant space is earning a fair return.

It should be noted that this particular ratio measures efficiency in the *use* of space — not the cost of space. If two firms earn equal profits and have plants of the same size, their space ratios are the same. It matters not if one pays twice the rent of the other, or if one plant includes facilities or amenities absent in the other.

Why would a manager measure against amount of space instead of cost of space? One answer is that space acquired long ago is sometimes carried on the books at unrealistically low values, or below-market rent is being paid on very long leases. This ratio is useful in those situations, as it can reveal inefficiencies in the use of space that otherwise are hidden. It is also a good ratio to review before expanding or moving to a new location, as it provides insight into the amount of space used in the past to earn certain levels of profit.

If comparisons are made between companies, it's important to first determine their relative profitability measured against something like sales or invested capital. Space ratio comparisons are meaningful only if underlying profitability for the compared firms is about the same.

Because this ratio is measured in dollars per square foot, the long-term graph is likely to reveal an upward bias resulting from growth (more profit coming from the same-size plant) or from inflation.

(verbal equation)

$$\text{RETURN ON SPACE} = \frac{\text{Net Profit After Taxes}}{\text{Floor Space}}$$

(acronymic equation)
RETSPACE = NETPROFAFTTAX / SPACE

(symbolic equation)
R29 = S30/S48

Notes — Chapter 3

1. *Depreciation* is used here in the broad sense and includes depletion and amortization.

2. Steve Kichen and Steven Ramos, "Margin for Improvement," *Forbes* (June 25, 1990), p. 234.

3. Roy W. Longstreet, *Viewpoints of a Commodity Trader* (New York: Frederick Fell, 1968), p. 20.

4. For an example of inflation accounting, see Sumner N. Levine, *The Dow Jones-Irwin Business and Investment Almanac* (Homewood, IL: Dow Jones-Irwin, 1983), p. 291.

5. *See AFFORDABLE GROWTH RATE (2)* in Chapter 2.

6. Thomas P. Murphy, "Commandments," *Forbes* (August 1, 1983), p. 178.

7. Dun & Bradstreet, *Industry Norms and Key Business Ratios, Desk Top Edition, 1990-91,* (Murray Hill, NJ: 1991), p. vi.

8. Robert J. R. Follett, *How to Keep Score in Business* (Chicago: Follett, 1978), p. 128.

9. The equation for estimating return on invested capital using total interest (where an allocation cannot readily be made between short-term and long-term obligations) is:

$$\textbf{RETURN ON INVESTED CAPITAL} = 100 \ X \ \frac{\text{Net Profit After Taxes + Total Interest Expense}}{\text{Total Capitalization}}$$

Where **Total Capitalization** =

$$\begin{array}{c}\text{Stockholders'}\\\text{Equity}\\\text{Last Year}\end{array} - \begin{array}{c}\text{Intangibles}\\\text{Last}\\\text{Year}\end{array} + \begin{array}{c}\text{Current}\\\text{Liabilities}\\\text{Last Year}\end{array} - \begin{array}{c}\text{Accounts}\\\text{Payable}\\\text{Last Year}\end{array} + \begin{array}{c}\text{Long-Term}\\\text{Liabilities}\\\text{Last Year}\end{array}$$

Last year's current liabilities reduced by last year's accounts payable usually results in last year's short-term borrowed capital.

10. Interest expense may be adjusted for the effect of income taxes using the following equation:

$$\textbf{Adjusted Interest Expense} = \text{Interest Expense } X \ \frac{\text{Net Profit After Taxes}}{\text{Net Profit Before Taxes}}$$

11. One good source for current interest rates is *Barron's Market Laboratory*, "Best-Grade Bond Index," *Barron's*.

12. For a discussion of business failure rates, *See* Louis Rukeyser, *Louis Rukeyser's Business Almanac* (New York: Simon and Schuster, 1988), p. 220.

Chapter 4
Debt and Capital Ratios

Every business needs money. It's required for start-up — to buy machines, equipment, land, and buildings. It's required after the business is operating — to finance inventories, receivables, and expansion. Without money, a business cannot be started. Without money, an existing business dies.

Some firms obtain this money entirely from equity investors, or from profits resulting from business success. Money obtained this way does not have to be repaid, and there is no interest cost. Less fortunate companies obtain the needed money by borrowing it from banks, or by issuing debt instruments such as notes and bonds. Banks and bondholders, unlike equity investors, *do* expect to be repaid — often on a fixed date. For this reason, the company's survival may hinge on its ability to meet such obligations.

There are good reasons and bad reasons to borrow. The reason is good if each borrowed dollar earns a positive return exceeding the cost of interest payments. The reason is likely to be bad if it originates in human weakness — ego, greed, poor planning, or a desire to provide life support to a failed project.

Experts on risk analysis for corporations distinguish between *business risk* and *financial risk*.[1] Business risk is the uncertainty of income that originates in the firm's product, means of production, customer base, and regulatory climate. Financial risk, on the other hand, represents *additional* uncertainty imposed on shareholders because the firm uses fixed-obligation debt securities to pay for its productive assets.

There was a time when people realized that lending and borrowing are inherently hazardous activities that should be undertaken cautiously, and only then to finance productive investments like factories, machinery, tools, bridges and roads that provide some means of repayment.[2] This thinking is unpopular today. Generations have been raised to believe that business success results from maximizing the use of other people's money, and borrowing is necessary if only to stay ahead of inflation. Although there is truth in these ideas, the important matter of financial risk is frequently disregarded. Should you question that the greater risk to business is the one associated with borrowed money, try to recall an economic crisis or well-publicized business failure that did not stem from or ultimately result in an inability to meet a debt obligation.

Even firms that do not rely on long-term borrowing must exercise tight control of their money, however obtained. This chapter describes 29 debt, cash, and other capital management ratios important to most businesses.

30 CURRENT RATIO

Definition: Current assets divided by current liabilities.

This ratio (sometimes called the liquidity ratio) is perhaps the best-known measure of financial strength on a specific date. The number of times current assets (cash, marketable securities, accounts receivable, inventory) cover current liabilities (accounts and notes payable, accrued expenses, and taxes) is an important expression of the company's solvency — that is, its ability to meet obligations as they come due.

A popular rule of thumb for this ratio is two (2:1).[3] Many consider this the minimum necessary for reliable cash flow, though some lines of business (having a major portion of assets in cash) traditionally operate at lower figures. Much higher ratios could mean that management is not aggressive in finding ways to put current assets to work.

Although liquidity is improved by reducing inventories and stepping up collection of receivables, this does not (by itself) alter the current ratio. It only changes the mix of the current asset accounts. The best way to solve chronic liquidity problems is to infuse new cash into the business (by borrowing or selling stock). Liquidity is usually examined monthly, or more often when the ratio is low. The year-end value may lack significance for firms experiencing large seasonal changes in activity. This ratio is traditionally expressed as a straight quotient — not a percentage.

(verbal equation)
$$\text{CURRENT RATIO} = \frac{\text{Current Assets}}{\text{Current Liabilities}}$$

(acronymic equation)
$$\text{CURRRATIO} = \text{CURRASSET} / \text{CURRLIAB}$$

(symbolic equation)
$$\text{R30} = \text{S5} / \text{S10}$$

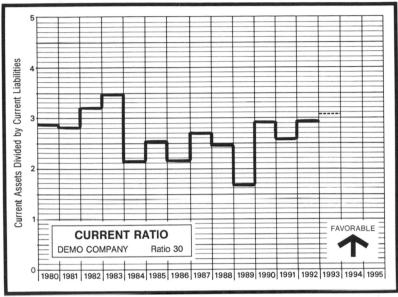

Figure 4-1. Sample graph of *Current Ratio* reveals variations in financial strength and ability to cope with contingencies.

31 QUICK RATIO

Definition: Quick assets (current assets less inventory) divided by current liabilities.

This ratio (sometimes called the acid test ratio) is perhaps the best measure of liquidity on a specific date, because it deals only with those assets that can be converted to cash in a short time. The so-called quick assets include cash, marketable securities, and accounts receivable — but not inventories (which are considered illiquid in the short term). This tough measure forces management to consider its ability to meet today's obligations if sales revenues should disappear, or if the business had to close its doors. A quick ratio between one-half and one (0.5:1 to 1:1) is considered satisfactory for most businesses if there is no reason to believe that anything will slow the collection of receivables and no negative year-to-year trends are apparent.[4]

Management has few options when dealing with a chronically-low quick ratio. Stepping up collection of receivables will improve the cash situation. Any action that increases profitability will help in the long run. The best immediate solution is to bring new money into the business.

This ratio is usually examined monthly, or more often when it is low. Because current assets and liabilities can change significantly on a daily basis, the year-end value may have little meaning. This measure also is traditionally expressed as a straight ratio — not a percentage.

(verbal equation)

$$\text{QUICK RATIO} = \frac{\text{Current Assets} - \text{Inventory}}{\text{Current Liabilities}}$$

(acronymic equation)
$$\text{QUICKRATIO} = (\text{CURRASSET} - \text{INVEN}) / \text{CURRLIAB}$$

(symbolic equation)
$$\text{R31} = (\text{S5} - \text{S4}) / \text{S10}$$

32 CURRENT DEBT TO EQUITY

Definition: Current liabilities divided by tangible stockholders' equity, multiplied by 100 to provide a percentage.

This measure of financial strength compares what is owed currently to what is owned. Because current debt is due *now*, the ratio is another important indicator of solvency and receives close attention of lenders. It answers the question, "How much of the investment the owners have in their business is claimed by current debt?"

The traditional danger point for this ratio is 80%, above which any unexpected interruption in cash flow might put the business in jeopardy. Some sources think a somewhat lower ratio of two-to-three (about 67%) is a better upper limit.[5] For small retail businesses, where most current assets are in inventory, 50% may be appropriate.[6] Relying too heavily on suppliers to provide capital is risky, and also involves loss of payment discounts. Increasing owner equity by selling more stock lowers the ratio, as does reducing current liabilities.

Intangible assets (good will, patents and trademarks, treasury stock, organization expenses) are deducted from net worth because of their illiquidity, and also because their real value is difficult to determine.

This ratio is usually examined monthly, or more often when it is high.

(verbal equation)

$$\text{CURRENT DEBT TO EQUITY} = 100 \times \frac{\text{Current Liabilities}}{\text{Tangible Stockholders' Equity}}$$

(acronymic equation)
CURRDEBTEQ=100∗CURRLIAB/(STOCKHOLDEQ−INTAN)

(symbolic equation)
R32=100∗S10/(S14−S7)

33 DEBT TO EQUITY

Definition: Total liabilities divided by tangible stockholders' equity, multiplied by 100 to provide a percentage.

This ratio, popular with lenders, compares the total of what is owed to what is owned. When the ratio exceeds 100%, it means that the capital provided by lenders exceeds that provided by the stockholders. Owners seeking leverage in their capitalization structure prefer a high ratio. For each dollar invested, the company is able to buy more assets, presumably leading to increased sales and a higher return on investment. Lenders, on the other hand, prefer to see a low ratio as insurance that the company is able to repay its debts.

Median values for the ratio (looking at different lines of business) vary from about 30% to more than 150%. In the case of industrial firms, many believe that values significantly above 100% require careful examination.[7] For a great many years (as a result of taxation policies which favor debt over equity), average values for this ratio have increased. Although business writers do frequently mention certain upper limits, such as 100% or even 300%, it can be argued that there really is no *definitive* danger point. The ability to effectively use leverage depends on the line of business, managerial skill, and luck. Managers committed to leverage might keep in mind, however, that many of the world's finest companies operate entirely without debt.[8]

Once the debt burden is undertaken, means to service it must be maintained. The higher the debt, the greater the risk that the company will find itself in trouble if sales cannot be maintained at normal levels.

(verbal equation)

$$\text{DEBT TO EQUITY} = 100 \times \frac{\text{Total Liabilities}}{\text{Tangible Stockholders' Equity}}$$

(acronymic equation)
DEBTEQ=100∗(CURRLIAB+LONGTERMLIAB)/(STOCKHOLDEQ−INTAN)

(symbolic equation)
R33=100∗(S10+S11)/(S14−S7)

34 DEBT TO ASSETS

Definition: Total liabilities divided by total assets, multiplied by 100 to provide a percentage.

This ratio, also called the debt ratio, compares what is owed to the value of assets used by the business. It is a capitalization ratio as well as a leverage ratio (telling lenders what percentage of the firm's assets are financed by borrowing). It is used to predict long-term solvency.

Debt varies greatly from firm to firm. In the 1970's the average debt ratio for manufacturing was about 33%. The figure is higher today. Risk of inability to repay debt is probably average when the debt ratio is average, but grows as the ratio moves upward. As long as some equity exists, the debt ratio is below 100%. If losses reduce assets to the point where they are exceeded by debt (ratio greater than 100%), stockholders' equity is assumed to have a negative value. Bankruptcy is a legal term, of course, but from a practical viewpoint the firm reporting a debt ratio greater than 100% is functionally bankrupt.

In addition to measuring leverage, this ratio monitors success in using debt to build the business. If the ratio climbs over time, a likely explanation is that borrowing is financing losses or unearned dividends.

(verbal equation)

$$\textbf{DEBT TO ASSETS} \ = \ 100 \ \text{X} \ \frac{\text{Total Liabilities}}{\text{Total Assets}}$$

(acronymic equation)
$$\textbf{DEBTASSET} = 100 * (\text{CURRLIAB} + \text{LONGTERMLIAB}) / \text{TOTASSET}$$

(symbolic equation)
$$\textbf{R34} = 100 * (\text{S10} + \text{S11}) / \text{S8}$$

35 TURNOVER OF WORKING CAPITAL

Definition: Net sales divided by working capital.

This ratio measures how effectively a company's working capital (current assets less current liabilities) is used to generate and process sales. When sales rise, inventories increase to match actual and anticipated orders. Payables and receivables also increase. Purchasing and credit-policy decisions must be made wisely if unexpected and serious cash shortages are to be avoided. This ratio continuously measures the complex relationship between buying and selling.

Maintaining the ratio at a low value insures availability of cash to sustain operations. But this may be an inefficient use of funds. Letting the ratio grow to a high value, on the other hand, could make the company vulnerable in an adverse business climate. The best managerial goal may be to hold the ratio more-or-less constant after first determining (by experience) what works best for the company. Median values for this ratio reported by line of business vary from two or three (certain types of retailing) to 18 or more (meat packing and gas transmission).

(verbal equation)

$$\textbf{TURNOVER OF WORKING CAPITAL} = \frac{\text{Net Sales}}{\text{Working Capital}}$$

(acronymic equation)

$$\textbf{TURNWORKCAP} = \text{NETSALES} / (\text{CURRASSET} - \text{CURRLIAB})$$

(symbolic equation)

$$\textbf{R35} = S16 / (S5 - S10)$$

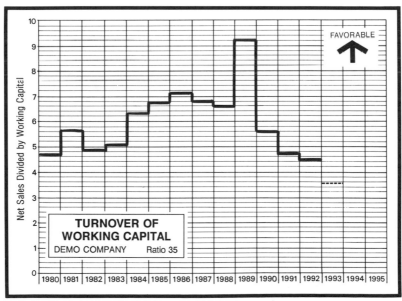

Figure 4-2. *Turnover of Working Capital* example graph for a small business shows reversal of a seven-year positive trend.

36 FIXED ASSET RATIO

Definition: Fixed assets divided by tangible stockholders' equity, multiplied by 100 to provide a percentage.

This indicator of financial strength inversely measures the liquidity of shareholder equity. The more a business ties up its net worth in land, buildings, leasehold improvements, machinery and furniture, the less it has available for working capital. Before embarking on plans to acquire long-term assets, management should ask questions like, "Can we lease it instead of buy it?" "Can we sub-contract it instead of make it?" Costs may be higher if these alternatives are adopted, but risk is reduced and financial strength maintained.

A ratio exceeding 75% may indicate over-investment and is worthy of careful examination.[9]   Higher values are sometimes suggested for manufacturers. In certain wholesale lines, average ratios are as low as 5%, indicating less need for investment in fixed assets. The reasonableness of the ratio for a particular business also depends on how the purchase of the asset is financed. If long-term loans are available, the company can safely tolerate a higher investment in fixed assets than would be the case if it relied on working capital to pay for the purchase.

Fixed assets are valued after depreciation. Intangibles are excluded from most calculations involving stockholder equity, including this one. Some may note that the title of this ratio suggests its purpose is to indicate what portion of net worth is tied up in fixed assets. So why not include intangibles in the denominator? The answer is that the ratio is commonly used as a measurement of liquidity — not fixed assets. A company with substantial intangibles on its books would report a lower fixed asset ratio if the intangibles were included. This could incorrectly suggest higher liquidity than is the case.

(verbal equation)

$$\text{FIXED ASSET RATIO} = 100 \times \frac{\text{Fixed Assets}}{\text{Tangible Stockholders' Equity}}$$

(symbolic equation)

$$\text{FIXEDASSETRATIO} = 100 * \text{FIXEDASSET} / (\text{STOCKHOLDEQ} - \text{INTAN})$$

(symbolic equation)

$$R36 = 100 * S6 / (S14 - S7)$$

37 FIXED ASSETS MIX

Definition: Fixed assets divided by total assets, multiplied by 100 to provide a percentage.

This ratio is also an indicator of financial strength, inversely measuring the liquidity of assets by comparing fixed assets to total assets.

Managers need to know what portion of their assets are tied up in long-term, relatively illiquid property such as land, buildings, and machinery. The higher the ratio, the less flexibility management has in meeting changing sales and market conditions.

Lenders are likely to become uncomfortable if the ratio moves higher than 50%. It can never reach 100%, because for that to happen, all of the company's other assets (cash, receivables, inventories, deposits, goodwill) would have to be gone. Even if a company is out of cash, has negative net worth, and is bankrupt, it probably has some inventory and some monies owed to it.

One way to lower the ratio is to sell off fixed assets. Production needs are then replaced by leasing and subcontracting. Although this may result in higher costs, it improves managerial flexibility and strengthens the balance sheet.

A variation of this ratio adds intangibles to fixed assets in the numerator. This is done to enhance its value as an inverse indicator of liquidity. Firms with substantial intangible assets (which are included in total assets) report lower values for the basic ratio. This suggests higher liquidity than is the case, because intangibles are illiquid just as fixed assets are illiquid. The variation that includes intangibles might be described as an illiquid asset ratio.

(verbal equation)

$$\text{FIXED ASSETS MIX} = 100 \text{ X } \frac{\text{Fixed Assets}}{\text{Total Assets}}$$

(acronymic equation)

$$\text{FIXEDASSETMIX} = 100 * \text{FIXEDASSET} / \text{TOTASSET}$$

(symbolic equation)

$$R37 = 100 * S6 / S8$$

38 EQUITY RATIO

Definition: Tangible stockholders' equity divided by the difference between total tangible assets and current liabilities, multiplied by 100 to provide a percentage.

This ratio, sometimes called the common stock ratio, describes how much of the company's capitalization is provided by shareholders. Lenders are particularly interested in the measurement because it shows the extent to which the owners of the company are sharing the risks. High ratios correlate with a higher likelihood that loans will be repaid.

If the company falls upon hard times and sustains losses, stockholders' equity decreases. Assuming debt stays about the same, the ratio declines. This is just another way of saying that business risk is assigned primarily to the owners, and when things go wrong, their relative stake in the capitalization of the company is reduced.

The upper limit to the ratio is 100%, which means that all of the capitalization is provided by investors.

The value of preferred stock is usually excluded from the numerator because, in most instances, its holders do not have a voice in the affairs of the corporation. But some reviewers choose to leave it in, reasoning that the purpose for computing the ratio is to disclose the total amount of investor equity relative to direct loans existing or anticipated.

Current liabilities are subtracted from total assets in the denominator to provide total capitalization. Some reviewers do not make this adjustment and simply use total tangible assets as the comparison base.

Intangible assets (difficult to value) are subtracted from numerator and denominator if they are significant. If there are no intangible assets, the denominator (total capitalization) can also be found by adding long-term liabilities and stockholders' equity.

Despite the variations in method of computation, this ratio is considered one of the most important in financial statement analysis, and a good indicator of long-term solvency.

(verbal equation)

$$\text{EQUITY RATIO} = 100 \times \frac{\text{Tangible Stockholders' Equity}}{\text{Total Tangible Assets} - \text{Current Liabilities}}$$

(acronymic equation)

$$\text{EQRATIO} = 100 * (\text{STOCKHOLDEQ} - \text{INTAN}) / (\text{TOTASSET} - \text{INTAN} - \text{CURRLIAB})$$

(symbolic equation)

$$R38 = 100 * (S14 - S7) / (S8 - S7 - S10)$$

39 SUPPLIER FINANCING OF ASSETS

Definition: Accounts payable divided by total assets, multiplied by 100 to provide a percentage.

Businesses are financed in many ways, the most well-known being investor equity and long-term borrowing. Suppliers also participate in the capitalization of businesses by extending credit (usually unsecured) for the purchase of merchandise for resale. Although this is thought of as short-term credit, it is likely (if payments are kept current) to be automatically and continuously renewed.

In the case of many small- and medium-size businesses, suppliers and customers enjoy close and mutually-dependent relationships. Credit terms may be extremely generous — much better than market. The customers are, in effect, beneficiaries of interest-free, unsecured, automatically renewable lines of credit. When this type of buyer-seller relationship is identified, the financing aspects should be monitored.

There are risks in supplier financing. Despite its possible long-term character, it *is* short-term credit. Any number of events have potential for causing its disruption or termination. The supplier may be acquired by a larger firm unwilling to continue in the same way. The buyer may fail to meets its payment obligations and lose the special privileges. It is these questions of uncertainty that explain why supplier financing is not generally acknowledged as a source of capital.

The ratio is useful in cash flow analysis, and when questions are asked about obtaining funds to accommodate growth. When needed asset increases cannot be fully financed by profits, borrowed funds, or new equity capital, it is reasonable to ask if supplier financing might possibly make up the difference.

Credit extended by sellers in the form of open accounts also shows up in the ratio *CURRENT DEBT TO EQUITY (32)*.

If accounts payable fluctuates significantly during the year, the calculation may have little meaning on a particular date. In that case it is better to use an average figure in the numerator.

(verbal equation)

$$\text{SUPPLIER FINANCING OF ASSETS} = 100 \times \frac{\text{Accounts Payable}}{\text{Total Assets}}$$

(acronymic equation)

$$\text{SUPPFINASSET} = 100 * \text{ACCPAY} / \text{TOTASSET}$$

(symbolic equation)

$$R39 = 100 * S9 / S8$$

40 DEPRECIATION RATE

Definition: Depreciation expense divided by fixed assets, multiplied by 100 to provide a percentage.

One of the first lessons learned by students of accounting is that depreciation has nothing to do with *actual* wear and tear of property. It is, at best, an imaginary number designed to allocate an asset's cost (less salvage) to the period during which it is used. Company treasurers usually seek maximum rates of depreciation on their tax returns (to decrease taxes and thus increase today's *real* profits). At the same time, they are likely to report minimum rates of depreciation to shareholders (to increase *stated* profits). This seeming contradiction is legal and commonplace.

So what is the point of calculating a depreciation rate in ratio analysis? One answer is that it can be a good relative indicator of how aggressive are a company's accounting policies. The higher the ratio, the more confidence a lender or investor can have that the company keeps a conservative set of books. Low ratios, on the other hand, could be a sign of earnings management. What is high or low, of course, depends on the company and the nature of its property. The numbers are always relative.

A problem with low rates of depreciation is that the figures become meaningless if extended useful lives are elected and inflation rates are high. Although the practice of maximizing book life improves short-term reported profits, investors could be in for earnings shock when the time comes to replace assets acquired years ago.

Because companies continually replace old property with new, current depreciation is most conveniently measured against the depreciated basis of the fixed assets (instead of cost). There is nothing wrong with making the comparison to cost, however, if the numbers are available and consistently applied. If land is included in the value of the fixed assets, it should be subtracted from the denominator.

(verbal equation)

$$\text{DEPRECIATION RATE} = 100 \ \text{X} \ \frac{\text{Depreciation Expense}}{\text{Fixed Assets}}$$

(acronymic equation)

DEPRRATE = 100 * DEPREXP / FIXEDASSET

(symbolic equation)

R40 = 100 * S24 / S6

41 INVENTORY TO CURRENT ASSETS

Definition: Inventory divided by current assets, multiplied by 100 to provide a percentage.

Components of the current assets account are cash, marketable securities, notes receivable, accounts receivable, merchandise inventories, certain supplies, and prepaid rent. In order to service customers efficiently and keep back orders at a minimum, management is often tempted to invest too great a portion of its current assets in merchandise. Where receivables (the other major component of currents assets) are self-liquidating, inventories often are not. This ratio measures the percentage of current assets tied up in inventory.

Ratios involving inventory are usually thought of as measures of efficiency and managerial performance. This ratio does fall into that category, but it may be a better indicator of asset allocation and liquidity because it makes the comparison to other assets instead of sales or cost of goods sold.

Once again, there is no *right* value for this ratio. Rather, management should determine what is normal for its ongoing operations and then be alert to changes when they occur. If the measure moves out of its historic range, the event should be viewed as a red flag requiring appropriate managerial investigation.

Whenever ratios involving inventory are examined, reviewers should ask questions about how the inventory is valued. Although cost ordinarily provides the most appropriate basis, managers often use other methods for tax reasons or to meet performance goals. The way in which age and obsolescence are taken into account may be more significant than the underlying pricing method used.

Some inventory ratios use averages in the numerator. This one uses the inventory value prevailing on the day the current assets are valued.

(verbal equation)

$$\begin{array}{c} \textbf{INVENTORY} \\ \textbf{TO} \\ \textbf{CURRENT ASSETS} \end{array} = 100 \text{ X } \frac{\text{Inventory}}{\text{Current Assets}}$$

(acronymic equation)

INVENCURRASSET = 100 * INVEN / CURRASSET

(symbolic equation)

R41 = 100 * S4 / S5

42 TIMES INTEREST EARNED

Definition: Net profit before taxes, plus interest expense, the sum divided by interest expense.

Commitments to lenders are payable strictly as specified in the debt instruments. In the unhappy event that earnings fail to meet expectations in a period, the company may find itself financially embarrassed. This is more likely to happen if it has relied on leverage as an operating strategy. This ratio measures the firm's coverage of its debt obligations.

A ratio value of one means that the company has earned just enough to pay its interest expense. From a lender's viewpoint this is unacceptable performance, as no cushion is left to protect against an earnings decline in some future period. Interest expense is not the only claim on gross earnings. Healthy profits (after payment of interest) are necessary to attract and hold investors, to pay dividends, and to finance expansion of the business.

Because businesses differ so much, there is no specific number that represents a safety limit for the ratio. About all that can be said is that when the ratio is above 10 it will probably be viewed as normal and receive scant attention of reviewers. But when it is below four or five, they may take a closer look.

Income before taxes is traditionally used for the measure because tax rates vary so much from company to company. And because this is a coverage ratio, interest expense is added back to profit in the numerator. That portion of leasing expense attributable to interest is sometimes added to interest expense in making the calculation. Another variation adds depreciation expense to the numerator because it does not represent an actual outlay of cash.

This ratio is traditionally expressed as a times quotient — not a percentage.

(verbal equation)

$$\text{TIMES INTEREST EARNED} = \frac{\text{Net Profit Before Taxes } + \text{ Interest Expense}}{\text{Interest Expense}}$$

(acronymic equation)
$$\text{TIMESINTEREARN} = (\text{NETPROFBEFTAX} + \text{INTEREXP}) / \text{INTEREXP}$$

(symbolic equation)
$$\text{R42} = (\text{S29} + \text{S22}) / \text{S22}$$

43 CASH FLOW TO DEBT MATURITIES

Definition: Net profit after taxes, plus depreciation expense, the sum divided by long-term debt maturities.

This ratio examines the company's ability to make its annual debt-retirement payments from cash generated by the business. Because they are bookkeeping entries and do not represent any actual use of cash, allowances for depreciation are added back to after-tax net profit in determining cash flow.

This ratio is of interest primarily to lenders, and when the company's capitalization includes substantial long-term obligations. There is no exact ratio which is considered adequate, but a value of two or higher (meaning that the business is generating twice the cash needed to make principal payments on its loans) apparently satisfies most lenders.

Not all of the cash flow will be available to pay off debt. Some of it may be needed for payment of dividends and some to replace depreciating assets. Nevertheless, the ratio is a useful indicator of maximum funds available to meet important obligations.

If the ratio falls as low as unity, it means the company's ability to grow has disappeared. The reason for this is that all of its cash is required to make debt payments. Nothing remains to buy equipment, or to increase inventory and receivables. The best solution then is to increase the equity base (sell stock).

Note that because accountants sometimes show that portion of long-term debt due in the current year as *current* debt, there are instances where the denominator may exceed the value for total long-term debt shown on the financial statement.

This ratio is also traditionally expressed as a times quotient — not a percentage. A variation uses before-tax profit in the numerator and, in addition to depreciation expense, adds back long-term debt interest.

(verbal equation)

$$\begin{matrix} \text{CASH FLOW} \\ \text{TO} \\ \text{DEBT MATURITIES} \end{matrix} = \frac{\text{Net Profit After Taxes } + \text{ Depreciation Expense}}{\text{Long Term Debt Maturities}}$$

(acronymic equation)

CASHFLOWDEBTMAT = (NETPROFAFTTAX + DEPREXP)/DEBTMAT

(symbolic equation)

R43 = (S30 + S24)/S32

44 DOOMSDAY RATIO

Definition: Cash divided by current liabilities.

At the beginning of this chapter, two solvency ratios are described — *CURRENT RATIO (30)* and *QUICK RATIO (31)*. The former looks at current assets relative to current liabilities. The latter does the same, but excludes inventories (reasoning that they are illiquid on a short-term basis).

DOOMSDAY is the most demanding of the solvency ratios. It assumes that in addition to inventory, accounts receivable and prepaid expenses are also illiquid. This leaves only *cash* in the numerator. It derives its name, of course, from the idea that if business were to cease on the day of measurement, only cash would be available to meet current obligations.

The practical use for this ratio is not to speculate about the possible illiquidity of short-term assets. Rather, for a particular company, it is a useful relative indicator of the adequacy of the firm's cash buffer. Monitored as often as daily, it can provide early warning of cash shortages and help avoid crisis situations in the meeting of short-term obligations.

Because very few businesses have reason to maintain cash positions close to their current liabilities, the value of the ratio is almost always less than unity. Differences in managerial style account for wide variations between companies in the relative size of the cash account. Nevertheless, lenders and investors sometimes look closely at this ratio to determine if a firm is operating too close to the edge.

When comparing the cash ratios of different companies or different time periods, averages are more meaningful than the figures prevailing on a specific date. The value on the last day of the year may have no significance at all.

If marketable securities can be liquidated within a few days, they are included in the numerator.

(verbal equation)

$$\text{DOOMSDAY RATIO} = \frac{\text{Cash}}{\text{Current Liabilities}}$$

(acronymic equation)

$$\text{DOOMSRATIO} = \text{CASH} / \text{CURRLIAB}$$

(symbolic equation)

$$R44 = S2 / S10$$

45 CASH TO TOTAL LIABILITIES

Definition: Cash divided by total liabilities, multiplied by 100 to provide a percentage.

Cash ratios are not very popular. One reason for this is that a company's money position varies dramatically from day to day. Many managers object to being examined on matters that are short-term in nature, and where various strategies are available to deal with each problem. Another reason is the belief that inventories and receivables are always there to be converted to cash when management desires. Although these observations are correct, cash ratios are nevertheless important because cash is the ultimate asset.

When W. T. Grant filed for bankruptcy in 1975, its working capital figures appeared satisfactory. What the figures did not show was the low quality of accounts receivable and a very serious shortage of cash.[10] Even if inventories are not overstated and receivables are fully collectible, time to convert them may be insufficient to meet creditor demand. Cash is cash.

Critics of this ratio might say that measuring cash to total liabilities makes no sense because only part of the long-term debt is due now. If viewed in terms of coverage, this is true. If viewed as an indicator of immediate liquidity relative to the company's size, however, total debt is a sensible measuring base.

Comparative information on levels of cash held by corporations is not easily obtained. Breakdowns of working capital can sometimes be found in annual reports in sections called, "Management Discussion and Analysis."

If marketable securities can be liquidated within a few days, they are included in the numerator.

(verbal equation)

$$\text{CASH TO TOTAL LIABILITIES} = 100 \ \text{X} \ \frac{\text{Cash}}{\text{Total Liabilities}}$$

(acronymic equation)

$$\text{CASHTOTLIAB} = 100 * \text{CASH} / (\text{CURRLIAB} + \text{LONGTERMLIAB})$$

(symbolic equation)

$$R45 = 100 * S2 / (S10 + S11)$$

46 CASH TO DISBURSEMENTS

Definition: Cash divided by average monthly disbursements, multiplied by 100 to provide a percentage.

Just as a family compares the balance in its checking account to its habitual level of spending, companies need to look at cash positions relative to expenditures.   If cash falls below a certain level, important purchases may have to be postponed and payments to creditors delayed.

This ratio is useful in preparing cash-flow budgets. After expenditures are projected for a future period, historical values for the ratio are used to estimate the amount of cash likely to be needed in the forthcoming period. If the cash-flow budget indicates a likely insufficiency, plans can be made to correct the situation. Cash can be increased by improving management of receivables and inventory, soliciting more cash and credit card sales relative to open account sales, obtaining or increasing a bank line of credit, slowing payments to suppliers, selling company stock, and so forth.

The denominator, average monthly disbursements, is found by adding the year's total expenses to the year's purchases, and then dividing the sum by 12. By using a monthly base, a manager is provided with a figure representing a percentage of one month's average cash outlay. Thus if average monthly expenditures are $157,000 and cash on hand is $46,000, the cash to disbursements ratio is **29.3%.**

The ratio can also be used to express coverage of a certain number of day's expenditures by multiplying the result by 21, which in the above example is about six business days. Of course, in most circumstances cash will also be coming in during the month. The ratio calculated in days, therefore, represents the lower limit of realistic coverage.

As with all ratios involving cash, the result of computation varies markedly from day to day as payments are made to suppliers and funds are received from customers. For some uses of the ratio, *average* cash values are more meaningful in the numerator than values at year end.

(verbal equation)

$$\textbf{CASH TO DISBURSEMENTS} \ = \ 100 \ X \ \frac{\text{Cash}}{\text{Average Monthly Disbursements}}$$

(acronymic equation)

$$\textbf{CASHDISB} = 100 * CASH / ((TOTEXP + PURCH) / 12)$$

(symbolic equation)

$$\textbf{R46} = 100 * S2 / ((S28 + S17) / 12)$$

47 CASH TO WORKING CAPITAL

Definition: Cash divided by working capital, multiplied by 100 to provide a percentage.

It's been pointed out before that a firm with apparently-adequate working capital might not be healthy at all if its cash is chronically low compared to all liabilities and an ongoing level of expense. This ratio reveals that situation exactly by telling what percent of reported working capital is in the form of cash.

How much cash to keep on hand is a matter of judgment. Some managers work very close to the line, insisting that virtually all available cash be earning profits (more advertising, inventory, or receivables). This somewhat risky strategy requires careful monitoring, perhaps on a daily basis. More conservative managers prefer to keep enough cash on hand to meet ordinary needs, plus a reserve.

The prospective purchaser of a small business might find it useful to measure this ratio before making an offer. If the result comes out much lower than for similar businesses, additional inquiries are in order. Particularly if the business is touted as being highly profitable, a buyer might wonder why the cash level is so low. Is the manager one of those adept individuals described above, or is there another explanation? An unusually low value *could* mean that the seller is strapped for cash, and the company is in trouble.

Another use for this ratio is to alert management to the existence of too much cash in its working-capital accounts. This often happens in successful enterprises where executives are concentrating fully on what they know best (innovation, production, or marketing). Opportunities to invest the cash bounty (in securities or the business itself) are sometimes overlooked.

As with all cash ratios, the value prevailing on the last day of the year may not be representative. Average figures should be used in the numerator when significant fluctuations are the pattern.

(verbal equation)

$$\textbf{CASH TO WORKING CAPITAL} = 100 \text{ X } \frac{\text{Cash}}{\text{Working Capital}}$$

(acronymic equation)

CASHWORKCAP = 100 * CASH / (CURRASSET − CURRLIAB)

(symbolic equation)

R47 = 100 * S2 / (S5 − S10)

48 Z-SCORE BANKRUPTCY MODEL

Definition: The sum of four factored ratios: 6.56 times Ratio A, plus 3.26 times Ratio B, plus 6.72 times Ratio C, plus 1.05 times Ratio D. Ratio A is working capital divided by total assets. Ratio B is retained earnings divided by total assets. Ratio C is net profit before interest and taxes divided by total assets. Ratio D is stockholders' equity divided by total liabilities.

This measure reflects the work of New York University's Professor Edward I. Altman. Altman studied the financial statements of 33 corporations that filed for bankruptcy and 33 control firms selected at random. Using a sophisticated statistical technique called multiple discriminant analysis (MDA), he discovered that bankruptcy is predictable up to two years prior to the event through ratio analysis.[11]

Using Altman's four-variable adaptation for private firms (the original research used five variables), the bankrupt group had Z-scores less than 1.10. The healthy non-bankrupt group scored above 2.60. Scores between 1.10 and 2.60 represent a gray area where bankruptcy could not be predicted.

Small-business managers using this measure should keep in mind that Altman's studies excluded corporations with total assets under $1-Million. Also, decision making based on Z-factors is biased toward short-term risk avoidance, and may not be entirely appropriate for companies needing to develop new products or new markets.[12] Changes in bankruptcy law might today allow firms to survive despite low Z-scores. Some believe that this model's original discriminant weights (6.56, 3.26, 6.72, and 1.05), while still able to discriminate, may have lost their ability to predict with a high degree of accuracy.[13] Such limitations should not deter a manager from making the computation if the firm's survival is in doubt.

Although Altman may not have intended that his predictor be used as a turnaround tool, it can be.[14] An appealing feature of the formula is that by changing *assets*, all but one of the ratios is modified. If a careful watch is kept on the Z-score and contingency plans are in place for increasing assets when needed, it is possible that bankruptcy might be averted for some companies in trouble. The model has also been suggested as a relatively simple method for evaluating credit applications.[15]

In calculating the Z-score using either the acronymic or symbolic equations below, don't overlook the correct order of execution for the computation steps: Multiplication, division, addition, subtraction. Operations within parentheses are performed first in the order just listed.

(verbal equation)

BANKRUPTCY MODEL =

$$6.56 \text{ X} \frac{\text{Working Capital}}{\text{Total Assets}} + 3.26 \text{ X} \frac{\text{Retained Earnings}}{\text{Total Assets}} + 6.72 \text{ X} \frac{\text{Net Profit Before Taxes} - \text{Interest Expense}}{\text{Total Assets}} + 1.05 \text{ X} \frac{\text{Stockholder Equity}}{\text{Total Liabilities}}$$

(acronymic equation)

BANKMODEL=6.56 ∗ (CURRASSET−CURRLIAB) / TOTASSET+3.26 ∗ RTDEARN / TOTASSET+
6.72 ∗ (NETPROFBEFTAX+INTEREXP) / TOTASSET+1.05 ∗ STOCKHOLDEQ / (CURRLIAB+LONGTERMLIAB)

(symbolic equation)

R48=6.56 ∗ (S5−S10) / S8+3.26 ∗ S13 / S8+6.72 ∗ (S29+S22) / S8+1.05 ∗ S14 / (S10+S11)

Notes — Chapter 4

1. Frank K. Reilly, *Investments* (Hinsdale, IL: Dryden Press, 1982), p. 224-227.

2. Ashby Bladen, "A Matter of Delicate Timing," *Forbes* (May 11, 1981), p. 330.

3. Jack Zwick, *A Handbook of Small Business Finance*, Small Business Management Series No. 15 (Washington, DC: Small Business Administration, 1975), p. 19.

4. John Downes and Jordan Elliot Goodman, *Barron's Finance & Investment Handbook* (Hauppauge, NY: Barron's Educational Series, 1990), p. 91.

5. Dun & Bradstreet, *Industry Norms and Key Business Ratios, Desk Top Edition, 1990-91* (Murray Hill, NJ: 1991), p v.

6. Richard Sanzo, *Ratio Analysis for Small Business*, Small Business Management Series No. 20 (Washington, DC: Small Business Administration, 1977), p. 59.

7. Downes and Goodman, p. 92.

8. Using Value Line's *VALUE/SCREEN II* investment software system and a database of 1,606 widely traded companies, a study by the author in 1991 found more than 6% of these companies to be entirely free of long-term debt.

9. Dun & Bradstreet, *Industry Norms and Key Business Ratios, Desk Top Edition, 1990-91*, p. v.

10. Harlan D. Platt, *Why Companies Fail* (Lexington, MA: Heath, 1985), p. 34-35. *See also*, Christopher Power, "Light in Dark Corners," *Forbes* (August 1, 1983), p. 133.

11. Edward I. Altman, *Corporate Financial Distress* (New York: Wiley, 1983) p. 117.

12. John T. King, "The ABC's of Z Factor," *INC.* (April, 1981), p. 12.

13. Gregory Mueller, *Financial Ratios as Predictors of Bankruptcy: A Multivariate Approach* (San Diego, CA: Thesis presented to the faculty of San Diego State University, 1975), p. 68.

14. Michael Ball, "Z Factor: Rescue by the Numbers," *INC.* (December, 1980), p. 45-48.

15. Barbara T. Killman, "More Practical Uses for Z Factor," *INC.* (February, 1981), p. 10.

16. For a critique of Z-Score, *See*, L. C. Gupta, *Financial Ratios for Monitoring Corporate Sickness* (New Delhi: Oxford University Press, 1983).

Chapter 5
Efficiency Ratios

Physicists define efficiency as the ratio of a machine's output to its input. The business metaphor substitutes profits for output and sales for input. Where the ideal machine produces output equal to its input (no friction losses), the ideal business produces profits equal to its sales (no product cost, expenses or taxes). In either case, efficiency is unity, or 100%. Ideal machines and ideal businesses, of course, do not exist. Some input is always lost in producing output. We speak of these ideal situations only to gain a better understanding of the meaning of efficiency.

In business, the managerial goal is to operate as efficiently as possible. This usually means keeping costs down. Expenses are measured (and then controlled) to insure that adequate profit remains after paying for all the activities required to produce those profits. Other measures of efficiency determine how well assets are utilized in producing profits.

Expenses are usually analyzed relative to sales, because when sales go up expenses go up to service those sales. One popular managerial goal is to maintain expenses at a more-or-less constant percentage of sales. Another goal is to protect profits — that is, reduce expenses appropriately whenever sales fall below expectations.

Any deviation from budget, past performance, or industry average in an expense ratio or asset-utilization ratio is a signal to management that something may be wrong. It suggests the need to find out why the deviation exists and to take appropriate action.

Although efficiency in business means (simplistically) getting things done at the lowest possible cost, there is an important caveat. Businesses are not machines. They are dynamic institutions involving people. This means that any time something is changed, there is risk of some unexpected and undesired result. Reducing service to customers, for example, is a well-known way to lower expenses. But what if the reduction in service results in lost customers and (ultimately) lower sales? Such an expense reduction can hardly be called efficient. And that is why business management is often described as an art. Who can know in advance and with certainty the exact impact on sales of any specific managerial decision?

This is not to suggest that the seeking of lower-cost ways to do things should be avoided. On the contrary, such activity is essential to the survival of most businesses. It does, however, point up the need to be knowledgeable, insightful, and even humble in the search. The 29 ratios described in this chapter dig beneath the surface to measure many of those things which, in total, account for the organization's efficiency.

49 TOTAL EXPENSE RATIO

Definition: Total expenses divided by net sales, multiplied by 100 to provide a percentage.

Sales are usually considered profitable if they result in a healthy premium to cost of goods sold. But that is only the first step to profitability (and often the easiest). Equally important is managerial success in controlling expenses.

One would like to believe that corporate spending decisions are based on hard facts and carefully-evolved strategies. Unfortunately, this is not always the case. It is no exaggeration to say that greed, habit, carelessness, incompetence, and ego gratification play important roles in business spending just as they do in personal spending. For this reason, well-managed companies usually prepare detailed plans which describe and quantify predicted expenses in each of many categories.

At the time these plans or budgets are made, managers usually have in mind a certain sales figure or range of sales expected for the coming year. It is in anticipation of this level of sales that the spending plans are made. Of course, if actual sales fall short of planned sales, spending levels must be adjusted if profit margins are to be maintained.

The numerator in the equations below is the sum of all items of operating expense, including interest. Cost of goods sold (sometimes considered an expense) is not included.

(verbal equation)

$$\text{TOTAL EXPENSE RATIO} = 100 \text{ X } \frac{\text{Total Expenses}}{\text{Net Sales}}$$

(acronymic equation)
$$\text{TOTEXPRATIO} = 100 * \text{TOTEXP} / \text{NETSALES}$$

(symbolic equation)
$$\text{R49} = 100 * \text{S28} / \text{S16}$$

50 EXPENSES TO GROSS PROFIT

Definition: Total expenses divided by gross profit, multiplied by 100 to provide a percentage.

Maintenance of desired profit levels has been cited as the reason for comparing expenses to realized sales. If sales deviate from predicted figures, management is challenged to modify expenses to keep the company's profits on track.

Comparing one company's success in controlling expenses to another's is virtually impossible if their gross profit percentages are different. Consider two firms: One is a wholesaler operating on a 22% margin with expenses equal to 16% of sales. The other, a retail store down the street, enjoys a 55% margin but spends 40% of sales on expenses. In terms of sales, the retailer's expenses are 2-1/2 times those of the wholesaler. But wait! If measured against revenue remaining after subtracting the cost of goods sold for each business, their expense levels are about the same (73%). Thus when comparing expense levels for firms with diverse margins, better understanding results when the expenses are measured against gross profit.

It is particularly important to monitor this ratio whenever prices are lowered to meet competition. Even if expenses relative to sales are maintained at a steady rate, they will rise relative to gross margin. The resulting falloff in profit might surprise a management dutifully maintaining expenses at a fixed proportion of sales.

A refinement of the ratio excludes marketing expense because higher margins in some lines are achieved only when large outlays are made for advertising and promotion.

The option of comparing to gross profit instead of sales should be considered for all of the line-item expense ratios which follow. This is particularly important when comparisons are made between different industries or lines of business.

(verbal equation)

$$\text{EXPENSES TO GROSS PROFIT} = 100 \times \frac{\text{Total Expenses}}{\text{Gross Profit}}$$

(acronymic equation)

$$\text{EXPGROSSPROF} = 100 * \text{TOTEXP} / \text{GROSSPROF}$$

(symbolic equation)

$$\text{R50} = 100 * \text{S28} / \text{S18}$$

51 EMPLOYEE COMPENSATION RATIO

Definition: Wages expense divided by net sales, multiplied by 100 to provide a percentage.

This is the first and possibly most important of the ratios that compare individual line items of expense to sales. It is important because employee compensation is the largest single category of expense for many companies. It follows that if profits are to be maintained at desired levels relative to sales, employee compensation needs to be controlled proportionately. This ratio measures that relationship.

For many reasons, employee compensation is one of the most difficult expenses to control. Companies often solve problems by hiring more workers — or better-qualified workers. This may be the right thing to do. But one immediate result is an increase in expenses relative to sales. This may exacerbate the original problem (if related to insufficient profits), or create such a problem.

Wages are accompanied by ancillary expenses which usually cannot be decoupled (group and unemployment insurance, employment taxes, personnel services, retirement plans, and record keeping). In addition, payroll is a "ratchet-up" expense. That is, managers find it easier to increase wages (raises or new hires) than to decrease wages (salary reductions or layoffs). This comes not from an inability to make objective determinations about needed reductions in staff or reductions in pay, but from the fact that wages equate to people. The layoff of loyal employees (including close associates and friends) does not come as easy to a manager as popular literature suggests. It is the human aspect of this expense category that makes it so difficult to control.

The ratio itself offers no solutions to these problems. It provides only a means for measuring how well management is coping with them. Once it is decided what level of wages is best for a business, the goal is to maintain the ratio more-or-less at that value despite changes in sales. In the ideal situation, a long-term graph of this ratio slopes gently downward as division of labor and learning-curve rewards are realized.

(verbal equation)

$$\text{EMPLOYEE COMPENSATION RATIO} = 100 \times \frac{\text{Wages Expense}}{\text{Net Sales}}$$

(acronymic equation)

$$\text{EMPCOMPRATIO} = 100 * \text{WAGEEXP} / \text{NETSALES}$$

(symbolic equation)

$$\text{R51} = 100 * \text{S19} / \text{S16}$$

52 MARKETING EXPENSE RATIO

Definition: Marketing/selling expense divided by net sales, multiplied by 100 to provide a percentage.

It's been said that marketing is everything done in the organization that leads to the acquiring, servicing, or retaining of customers. Some include the product itself in this definition, as well as its price. Ratio analysts and accountants, however, are more likely to view marketing relative to the cost of the various activities: things like salaries and commissions for salespeople, advertising, publicity, trade shows, catalogs and literature.

This ratio measures what portion of sales the company spends to promote the sale of its goods or services. Because marketing overtures take time to work out (what is spent this year may not affect sales until next year), the ratio does not satisfactorily measure the effectiveness of marketing in the short run. There are better ways to do that. The measure is valuable as a budgeting tool. Firms typically reinvest a certain percentage of sales in their marketing programs, and monitor this ratio as a way of controlling those expenditures.

Low marketing ratios which persist over time may indicate highly efficient marketing programs, or businesses with less need to rely on overt marketing activities to generate sales. High ratios, on the other hand, may signal a less responsive market, lack of success in marketing activities, or management's desire to emphasize sales growth over profitability.

This is a good example of those ratios for which there is no right or wrong value. When analyzing a company's chart, remember that higher values are not necessarily better than lower values. Marketing expense is a dynamic cost insofar as its effect on profits is concerned. In the short run, higher marketing expense reduces profit. But if the programs result in an increase in sales, the long-term result may be an increase in profits. The managerial challenge is to find (often by trial and error) the optimum level of marketing expenditure which works best in the long run.

(verbal equation)

$$\text{MARKETING EXPENSE RATIO} = 100 \times \frac{\text{Marketing/Selling Expense}}{\text{Net Sales}}$$

(acronymic equation)

$$\text{MARKEXPRATIO} = 100 * \text{MARKEXP} / \text{NETSALES}$$

(symbolic equation)

$$R52 = 100 * S20 / S16$$

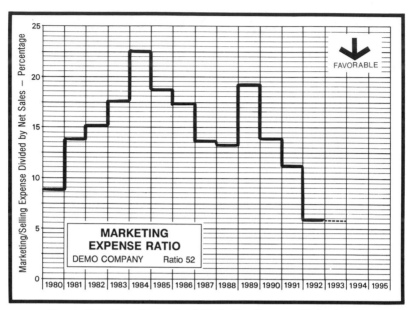

Figure 5-1. Sample graph of *Marketing Expense Ratio* shows portion of sales spent to create and maintain those sales.

53 RENT EXPENSE RATIO

Definition: Rent expense divided by net sales, multiplied by 100 to provide a percentage.

This ratio shows how economically space is matched to production. It is an important line-item ratio because rent (or its equivalent) is a significant expense for most businesses. Note that this ratio calculates cost of space relative to sales. It does not measure how well the space is used from an architectural point of view. For example, a firm leasing in a rural area might report a rent expense ratio that is a small fraction of the one reported by a similar firm operating in the city. At the same time, the city operation might be making better use of its space. Architectural efficiency in the use of space is better measured against area than cost.

If the firm owns its facilities, the numerator may represent occupancy cost. Depreciation of buildings, real estate taxes, and possibly an imputed leasehold value for the raw land is substituted for rent. Another variation adds utilities, maintenance, and insurance — to measure total occupancy cost relative to sales.

Ideally, the long-term graph of this ratio slopes gently downward if the business is growing. This results from more efficient use of the facilities and the rewards of leasing in larger, more economic units. For small businesses, or businesses that are not growing, the opposite may be true. Inflation, environmental concerns, and government restrictions may raise the rental cost of improved real estate faster than a company's sales can grow.

(verbal equation)

$$\textbf{RENT EXPENSE RATIO} = 100 \ X \ \frac{\text{Rent Expense}}{\text{Net Sales}}$$

(acronymic equation)
$$\textbf{RENTEXPRATIO} = 100 * RENTEXP / NETSALES$$

(symbolic equation)
$$\textbf{R53} = 100 * S21 / S16$$

54 INTEREST EXPENSE RATIO

Definition: Interest expense divided by net sales, multiplied by 100 to provide a percentage.

Some companies depend heavily on borrowed money to finance long-term growth and even daily operations. Others rely more on equity capital and cash flow from profits. Whichever the case may be, this ratio studies the interest cost of borrowing relative to the size of the company (measured by sales).

If a firm depends primarily on equity capitalization, comparing interest expense to sales may not be an important exercise. But where borrowing is significant and leverage high, management should give this ratio close scrutiny on a regular basis.

An interesting way to think about this ratio is as an alternative to profits. If management borrows and incurs interest expense equal to 3% of sales, for example, it means that before-tax profit (as a percentage of sales) would have been greater by three percentage points if management had not borrowed. Many companies operate without debt, relying instead on a larger equity base and profits (which are enhanced by not borrowing) to provide capital.

(verbal equation)

$$\text{INTEREST EXPENSE RATIO} = 100 \times \frac{\text{Interest Expense}}{\text{Net Sales}}$$

(acronymic equation)
$$\text{INTEREXPRATIO} = 100 * \text{INTEREXP} / \text{NETSALES}$$

(symbolic equation)
$$R54 = 100 * S22 / S16$$

55 INSURANCE EXPENSE RATIO

Definition: Insurance expense divided by net sales, multiplied by 100 to provide a percentage.

This ratio measures management's success in keeping insurance costs reasonably in line with sales. It is also an indirect indicator of the extent to which the business assumes responsibility for its own risks through self-insurance.

There was a time when insurance expense for most businesses was a relatively constant percentage of sales. In recent years, however, risks and costs have spiraled upward. Much of this originates in worsening unsolved problems in the society, bigger government, a propensity to litigate, and negative attitudes toward business.

When increases in relative insurance cost become significant, an overall review of the firm's protection program is needed. Such a review starts with recognizing the important risks. Management then decides what portion of these risks can be assumed by the company. Finally, proposals from a number of suppliers are obtained for those remaining risks which the company is unwilling to assume. It should be kept in mind that no amount of insurance covers all risks. It always comes down to balancing risks against the cost of protection, and operating the business intelligently to reduce exposure.

Employee group insurance is not included in the numerator. It is best assigned to an employee compensation account and monitored separately. Only insurance that protects the company against the risks of being in business (property, casualty, liability) should be included in the insurance expense account.

If a company does decide to assume more of its own risks (through self-insurance), this ratio will show the result as a lowering of insurance cost relative to sales.

(verbal equation)

INSURANCE EXPENSE RATIO $= 100 \times \dfrac{\text{Insurance Expense}}{\text{Net Sales}}$

(acronymic equation)

INSUREXPRATIO$=100*$INSUREXP$/$NETSALES

(symbolic equation)

R55$=100*S23/S16$

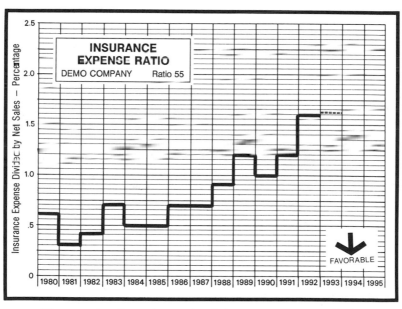

Figure 5-2. Example graph of *Insurance Expense Ratio* suggests managerial difficulty controlling costs. Another explanation is increasing risk associated with societal changes (crime, anti-business attitudes, and a propensity to litigate).

56 DEPRECIATION EXPENSE RATIO

Definition: Depreciation expense divided by net sales, multiplied by 100 to provide a percentage.

Depreciation is the accounting function that spreads the cost of equipment or a facility (less salvage) over its expected useful life. Investments in such assets need to be written off over the period of their use because (in the words of a wise professor), "All machinery is on an irresistible march to the junk heap, and its progress, while it may be delayed, cannot be prevented by repairs."[1]

Actual wear and tear (or change in market value) is not involved, nor does the act of depreciating an asset use up any cash. For these reasons, *controlling* depreciation to protect profits means only to protect *reported* profits. An examination of the depreciation ratio reveals more about a company's depreciation policies than its success in controlling expenses.

Myriads of depreciation methods exist (straight-line, declining balance, sum-of-years'-digits, unit-of-output, etc.). Each has its origins in the needs of particular industries or the ever-changing tax codes. The historic aim of realistically allocating cost to useful life is today probably less important than the management of earnings and income taxes.

As mentioned previously, the depreciation figure a company shows on its tax returns is likely to differ from the one it reports to shareholders. The reason for this is that the goal in tax accounting is to minimize taxes. The goal in shareholder reporting is either to minimize depreciation expense (make profits look good), or provide realistic write-offs without consideration of their impact on reported earnings. The choice is made by management. Differences between tax computations for depreciation and shareholder (per books) computations are sometimes revealed in footnotes to accounting reports.

(verbal equation)

$$\text{DEPRECIATION EXPENSE RATIO} \ = \ 100 \ X \ \frac{\text{Depreciation Expense}}{\text{Net Sales}}$$

(acronymic equation)
DEPREXPRATIO$=100*$DEPREXP$/$NETSALES

(symbolic equation)
R56$=100*$S24$/$S16

57 BAD DEBTS EXPENSE RATIO

Definition: Bad debts expense divided by net sales, multiplied by 100 to provide a percentage.

Whereas the *EMPLOYEE COMPENSATION RATIO (51)* accurately reflects management's success in controlling expenses and the *DEPRECIATION EXPENSE RATIO (56)* does not, this ratio lies somewhere between. In the sense that decisions to write off questionable accounts come as often from management policy as from transaction events, the ratio is similar to the depreciation ratio. But in the sense that write-offs reflect the company's ability to profitably choose to whom and to what extent credit is extended, the ratio does measure control of an important expense. Unfortunately, it is difficult for the reviewer to know which is the case.

Companies practicing conservative accounting write off questionable accounts as soon as possible. Although this reduces reported earnings, it also reduces taxes. Additionally (and perhaps more important), management is reminded of the risks involved in extending credit too liberally. Writing off an account does not mean that attempts to collect it cease. There is probably no such thing as too early a write-off of a questionable account.

A high value for the ratio can reflect negatively on the company's credit-extension policies, but it also suggests honest accounting. If the ratio is very low, the reviewer should ask for an aging schedule. Through intention or neglect, the company may have avoided writing off accounts unlikely to be collected. Because bad debt ratios are based on averages, they may mask the true composition of the receivables. Aging schedules, on the other hand, break the accounts down according to how many days they are past due (under 30, 31-60, 61-90, over 90, and so forth). This simplifies the collection effort by continuously identifying which accounts are problems.

(verbal equation)

$$\text{BAD DEBTS EXPENSE RATIO} = 100 \times \frac{\text{Bad Debts Expense}}{\text{Net Sales}}$$

(acronymic equation)

$$\text{BADBEBTEXPRATIO} = 100 * \text{BADDEBTEXP} / \text{NETSALES}$$

(symbolic equation)

$$\text{R57} = 100 * \text{S25} / \text{S16}$$

58 UTILITIES EXPENSE RATIO

Definition: Utilities expense divided by net sales, multiplied by 100 to provide a percentage.

Utilities expense is broadly defined as the cost of services required to support the physical plant. Typical components are electricity, gas, water, security, garbage collection, and fumigation. Small businesses sometimes include telephone expense in this category. Utilities expense differs from other types of overhead in that the services are provided by outside organizations — usually public utilities.

This is another category of expense that is difficult to control. Although energy use and telephone service may be cut back to some degree in response to managerial review, most of the expenses in this category are outside of the company's control. This is because rates are typically set by governmental commissions, and also because some minimum level of service is usually required, even if the plant is not functioning.

Manufacturing companies using large amounts of energy to create a finished product do not classify fuel costs as overhead. For these firms, energy is an integral component of the cost of goods sold. Changes in price between different fuel sources (natural gas, electricity, oil) often dictate major changes in manufacturing equipment and methods.

A good time to think about energy conservation is when a facility is constructed. Up-front dollars invested in insulation and other architectural amenities which reduce energy use should be more than repaid over the long term in a reduced value for this ratio. Even when leasing, inquiries should be made about energy efficiency. An apparently lower rent for a facility might not be a bargain if more energy is required to keep it warm in winter and cool in summer.

(verbal equation)

$$\textbf{UTILITIES EXPENSE RATIO} = 100 \ X \ \frac{\text{Utilities Expense}}{\text{Net Sales}}$$

(acronymic equation)
UTILEXPRATIO=100∗UTILEXP/NETSALES

(symbolic equation)
R58=100∗S26/S16

59 DESIGNATED EXPENSE RATIO

Definition: Any designated line item of expense divided by net sales, multiplied by 100 to provide a percentage.

This is an unspecified ratio included only to demonstrate that any expense item on the income statement may be compared to sales. As with the other expense ratios, the purpose of making the comparison is to aid in the control of that expense (relative to sales) in order to protect profits.

Every business is unique. Therefore, the importance of a particular expense varies. A company relying on telephone marketing, for example, might keep a close watch on that expense relative to the results it produces (sales). Similarly, a firm serving customers located in diverse regions of the world could choose to monitor travel cost relative to sales.

Other examples of possible designated expense line-items are automobile, gifts and entertainment, legal and professional, health insurance, supplies, contract labor, personal selling, postage, shipping and delivery. Whatever the nature of the expense, management has the opportunity to include it in its list of accounts, break it out on the income statement, and create a ratio comparing it to net sales.

Although line-item ratios normally relate to expenses (costs of doing business), they are also used to report on components of cost of goods sold. In manufacturing, it is common practice to break out the many cost components of the finished product — purchased goods, raw materials, fuel, factory labor, factory overhead, and so forth.

(verbal equation)

DESIGNATED EXPENSE RATIO $= 100$ X $\dfrac{\text{Designated Line Item of Expense}}{\text{Net Sales}}$

(acronymic equation)
DESIGEXPRATIO $= 100 * \text{DESIGEXP} / \text{NETSALES}$

(symbolic equation)
R59 $= 100 * S27 / S16$

60 REMAINING EXPENSE RATIO

Definition: Remaining expenses divided by net sales, multiplied by 100 to provide a percentage.

This ratio captures all of the other expenses not considered sufficiently significant to warrant an individual comparison to sales. In this book, expense ratios for wages, marketing, rent, interest, insurance, depreciation, bad debts, and utilities are defined. Allowance has also been made for designated expense line items important to individual businesses. Any number of these individual items may be identified and measured, depending on company needs. Everything left over is called remaining expense.

Because the components of remaining expense vary from company to company, cross-firm relating of the ratio should not be attempted. But for any one business, comparisons to prior years or to a budget reveal whether or not these miscellaneous expenses are adequately controlled relative to sales.

Expenses that typically find their way into this category are those mentioned in the previous ratio. If they are important to a company, they are broken out separately. If not, they are included here. Particularly in small businesses, such a miscellaneous category takes care of things like publications, dues, memberships, and small tools.

In the equations below, remaining expense is found by subtracting all of the individually-studied expenses from total expenses. This approach is somewhat cumbersome, but it does eliminate the need for another input statistic. An alternate method assigns remaining expense its own input number.[2]

(verbal equation)

$$\text{REMAINING EXPENSE RATIO} = 100 \times \frac{\text{Remaining Expense}}{\text{Net Sales}}$$

(acronymic equation)

$$\text{REMEXPRATIO} = 100 * (\text{TOTEXP} - \text{WAGEEXP} - \text{MARKEXP} - \text{RENTEXP} - \text{INTEREXP} - \text{INSUREXP} - \text{DEPREXP} - \text{BADDEBTEXP} - \text{UTILEXP} - \text{DESIGFXP}) / \text{NETSALES}$$

(symbolic equation)

$$\text{R60} = 100 * (S28 - S19 - S20 - S21 - S22 - S23 - S24 - S25 - S26 - S27) / S16$$

61 EXPENSE GROWTH

Definition: The difference between this year's total expenses and last year's total expenses, divided by last year's total expenses, multiplied by 100 to provide a percentage.

Profitability begins with pricing. If selling prices are adequate relative to buying prices, the result is a healthy gross margin. But this is convertible to the bottom line only if expenses are adequately controlled. Comparing individual expenses to sales is one way they are monitored. Another way is to compare percentage changes in total expenses to percentage changes in sales.

This growth statistic is therefore most useful when viewed side-by-side with *GROWTH IN NET SALES (1)* for the same period. If sales have increased, it's likely that expenses have also increased (to support those sales). The question is whether they increased at a faster or slower rate than did sales. If *faster*, then profit growth is restricted relative to sales. If *slower*, then profits have received a leveraged boost. On the other hand, if sales decrease in the period, expenses must decrease at least proportionately if profit margins are to be maintained.

The budget of a well-managed company usually specifies a certain rate of growth for expenses. To be viable, the number chosen must take anticipated sales into account. Ideally, expenses should grow at about the same rate (or slightly slower) than sales.

Exceptions apply when expenses are constricted to increase profitability, or when they are increased without regard to anticipated sales in order to achieve non-financial goals. It is common for fast-growing companies to increase marketing or research expenditures faster than sales are increasing. Such "pump priming" investments in the company's future are warranted if they result in a sufficiently-increased level of sales in future periods.

(verbal equation)

$$\textbf{EXPENSE GROWTH} = 100 \times \frac{\text{Total Expenses} - \text{Total Expenses Last Year}}{\text{Total Expenses Last Year}}$$

(acronymic equation)

$$\textbf{EXPGROW} = 100 * (\text{TOTEXP} - \text{TOTEXPLASTYEAR}) / \text{TOTEXPLASTYEAR}$$

(symbolic equation)

$$\textbf{R61} = 100 * (S28 - S28LY) / S28LY$$

62 BUDGET COMPLIANCE (EXPENSES)

Definition: Actual total expenses divided by budgeted total expenses, multiplied by 100 to provide a percentage.

Three budget compliance ratios are described in this book — sales, profits, and expenses. Each is intended to measure success or lack of it in one aspect of company planning.

This ratio keeps track of a management's proficiency in living up to its own *spending* plans. If thoughtful advance planning determined that certain expense levels would be adequate in a forthcoming period, and now they are not, then it is appropriate for someone to inquire into the reasons. Although contingencies or unexpected bursts of sales may make exceeding an expense budget necessary and prudent in occasional years, a good profit-protecting goal is to maintain this ratio between 90 and 100%.

Something is wrong if the ratio consistently exceeds 100%. Planners may be overly optimistic, or they may intentionally be submitting too-low numbers to avert inquiries. On the other hand, if the ratio is consistently *low*, it probably means that those preparing the budgets are too cautious. They may be budgeting expenses unrealistically high as a form of self-protection.

The question of whether or not budgets should limit management's right to act is an eternal one. The liberal view says that the budget plan is a document from the past — new information and today's requirements should allow for appropriate deviations. The contrary view stresses the hazards of short-range thinking, recognizing how easily human emotions can disrupt the execution of carefully thought-out plans. An intelligent resolution to this dilemma is to provide for interim-period budget reviews. There is nothing wrong with revising a budget if the same amount of diligence and careful consideration is given to the changes as was given to the original plan.

(verbal equation)

$$\text{BUDGET COMPLIANCE (EXPENSES)} = 100 \times \frac{\text{Total Expenses}}{\text{Budgeted Total Expenses}}$$

(symbolic equation)

$$\text{BUDGCMPLEXP} = 100 * \text{TOTEXP} / \text{BUDGTOTEXP}$$

(symbolic equation)

$$\text{R62} = 100 * \text{S28} / \text{S42}$$

63 RENT TO SPACE

Definition: Rent expense divided by area (in square feet) of rented floor space.

Rent, the cost of controlling real property to carry out the business function, is a significant expense for most businesses. When this cost is expressed relative to the space occupied, comparisons between firms and other time periods are possible.

Commercial and industrial rents are usually quoted this way — dollars per square foot. When making comparisons, however, it is important to know exactly what is provided. Where the rent for a small office might include utilities and even janitorial service, larger spaces are usually priced on a net basis, free even of real estate taxes. This means that the lessee pays considerably more than the quoted net rate. Rents are sometimes tied to price indices such as the CPI, and may also be contingent on a sharing of revenues derived from the business function.

In addition to asking what is included, prospective tenants should look carefully at other less-obvious features of the property. Is the building well located to serve customers? Is it well insulated? Is the zoning appropriate? What about security, parking, and public transportation?

This rent ratio is consulted by managers when the time comes to lease additional space or negotiate leases. It is a measure of cost efficiency but not architectural efficiency. Recently-built properties (and properties located in urban areas) are typically more costly to rent than older properties or properties located in rural areas. Rents in urban areas are higher because land costs and taxes are higher. Newly built properties usually cost more to rent because landlords' costs are higher (inflation).

If a company owns its business property, a similar ratio may be created using applicable components of depreciation, insurance, real estate taxes, and imputed land-rental cost in the numerator.

(verbal equation)

$$\textbf{RENT TO SPACE} \ = \ \frac{\text{Rent Expense}}{\text{Floor Space}}$$

(acronymic equation)

RENTSPACE = RENTEXP / SPACE

(symbolic equation)

R63 = S21 / S48

64 TURNOVER OF ASSETS

Definition: Net sales divided by total assets.

This business ratio (sometimes called investment turnover) measures how many times the company's assets are used in the year to create and process sales. Like other turnover ratios, it is an indicator of efficiency and managerial performance.

In making comparisons to similar businesses or other time periods, low ratios indicate insufficient sales or the need to reduce unproductive assets. High ratios point to an ability to create and process sales at low cost. A long-term upward trend in the ratio demonstrates management's success in developing its markets and in reaping the rewards of division of labor. A downward trend signals deteriorating efficiency, or accumulation of assets not contributing to current production or an increase in revenues.

If management undertakes a deliberate expansion of sales (new products, entry into virgin territories, or an aggressive advertising campaign), the reciprocal of this ratio may prove useful in estimating the amount of additional capital that is required. Based solely on the history of the particular business and its market, the inverted ratio (assets to sales) provides management with a realistic number on which to base capital needs.

A variation of the ratio, fixed assets turnover, compares net sales to fixed assets instead of total assets. The difference could be important if a company has substantial intangibles or current assets and the purpose for computing the ratio is to learn more about how efficiently the company uses its plant capacity.

(verbal equation)

$$\textbf{TURNOVER OF ASSETS} \ = \ \frac{\text{Net Sales}}{\text{Total Assets}}$$

(acronymic equation)

TURNASSET – NETSALES / TOTASSET

(symbolic equation)

R64 = S16 / S8

65 CASH SALES MIX

Definition: Cash sales divided by net sales, multiplied by 100 to provide a percentage.

Although this ratio uses "sales" in its title and equations, it is not a sales ratio.   Rather, it is a money management and marketing tool measuring the percentage of revenues paid in full at the time of sale.

There was a time when certain lines of business sold mostly on credit and certain other lines sold for cash. The nature and timing of payments was linked to the type of business. This is less true today for many reasons.   Distinctions between wholesale and retail have blurred. Geographical territories have all but disappeared. Sellers demand cash from unknown buyers, and buyers willingly pay in advance when price or product are superior.   Another reason is the credit card.   Originally thought of as a consumer buying tool, "plastic" has found its way into routine business transactions. And despite the word credit, sales paid by card are (from the seller's point of view) cash sales. This is true because payment is obtainable shortly after the sale from a merchant bank (less a small discount, of course).

Advantages to the seller in obtaining cash or a credit-card voucher at time of sale are many. Proceeds may be immediately reinvested in new merchandise.   Working capital is no longer tied up in unproductive receivables. Credit risk is largely eliminated.

Although selling on credit will always be appropriate for large businesses and in certain lines of small business, managers not so limited can do many things to increase the cash-up-front portion of total sales. The acceptability of payment by credit card can be advertised. Cash-in-advance discounts can be offered. Special promotions can be tied to a requirement that all purchases by paid in advance.

If a separate record of cash sales is not maintained, the figure can be found by subtracting credit sales from net sales.

(verbal equation)

$$\textbf{CASH SALES MIX} \; = \; 100 \; \text{X} \; \frac{\text{Cash Sales}}{\text{Net Sales}}$$

(acronymic equation)

$$\textbf{CASHSALESMIX} = 100 * (\text{NETSALES} - \text{CREDSALES}) / \text{NETSALES}$$

(symbolic equation)

$$\textbf{R65} = 100 * (S16 - S39) / S16$$

66 COLLECTION PERIOD

Definition: Accounts receivable divided by average daily credit sales.

This ratio (sometimes called "days sales outstanding," or DSO) is the traditional measure of success in skillfully offering credit and collecting open accounts. The longer the DSO, the more attention management needs to pay to its accounts receivable and policies on extension of credit. The existence of so many books, seminars, and university courses on collections attests to its importance. In virtually all businesses, sales go up as credit-extension standards go down. This often tempts managers to lower the quality of receivables to meet sales goals.

The ratio looks at the collection period at one point in time — when accounts receivable are measured. If the figure for receivables is not representative of the year as a whole (or if the company's sales are growing or contracting), the DSO will vary significantly even if actual collection patterns are unchanged.[3]

Probably the best way to monitor the quality of receivables is to age them — set them out in columns according to how long they are outstanding. When the ratio of "past 90 days" to "under 30 days" rises, a reasonable conclusion is that the quality of receivables has declined.

A collection period more than 30 days greater than the company's usual selling terms is the traditional warning figure. Thus, for a firm selling "net 30 days," a value less than 60 indicates normal collections.[4] Some, however, consider the collection period excessive if it exceeds normal selling terms by even 10 to 15 days.[5] When money is tight and debtors are slowing their payments, the collection period is likely to increase, regardless of any action management takes to improve things.

The denominator, average daily credit sales, is found by dividing the year's credit sales by 365. Variations divide credit sales by 360 (12 uniform months of 30 days each) and sometimes 260 (52 uniform weeks of 5 working days each). Averaging periods of less than a year are often used in an attempt to obtain greater accuracy. This ratio is expressed in *days* and not as a percentage.

(verbal equation)

$$\text{COLLECTION PERIOD} = \frac{\text{Accounts Receivable}}{\text{Average Daily Credit Sales}}$$

(acronymic equation)

$$\text{COLLPRD} = \text{ACCREC} / (\text{CREDSALES} / 365)$$

(symbolic equation)

$$\text{R66} = \text{S3} / (\text{S39} / 365)$$

67 PAYMENT PERIOD

Definition: Accounts payable divided by average daily purchases.

This measure is similar to the one relating to collections. But instead of showing how long customers take to pay their bills, it shows how long the company takes to pay its own. The managerial trade-off in this ratio is between preservation of operating cash and the firm's credit reputation.

If supplier terms are 30 days and the payment period is 15 or 20 days, payments are being made too soon. Some may laugh and say that this would never happen. But it does, particularly if a company's cash is ample and its bookkeeper a zealous worker. The obvious answer is to slow payments a bit and put some of this cash to work, perhaps in an interest-paying account.

In the opposite situation, when the payment period is 60 days or more, the firm is probably building a reputation as a "slow pay" and a credit problem. Bending payment rules may work in the short run, but over time the company suffers in ways that defy measurement.

Credit experts recommend being forthright with suppliers when there is a need to slow payments. Explaining why there is a problem and making a partial payment is likely to be more favorably received than silence. As long as money keeps coming in, most suppliers continue to ship.

Average daily purchases are found by dividing annual purchases by 365. As with the previous ratio, some reviewers divide by 260 (annual working days) or use much shorter averaging periods to improve accuracy. This measure is also expressed in days and not as a percentage.

(verbal equation)

$$\text{PAYMENT PERIOD} = \frac{\text{Accounts Payable}}{\text{Average Daily Purchases}}$$

(acronymic equation)

$$\text{PMTPRD} = \text{ACCPAY} / (\text{PURCH} / 365)$$

(symbolic equation)

$$R67 = S9 / (S17 / 365)$$

68 EXPENSE CONTROL RATIO

Definition: Percentage change in net sales reduced by percentage change in total expenses.

The relationship shows the number of percentage points sales have changed during the year in excess of the number expenses have changed. A positive number (healthy) means that sales grew faster than expenses. A negative number (usually unhealthy) means the opposite. The ratio is useful to fast-growing companies. Management's cost-control goal is to keep the value of the ratio at or above zero.

Because there may be good reasons for increasing expenses faster than sales in certain years, a running average of the ratio often provides the best insight into what is happening. But in the absence of special circumstances, a negative number usually signals falling profitability.

The ratio is calculated simply by subtracting *EXPENSE GROWTH (61)* from *SALES GROWTH (1)* — both are percentages. The ratio also works for companies with flat or declining sales. If profit rates are to be maintained, expenses must also be held flat, or forced to decline at the same rate as sales.

(verbal equation)

EXPENSE CONTROL RATIO = SALES GROWTH − EXPENSE GROWTH

(acronymic equation)

EXPCNTLRATIO = SALESGROW − EXPGROW

(symbolic equation)

R68 = R1 − R61

69 INVENTORY TURNOVER

Definition: Cost of goods sold divided by average inventory.

Because this ratio is based on averages, it does not literally measure number of times goods are purchased and sold in a year. Rather, it is a popular indicator of operating efficiency, appraising how well management controls capital committed to inventory. An increasing inventory may be a healthy concomitant to growing sales, or an accumulation of goods resulting from reduced sales and inefficient purchasing. This "times" turnover ratio helps reveal which is the case.

Firms with high gross profit usually have lower inventory turnover, and vice-versa. The ratio for a retail jewelry store might be less than three, where the ratio for a nearby discount store could be greater than 15.

Net sales are sometimes used in the numerator instead of cost of goods sold. It doesn't matter very much which way turnover is measured if it's done consistently. When comparing one business to another, net sales may be the better yardstick because cost of goods sold varies considerably between firms.

Cost of goods sold is found by subtracting gross profit from net sales. Average inventory is determined by adding opening and closing figures and dividing by two, or (for greater accuracy) by averaging a series of more-frequent inventory reports.

(verbal equation)

$$\textbf{INVENTORY TURNOVER} = \frac{\text{Cost of Goods Sold}}{\text{Average Inventory}}$$

(acronymic equation)

$$\textbf{INVENTURN} = (\text{NETSALES} - \text{GROSSPROF})/((\text{INVEN} + \text{INVENLASTYEAR})/2)$$

(symbolic equation)

$$\textbf{R69} = (\text{S16} - \text{S18})/((\text{S4} + \text{S4LY})/2)$$

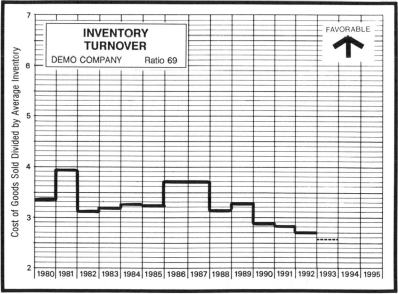

Figure 5-3. *Inventory Turnover* sample graph shows how well management controls the capital it has committed to inventory.

70 INVENTORY IN DAYS SALES

Definition: Inventory divided by average daily sales.

What does it mean to a manager to read a report showing that the business has $563,000 in inventory? Not much if sales are fluctuating. Inventory must be *compared* to something. By converting the inventory value to the theoretical number of days it meets sales needs, management is provided a measure that is understandable in an environment of changing sales.

An increase means that purchasing has taken place at a faster rate than sales, or that sales have declined and inventories have not contracted proportionately. A decrease means just the opposite — that purchasing has not kept up with sales. In the ideal situation the ratio is a constant. This is true even for a growing business. If management has means in place to reliably monitor and carry out the purchasing function, then on average, inventories measured in days sales need not vary much.

The ratio is enhanced if aged and obsolete inventory is systematically written off. It's true that write-offs increase cost of goods sold and reduce before-tax profits. But lower before-tax profits also reduce income taxes, and that is desirable. The write-off of unproductive inventory does not mean that the goods must be thrown out.   Small business owners sometimes miss this point, preferring to keep inventory values high so reported profits will be high (or perhaps hoping that a potential buyer of the business will be persuaded to pay more for it).

Average daily sales are typically calculated by dividing annual net sales by 365. Because this is a good ratio to monitor more frequently than once a year, some managers base the ratio on sales for the most recent month or quarter, dividing those figures by 30 or 91 to provide average daily sales.

This measure is expressed in days and not as a percentage.

(verbal equation)

$$\text{INVENTORY IN DAYS SALES} = \frac{\text{Inventory}}{\text{Average Daily Sales}}$$

(acronymic equation)
$$\text{INVENDAYSALES} = \text{INVEN} / (\text{NETSALES} / 365)$$

(symbolic equation)
$$\text{R70} = \text{S4} / (\text{S16} / 365)$$

71 INCOME TAX RATE

Definition: Income taxes divided by net profit before taxes, multiplied by 100 to provide a percentage.

As the saying goes, "The only things certain in life are death and taxes." The statement may be true, but it betrays a cultural complacency inappropriate to the challenge of business. There are always things that can be done to legally reduce taxes.

This simple ratio tells what percent of net profit is taken as income tax by government (federal, state, city). In 1992 the federal rate for corporations was 34%, subject to complex adjustments and credits. Income taxation is taken for granted in the United States, but because it penalizes success many doubt it is the best system. Inefficient, unprofitable companies pay nothing and are, in effect, subsidized by government. Some believe that all taxes on corporate income reduce productivity and competitiveness (because they are passed along as higher prices).

Advocates of a value-added system (where the tax is levied differentially at each stage of the manufacturing and distribution cycle) argue that it not only rewards efficiency, but each player (winner or loser) pays for a fair share of government services and the nation's social needs. Business tax rates and policies are, of course, politically determined.

The primary purpose for calculating the ratio is to make sure it receives the attention of the company's owners and managers. The higher the rate, the more likely something can be done to reduce it. Legal reduction of taxes is possible using a practice called *earnings management*. The idea is to find ways (unrelated to daily operations) to reduce short-term reported profits. Possibilities include accelerating depreciation rates, aggressively writing off doubtful accounts and inventory, transferring income to future accounting periods, and maximizing productive expenses in the current period.[6] A good tax accountant should have many ideas, and knows what is allowed by law.

If the value for income taxes paid (or allowed for) is not available to the reviewer, the figure is found by subtracting net profit after taxes from net profit before taxes.

(verbal equation)

$$\text{INCOME TAX RATE} = 100 \ X \ \frac{\text{Income Taxes}}{\text{Net Profit Before Taxes}}$$

(acronymic equation)

$$\text{INCTAXRATE} = 100 * (\text{NETPROFBEFTAX} - \text{NETPROFAFTTAX}) / \text{NETPROFBEFTAX}$$

(symbolic equation)

$$\text{R71} = 100 * (\text{S29} - \text{S30}) / \text{S29}$$

72 BACK ORDER RATIO

Definition: Value of back orders divided by average monthly sales, multiplied by 100 to provide a percentage.

This ratio keeps track of business "in the house" that has not been fulfilled. An increase might point to the need for more personnel in production or shipping, for better management of inventory, or for more effort in expediting deliveries from suppliers.

The back order ratio is an important measure of how well the company treats its customers. As the ratio grows, customers are likely to be less satisfied. At the same time, internal efficiency falls because of the need for multiple shipments, duplicated paperwork, and time spent responding to expediting requests. Back orders tend to go up when marketing efforts are increased or in an economic upturn, and go down when marketing is contracted or the economy cools. Unfortunately, it is just when the back order ratio is signalling trouble (good times) that management may fail to examine the number.

Back orders (the numerator) are valued at selling prices to customers. Whether presented as a year end or monthly statistic, by convention the denominator in the ratio is one month's average sales.

(verbal equation)

$$\text{BACK ORDER RATIO} = \frac{\text{Back Orders}}{\text{Average Monthly Sales}}$$

(acronymic equation)
$$\text{BACKORDRATIO} = 100 * \text{BACKORD} / (\text{NETSALES} / 12)$$

(symbolic equation)
$$R72 = 100 * S44 / (S16 / 12)$$

73 EMPLOYEE TURNOVER

Definition: Number of annual terminations divided by average number of employees, multiplied by 100 to provide a percentage.

An important cost for most businesses is that incurred in training its employees. Whether through formal programs or on-the-job experience, months or years may be required before a typical employee achieves optimum job performance. Each time a trained employee leaves the firm (for whatever reason), the company incurs a hidden cost that does not appear on any financial statement.

Although a high turnover ratio sometimes results from the firm's falling on economic hard times, it may also signal inadequate attention paid to the hiring process, an unsatisfactory compensation program, or a management insensitive to important needs of its employees.

When the ratio is used to measure managerial success in keeping turnover low, it is assumed that each termination is matched by a later hire. If permanent reductions in staff are the cause of the terminations, however, adjustments in the statistics may be needed to reflect that fact.

The denominator in the ratio represents average number of workers employed during the year. Statistics for both numerator and denominator should be maintained in full-time equivalents.

(verbal equation)

$$\textbf{EMPLOYEE TURNOVER} \ = \ 100 \ X \ \frac{\text{Employee Terminations}}{\text{Employees}}$$

(acronymic equation)
$$\textbf{EMPTURN} = 100 * \text{EMPTRMN} / \text{EMP}$$

(symbolic equation)
$$\textbf{R73} = 100 * S36 / S46$$

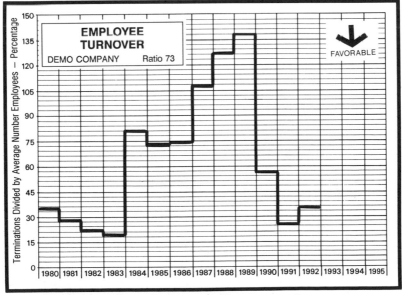

Figure 5-4. Example *Employee Turnover* graph measures efficiency in the management of human resources.

74 ORDERS PER EMPLOYEE

Definition: Number of transactions divided by average number of employees.

This measure of productivity keeps track of how many orders, shipments, or jobs are processed per employee, without regard to the value of sales or the wages paid for their fulfillment. It is useful when looking for evidence of improved efficiency resulting from installation of labor-saving devices or changes in method or work flow. The ratio has an important quality — neither of the numbers used in its calculation appear on the company's financial statements. It has potential, therefore, to reveal conditions otherwise overlooked.

The calculation uses total number of employees (including supervisors and managers). Variations count only production workers. Although the ratio title refers to orders, for most businesses number of transactions is easier to calculate (by referring to serially-numbered invoices or sales tickets). It doesn't matter very much what indicator of productive output is used, as long as it is representative and consistently applied.

(verbal equation)

$$\textbf{ORDERS PER EMPLOYEE} \ = \ \frac{\text{Transactions}}{\text{Employees}}$$

(acronymic equation)
$$\textbf{ORDEMP} = TRANS / EMP$$

(symbolic equation)
$$\textbf{R74} = S33 / S46$$

75 DEFLATED WAGE GROWTH

Definition: The difference between this year's deflated average wage and last year's average wage, divided by last year's average wage, multiplied by 100 to provide a percentage.

Business managers periodically compute (and carry in their heads) the average annual wage paid to their employees. The number is called upon in hiring, in preparing bids, when planning wage increases, and when the time comes to structure next year's budget. *Growth* in average wages is also monitored, to maintain control over what is a significant area of expense for most businesses. Whenever wage growth exceeds sales growth, profits are likely to suffer.

A limitation of the simple growth calculation is that it is skewed by inflation. This is easily overcome by applying a price-level deflator to the year's average wage. The deflator is defined as last year's value for a suitable price index divided by this year's value. Multiplying this year's average wage by the deflator and using it in the growth equation reveals structural changes in wages that otherwise might be masked by changes in the price level. Structural changes are those resulting from automation and technology, age of the work force, or managerial policies related to compensation. The deflator is not difficult to compute, and any desired price index may be used if it is applied consistently.

The actual value of this ratio may be less important than its sign. If positive, it means that the average wage is growing faster than inflation. If negative, the possibility exists that employees are suffering a decline in real earnings. There may be good reasons for each possibility. The important thing is to recognize what is happening.

The average wage is found by dividing total wages expense by average number of employees. If the company employs part-time workers, the numbers should be computed in full-time equivalents.

Including all wages in the equation (line workers as well as executives) does not necessarily limit the usefulness of the ratio, because for most businesses there are many more "workers" than "bosses." For larger companies, however, it may be advantageous to calculate the average wage (and constant dollar growth) for separate departments or activities (such as production, engineering, data processing, and so forth).

(verbal equation)

$$\text{DEFLATED WAGE GROWTH} = 100 \times \frac{\left[\text{Average Wage} \times \dfrac{\text{Price Index Last Year}}{\text{Price Index}} \right] - \text{Average Wage Last Year}}{\text{Average Wage Last Year}}$$

(acronymic equation)

DEFLWAGEGROW=
100∗((WAGEEXP/EMP)∗PRICEINDEXLASTYEAR/PRICEINDEX−
(WAGEEXPLASTYEAR/EMPLASTYEAR))/(WAGEEXPLASTYEAR/EMPLASTYEAR)

(symbolic equation)

R75=100∗((S19/S46)∗S50LY/S50−(S19LY/S46LY))/(S19LY/S46LY)

76 ASSETS PER EMPLOYEE

Definition: Total assets divided by average number of employees.

Here is a ratio to measure the amount of "support" given employees to help them improve productivity. Increases in total assets (labor-saving equipment, plant size, or working capital) relative to a fixed number of employees usually results in higher efficiency.

The ratio keeps track of how much investment the company has made for each employee. Whether or not the investment does in fact result in higher overall efficiency is revealed by other measures, such as *RETURN ON ASSETS (20)* and *TURNOVER OF ASSETS (64)*. The first looks at profits and the second sales — both relative to assets.

If increasing assets does not ultimately result in more sales and profits, then management might ask itself if it has used good judgment in adding to its investment.

It may be inappropriate to include all assets in the numerator. An intangible such as goodwill (having origins in an acquisition of assets at more than book value) is not likely, on its own, to contribute much to productivity.

Calculating the ratio at year end is usually satisfactory. However, if a significant change in total assets has occurred during the year, an average of opening and closing figures is used. Changes in the general price level typically result in an upward bias for this ratio.

Assets per employee is measured in dollars — not as a percentage. Number of employees is an average for the year measured in full-time equivalents.

(verbal equation)

$$\textbf{ASSETS PER EMPLOYEE} \ = \ \frac{\text{Total Assets}}{\text{Employees}}$$

(acronymic equation)
ASSETEMP= TOTASSET / EMP

(symbolic equation)
R76= S8 / S46

77 FLOOR SPACE PER EMPLOYEE

Definition: Number of square feet of floor space divided by average number of employees.

Plant expense has increased sharply in recent decades, on an absolute basis and also when compared to many other costs of doing business. This comes from the fact that our planet is fixed in size relative to an expanding population, and also from increasingly higher standards established for the safety and comfort of workers and customers.

Because plant costs are relatively higher than in the past (and rising), managers must be very careful not to waste space. This can be achieved by careful planning which provides the optimum amount of room each worker needs to safely do the job — but no more. Potentially in conflict with this is the requirement that employees work in environments that are psychologically appealing — open, light, airy, quiet, and sometimes private, as the case may be. Finding a good compromise can be vexing to managers. Sometimes the best solution is to call upon professional factory/office designers.

One business can be compared to another if the kinds of things done are similar (assembly lines, offices, repair shops, warehousing, and so forth). Large companies sometimes establish space standards for various job functions. Scores of closely spaced desks or workstations in one large room may be the standard for one activity, and spacious private rooms (with view) for another.

The ratio is an architectural measurement — not a cost measurement. If one plant is newer than another, or located in an urban area compared to a rural area, relative costs are not revealed. Only mechanical efficiency (number of square feet per employee) is measured.

A variation of the ratio looks at parking lot space. Modern stores, offices, and factories require dedication of large amounts of costly land (and sometimes buildings) for this purpose. The spaces need to be located close to the facility (so that employees and customers need not walk too far). Allocations per vehicle also need to be sufficiently generous in size so that door and fender bumping are minimized. But even a few square feet per vehicle adds up to many thousands of dollars in initial land cost, improvements, taxes, and security. As before, the goal is to find a good compromise. Measuring parking space against number of employees (or customers) is a good first start.

These ratios are calculated from numbers not likely to be found on the company's financial statement.

(verbal equation)

FLOOR SPACE PER EMPLOYEE = $\dfrac{\text{Floor Space}}{\text{Employees}}$

(acronymic equation)
SPACEEMP=SPACE/EMP

(symbolic equation)
R77=S48/S46

Notes — Chapter 5

1. Henry R. Hatfield, *Accounting: Its Principles and Problems* (Lawrence, KS: Scholars Book Co., 1971), p. 130.

2. Readers may prefer to assign remaining expense its own acronymic variable name (such as **REMEXP**) and use it in the numerator of the equation.

3. *See* Charles W. Kyd, "Formula for Disaster?", *INC.* (November, 1986), p. 123.

4. John Downes and Jordan Elliot Goodman, *Barron's Finance & Investment Handbook* (Hauppauge, NY: Barron's Educational Series, 1990), p. 91.

5. Richard Sanzo, *Ratio Analysis for Small Business*, Small Business Management Series No. 20 (Washington, DC: Small Business Administration, 1977), p. 13.

6. For an example of how depreciation rates affect tax rates, see Ray H. Garrison, "The Depreciation Tax Shield," *Managerial Accounting* (Homewood, IL: Richard D. Irwin, 1991), p. 659.

Chapter 6
Marketing Ratios

When scholars and credit agencies report on the causes of business failure, they often cite "insufficient sales." Managers know this well — that healthy sales are essential to business success and survival. They also know that sales do not originate in a vacuum. Marketing activities, in one form or another, are required to create, maintain and increase these essential sales.

Marketing philosophies differ significantly between companies. In some organizations, programs are carefully thought out, documented, tested, executed, and measured. In others, a seat-of-the-pants style leads to decisions based on personal preference or perceived company needs. Whatever the style, one or a combination of four philosophies usually guides the spending decisions and selection of programs.

The first of these emphasizes only the results of marketing. It is a brute-force approach. Newcomers to business (anxious to build sales to desired levels as quickly as possible), typically begin this way. They concentrate almost exclusively on bringing in the business — not the cost. Overlooked is a simple truth, understood by those who have tried and failed, that sales can almost always be increased to satisfactory levels — but at a *price*. If that price is reasonable compared to results, all is well. But more often than not, particularly for new businesses, the cost required to achieve *desired* sales exceeds expectations and the programs prove unsustainable.

A second philosophy (also popular in small business) uses a budget to determine marketing expenditures. In this method, the amount spent on this year's programs is a certain percentage (say, 10%) of last year's sales. Advocates of this approach like its simplicity and the fact that when business is poor and customers are not responding, an automatic cutback and consequent cost-saving takes place. Of course, this may be the time when more, not less, marketing is needed. The budget method is conservative and often works well, but many say it is a case of the tail wagging the dog. Opportunities are regularly lost by advocates of this philosophy. Further, it is not goal oriented, and fails to address questions of how desired results will be achieved.

Another philosophy is investment oriented. The thinking is that for each dollar spent on marketing there should be some measurable reward (in increased sales and profits). Advocates of investment marketing spend a lot of time testing different advertising media, monitoring and rewarding sales staff, and looking for new cost-effective ways to bring in enough business to pay for the programs *plus a profit*. The method works well for direct-response companies. But it is less applicable where very long-term strategies are required. Auto manufacturers, for example, look far beyond this year's sales or next year's sales, and must expend marketing money now in ways that enhance revenue streams years into the future.

This leads to a fourth philosophy — acquisition and retention of customers. The strategy (sometimes called *internal marketing*) builds the business itself by building the customer base. Instead of focusing on the needs of the company, emphasis is placed on those of the client — quality products, attractive styling, competitive pricing, convenient locations, clean facilities, and sensitive after-sale service. By giving highest priority to attracting and holding customers who buy over and over again, the company's long-term marketing expenditures are significantly reduced.

This chapter includes 13 ratios typical of those used to measure marketing results. More so than for any other group, marketing ratios often need to be revised and sometimes invented to meet the needs of individual businesses. The ratios that follow, therefore, are only representative. Many have their origins in the direct mail industry. Marketing managers in other lines, however, will likely see in them possibilities for variations tuned to the needs of their own businesses.

78 AVERAGE ORDER SIZE

Definition: Net sales divided by number of transactions.

The best-prepared plans for growth in sales and profits may go awry if insufficient attention is paid to average order size (AOS). Whether sales are handled by a clerk in a store, by telephone, or through a catalog, the effort (and cost) of soliciting such sales is about the same for products with high or low ticket value.

Desired net sales are achieved not just by soliciting customers in a certain way at a certain frequency, but by offering combinations of products and services with the right average price. A firm needing to increase sales 25% to meet its profit goals, might in some circumstances accomplish this by offering higher-quality, higher-priced products. Properly handled, such a strategy may require no changes in plant, equipment, employees, or marketing methods.

AOS can be increased not just by offering higher-ticket products, but by upgrading through personal selling, and by coupling the sale of one item to another. "Buy a shirt *and* a pair of trousers and we'll throw in a tie — no charge!"

Managers use the average order size ratio to select new products, to allocate display and advertising space, and as an indicator of their customers' propensity to spend.

(verbal equation)

AVERAGE ORDER SIZE $= \dfrac{\text{Net Sales}}{\text{Transactions}}$

(acronymic equation)
AVERORDSIZE = NETSALES / TRANS

(symbolic equation)
R78 = S16 / S33

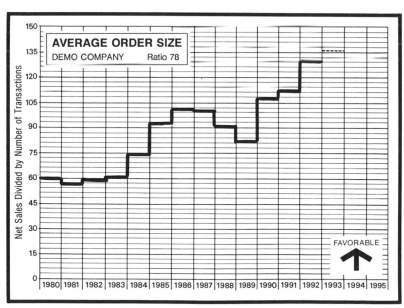

Figure 6-1. Sample graph of *Average Order Size* shows inflation and/or a policy of marketing higher-ticket merchandise.

79 DEFLATED AOS CHANGE

Definition: This year's deflated average order size reduced by last year's average order size.

One definition of money is that it be a standard against which the value of goods and services are measured. When we speak of dollars per bushel or cents per gallon, a constant reference is implied. But governments do not safeguard the integrity of monetary units as they do standards of size and weight.

Thus efforts to maintain or increase average order size often fail in times of inflation. The illusion of success may be there, but if the rate of inflation exceeds the gains, nothing is accomplished. The purpose of this ratio is to provide a dollar measurement of *real* change in AOS over the year. Example: A firm's AOS is $126. The next year it is $131. On the surface, order size has increased by $5. But if the rate of inflation is 7.1%, the figure needs to be deflated by that percentage. The result is a constant dollar AOS of $121.70 for the second year. The real change is negative, therefore, in the amount of $4.30. This is not progress.

A positive value for the ratio means that a company's average order has increased, despite inflation. A negative number means the opposite. Even if a firm has no need to change its prices or product mix to achieve higher AOS, it does need to protect itself against the destructive forces of inflation. If costs are increasing, prices need to be increased proportionately (or more) to maintain profit margins. Zero or negative values for this ratio suggest profitability problems in the future.

Note that in the equations below, two of the input numbers are previously-computed ratios. Using available numbers eliminates the need to calculate the AOS again and results in a simple equation. Alert readers may wonder why this constant dollar ratio is not measured as a percentage change (as with similar sales and profit ratios). Either method is satisfactory. Absolute change (instead of percentage change) was chosen for this ratio simply to illustrate possibilities.

(verbal equation)

$$\text{DEFLATED AVERAGE ORDER-SIZE CHANGE} = \left[\text{AVERAGE ORDER SIZE} \times \frac{\text{Price Index Last Year}}{\text{Price Index}} \right] - \text{AVERAGE ORDER SIZE LAST YEAR}$$

(acronymic equation)
DEFLAVERORDSIZECH=
AVERORDSIZE * (PRICEINDEXLASTYEAR / PRICEINDEX) − **AVERORDSIZELASTYEAR**

(symbolic equation)
R79 = R78 * (S50LY / S50) − **R78LY**

80 ORDER GROWTH

Definition: The difference between this year's number of transactions and last year's number of transactions, divided by last year's number of transactions, multiplied by 100 to provide a percentage.

Business growth is usually monitored by looking at net sales. Another (equally valid) measure of the firm's activity is number of orders received and processed. Measuring growth against order activity (rather than sales) may be preferable for new or fast-growing companies, because they are concentrating on acquisition and retention of customers.

When this is management's strategy (building a base of individuals or firms likely to buy over and over again), it may be necessary (in the early years) to emphasize lower-ticket, lower-profit products and services. This attracts new customers and provides "growth," though not necessarily in net sales. A case in point is any direct marketing business where customers are acquired (often at a loss) to create a mailing list.

Sometimes the reverse is true. A firm may be receiving and processing too many small orders with a resultant loss of profitability. Whenever growth in number of orders differs materially from growth in sales (both measured as percentage changes from the prior year), it pays to find out why. If order growth is higher, average order size is falling. If sales growth is higher, average order size is rising. A problem is suggested only when the event is a surprise to management.

The statistic is measured in number of orders received or filled, packages shipped, or by a count of sales tickets. It doesn't matter much how number of transactions is defined, as long as the method used is consistent.

(verbal equation)

$$\text{ORDER GROWTH} = 100 \times \frac{\text{Transactions This Year} - \text{Transactions Last Year}}{\text{Transactions Last Year}}$$

(acronymic equation)

$$\text{ORDGROW} = 100 * (\text{TRANS} - \text{TRANSLASTYEAR}) / \text{TRANSLASTYEAR}$$

(symbolic equation)

$$\text{R80} = 100 * (\text{S33} - \text{S33LY}) / \text{S33LY}$$

81 CUSTOMER GROWTH

Definition: The difference between this year's number of customers and last year's number of customers, divided by last year's number of customers, multiplied by 100 to provide a percentage.

Most managers recognize the need to make a plan for company growth and to express that plan as an annual rate of increase in sales. But unless such a plan includes means for increasing the size of the customer base, the likelihood of realization may be low.

An axiom of business is that you will be more successful in selling to someone who has bought from you before than to a stranger. That is why it is so important that companies interested in growth keep track of their progress in building a customer list of firms or individuals with that greater propensity to buy, based on habit or prior satisfaction.

Although many companies do not maintain formal mailing lists of customers, most do have the information in accounts receivable records or in the files of their sales people. Mail-order companies pay great attention to progress in building these lists.

A proof that customer lists are valuable is found in their ready salability to others. Many direct-marketing companies attribute a substantial portion of net income to the sale or rental of these names and addresses. Buyers of the lists are often in quite different lines of business. What is most valuable about these prospects is their recently confirmed propensity to buy (anything).

This customer-focused ratio reveals bedrock growth not likely to be clouded by economic conditions or temporary aberrations in market acceptance of a company's products or services. A good managerial goal for growth companies is to achieve annual percentage increases in number of customers that match planned percentage growth in sales.

(verbal equation)

$$\text{CUSTOMER GROWTH} = 100 \times \frac{\text{Customers this Year} - \text{Customers Last Year}}{\text{Customers Last Year}}$$

(acronymic equation)
$$\text{CUSTGROW} = 100 * (\text{CUST} - \text{CUSTLASTYEAR}) / \text{CUSTLASTYEAR}$$

(symbolic equation)
$$\text{R81} = 100 * (\text{S45} - \text{S45LY}) / \text{S45LY}$$

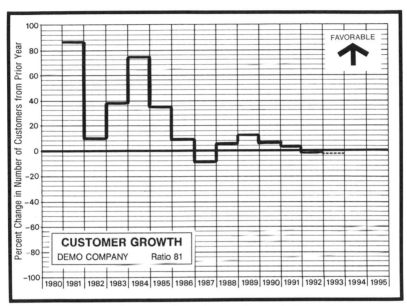

Figure 6-2. *Customer Growth* example graph shows changes in the customer base.

82 SALES PER CUSTOMER

Definition: Net sales divided by average number of customers.

This ratio is similar to the one that measures order size. It concerns itself, however, not with the value of an average transaction, but with how much is purchased annually by each customer.

The most important use for this ratio is to convert plans for sales growth into plans for acquiring new customers. It is one thing to decide that a company needs a 12% increase in sales next year to meet its goals, but quite another to implement the decision. A first step can be calculation of this ratio to reveal, on average, about how many new customers are needed. Then it becomes a question of how they will be acquired — through additional sales staff, advertising, special offers, an acquisition?

It is true that in the short run, newly acquired customers may not purchase up to the level indicated by the ratio. The reason for this is that a period of time is required before buyers convince themselves that the new firm can be trusted. They must decide (for a variety of practical reasons) if this is a company they wish to deal with on a regular basis. Eventually, though, if nothing happens to drive these customers away, human psychology contributes to an increase in the buying rate.

Average number of customers is most easily determined by adding opening and closing numbers and dividing by two.

This measure is expressed in dollars — not as a percentage.

(verbal equation)

$$\textbf{SALES PER CUSTOMER } = \frac{\text{Net Sales}}{\text{Customers}}$$

(acronymic equation)
$$\textbf{SALESCUST} = NETSALES / ((CUST + CUSTLASTYEAR)/2)$$

(symbolic equation)
$$\textbf{R82} = S16 / ((S45 + S45LY)/2)$$

83 CUSTOMER SOLICITATION RATIO

Definition: Number of solicitations directed to customers divided by total number of solicitations, multiplied by 100 to provide a percentage.

This ratio measures the extent to which the company directs its sales efforts to existing customers. It is very important in direct-response businesses, for example, where mailings of catalogs to known customers pull two, three, or even ten times as many orders as those sent to cold prospects. There are several reasons for the greater rate of return. One is that the customer knows and (presumably) trusts the company. Another is habit. Most buyers are comfortable doing what has been done before.

Solicitations can be in the form of telephone calls, personal visits by a sales representative, or mailings. Whatever the form of canvasing, the principal is the same — those who have bought before are more likely to buy this time.

For new businesses (with no existing customer base) the ratio is zero. As the business grows and the customer list grows, a greater proportion of the overt marketing effort can be directed to the known customers, with a likely increase in profitability.

A ratio of 100% is the long-term goal of many small businesses. The strategy is to build the base in early years with minimal emphasis on profit. Then, when the base is large enough, higher returns are achieved by limiting sales efforts to known customers. Of course, due to inevitable attrition of the base, *some* prospecting is always required just to stay even.

(verbal equation)

$$\textbf{CUSTOMER SOLICITATION RATIO} = 100 \text{ X } \frac{\text{Solicitations to Customers}}{\text{Total Solicitations}}$$

(acronymic equation)
$$\textbf{CUSTSOLICRATIO} = 100 * \text{SOLICCUST} / \text{SOLIC}$$

(symbolic equation)
$$\textbf{R83} = 100 * S38 / S37$$

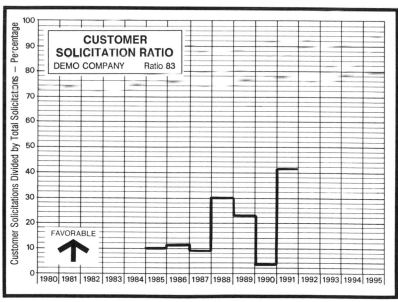

Figure 6-3. Sample chart of *Customer Solicitation Ratio* shows the percentage of mailings directed to existing customers.

84 CUSTOMER SPACE RATIO

Definition: Number of customers divided by number of square feet of floor space.

It is not uncommon for managers to compare the size of their physical plant to net sales. The thinking is that once a certain amount of floor space has been purchased or leased, the business activity must generate some relative amount of revenue. If it cannot, disposal of all or part of the facilities may be necessary.

Looking at number of customers this way also makes sense. Why? Because modern theory says that an important goal of marketing is the acquisition and satisfaction of customers. (Do that well and sales growth takes care of itself!) This ratio, therefore, provides the manager with another way to see just how well the company is matching business activity (measured by number of customers instead of sales) to space.

Is it a marketing ratio or an efficiency ratio? Both. In the sense that it focuses attention on maintaining or increasing the customer base, it is a marketing ratio. Used to detect physical facilities poorly matched in size to business activity, it measures efficiency.

There is no "right" value for the ratio. Rather, it is a relative indicator (best examined over time) to reveal that changes are taking place. A falling value means that the company is losing customers or prematurely increasing the size of its plant. A rising ratio signals an increase in customers or a reduction in space.

The measure varies widely depending on the type of business. For a research company with a single customer, the calculation may yield an extremely small number. A mail-order company, on the other hand, may service a large number of customers for each square foot of space utilized. For this reason, the measure is used primarily to detect change within one company.

This is another ratio using input numbers not found on the company's financial statements. It has the capability, therefore, to detect dynamic features of the business which might not show up elsewhere.

(verbal equation)

$$\text{CUSTOMER SPACE RATIO} = \frac{\text{Customers}}{\text{Floor Space}}$$

(acronymic equation)
CUSTSPACERATIO = CUST / SPACE

(symbolic equation)
R84 = S45 / S48

85 MARKETING GROWTH

Definition: The difference between this year's marketing expense and last year's marketing expense, divided by last year's marketing expense, multiplied by 100 to provide a percentage.

How much money should be spent on marketing? This question comes up again and again in business offices around the world. Some say the best answer is to allocate a fixed percentage of last year's sales to this year's advertising and promotion. Others say this is nonsense — marketing expenditures should be made solely to accomplish specific long-term goals, such as customer acquisition and retention. A slightly different view sees marketing as an investment which must provide measurable near-term rewards in the form of increased sales.

Whichever of these philosophies is adopted, it is reasonable to assume that over time marketing expenditures must grow if sales are to grow, and perhaps proportionately. This ratio, therefore, reports on management's current attitude about the need to increase or decrease marketing. When the number exceeds the company's average sales growth rate, it indicates an aggressive attitude toward marketing. When it falls below the average growth rate, it signals a retrenchment.

Most marketing programs take time to work out, so changes in the ratio in a given year do not necessarily result in comparable changes in sales in the same year. In fact, planners in mature companies are often surprised when a retrenchment in advertising or selling results in only a modest fall-off in sales. This is explained by the fact that companies and individuals act habitually, finding it more convenient to buy this time where they bought last time. Marketing retrenchment does result in loss of customers and sales, but the effects are often gradual.

(verbal equation)

$$\text{MARKETING GROWTH} \;=\; 100 \;\times\; \frac{\text{Marketing Expense This Year} \;-\; \text{Marketing Expense Last Year}}{\text{Marketing Expense Last Year}}$$

(acronymic equation)

$$\text{MARKGROW} = 100 * (\text{MARKEXP} - \text{MARKEXPLASTYEAR}) / \text{MARKEXPLASTYEAR}$$

(symbolic equation)

$$\text{R85} = 100 * (\text{S20} - \text{S20LY}) / \text{S20LY}$$

86 AVERAGE RETURN ON MARKETING

Definition: Average net sales divided by average marketing expense.

This ratio measures the overall effectiveness of marketing programs by relating net sales to the expenditures for advertising, promotion, and selling which created those sales. It is particularly useful in direct response businesses where revenues are generated primarily by overt marketing activities.

Although the value of the ratio is theoretically meaningful using one year's statistics for sales and marketing expense, a number of factors distort the measurement. The results of a particular marketing activity may not show up for months or even years after its initiation. Purchases by repeat customers may be unrelated to this year's marketing programs. Non-financial aspects of marketing (attitudes of staff, location, customer service) are not measured. Near year-end marketing expenditures may be incapable of impacting this year's sales. For all of these reasons, it is best to use input numbers which cover a multi-year period. This increases the likelihood that the measured return is indicative of the overall effectiveness of the company's marketing programs.

A disadvantage to using ratios based on averages, of course, is that results of changes in strategy are slow to show up. By the time the measurements are made, the people who made the original decisions may be gone, and the strategies already abandoned. For this reason, average marketing ratios are most profitably employed by stable companies using consistent programs. Keeping these disadvantages in mind, however, this return ratio may be one of the few means by which marketing managers can objectively measure long-term success in what they are doing.

The results are sometimes made more meaningful by selecting a set of marketing-expense statistics originating in periods several months earlier in time than the corresponding sales figures. Such an offset provides opportunity for marketing program changes to be felt, and eliminates some of the distortions caused by large expenditures that may have occurred near the end of an accounting period.

A reciprocal of the ratio is sometimes easier to understand. If the average return is five, for example, inverting the number tells us that the company spends 20% of its sales dollar on marketing to maintain average sales. Managers preparing budgets can "plug in" this number to see if it makes sense, and to identify the need for better programs.

A theoretical break-even value for the ratio is found by subtracting all expenses except marketing from gross profit. This number is then expressed as a percentage of sales. Dividing it into 100% tells what return is needed to break even.

Marketing managers use different averaging periods and time offsets in the formulas, depending on the particular circumstances of their companies. In the demonstration equations below, sales and expenses are averaged over two years. More sophisticated equations are likely to provide better results.

This is another of the times ratios — not a percentage. It expresses how many sales dollars (on average) are received for each marketing dollar expended.

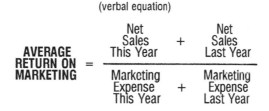

(verbal equation)

$$\text{AVERAGE RETURN ON MARKETING} = \frac{\text{Net Sales This Year} + \text{Net Sales Last Year}}{\text{Marketing Expense This Year} + \text{Marketing Expense Last Year}}$$

(acronymic equation)
AVERRETMARK=
(NETSALES+NETSALESLASTYFAR)/(MARKEXP+MARKEXPLASTYEAR)

(symbolic equation)
R86=(S16+S16LY)/(S20+S20LY)

87 AVERAGE ORDER RESPONSE

Definition: Average number of transactions divided by average number of solicitations, multiplied by 100 to provide a percentage.

A key success measure for direct-response businesses, this ratio tells relatively how many prospects were motivated by the firm's canvasing efforts to place orders. By changing product, offer, price, or list, the company continually works to increase order response and profits. What constitutes a satisfactory response depends entirely on the arithmetic of the offer. Where 1% might be profitable for one direct mailing, 5% could lose money on another. Note that this ratio measures response in terms of number of orders — not dollar sales.

Companies soliciting sales by means other than mail (telephone, magazine, newspaper, TV) compute the ratio using number of prospects contacted or number of media insertions placed.

Mail-order managers like to measure response to their mailings individually in order to optimize the many variables involved. Drawing conclusions from one mailing is risky, however. Market vagaries and general economic conditions may cloud the results. The reviewer must always consider when the solicitations were made and whether or not orders may be coming from other sources or other time periods. It is for this reason that coding is frequently used on mailing pieces and in media advertisements to relate realized orders to their marketing sources.

All of the admonitions expressed for the previous ratio apply to this one as well. Although it can be used to measure the results of a single mailing or a single year, this is difficult to do using readily available statistics. On the other hand, if average numbers are used, it is possible to determine historical response applicable to one business over an extended time period. Knowing such a number is extremely useful in planning and when making short-term judgments about specific mailings or programs.

Consider this analogy: A fishing company wants to know how many tons of fish it is likely to catch each time one of its boats puts to sea. Obviously, on any individual run, the result depends on many factors (the fish, the weather, the location, the equipment, the skill of the crew). But if records are maintained for all boats over a number of seasons, useful average yields are revealed. These numbers can be valuable in comparing varying fish prices with decisions to employ and even expand the company's fleet.

A two-year averaging period is used in the equations below. Other periods may be profitably used depending on the availability of information and company needs. A longer averaging period usually results in a more dependable number. That is, variations in markets and timing are smoothed out.

(verbal equation)

$$\text{AVERAGE ORDER RESPONSE} = 100 \times \frac{\text{Transactions This Year} + \text{Transactions Last Year}}{\text{Solicitations This Year} + \text{Solicitations Last Year}}$$

(acronymic equation)

$$\text{AVERORDRESP} = 100 * (\text{TRANS} + \text{TRANSLASTYEAR}) / (\text{SOLIC} + \text{SOLICLASTYEAR})$$

(symbolic equation)

$$\text{R87} = 100 * (\text{S33} + \text{S33LY}) / (\text{S37} + \text{S37LY})$$

88 AVERAGE SALES RESPONSE

Definition: Average net sales divided by average number of solicitations.

This measure differs from *AVERAGE ORDER RESPONSE (87)* in that it looks not at the number of orders received, but at their value. In the final analysis, the company prospers or fails on the basis of its sales revenues compared to costs. Certain changes in marketing strategy (such as selling higher-priced merchandise) which might result in no change in average order response, could produce a much higher average sales response. For that reason, average sales response deserves as careful an examination as average order response.

As with the previous two ratios, it is important that the measured sales be reasonably matched to the mailings or solicitations believed to have created those sales. Coding helps, as does the offsetting in time of mailing statistics to match likely response periods. Once again, averaging of more than one year's information provides a historical value for the ratio useful in planning.

The general rule is that over the long run, a sufficient value of orders must be received not just to pay for the canvasing effort, but to pay a fair share of overhead and return a profit. Some firms accept unprofitable sales response in early years in order to build a cadre of loyal customers able to provide higher (and presumably profitable) sales response in later years.

Note that this measure is valued in dollars. It provides the average return in sales for each solicitation (catalog or other mailing piece, magazine advertisement, telephone call, etc.). As before, a two-year averaging period is used in the demonstration equations.

(verbal equation)

$$\begin{matrix} \text{AVERAGE} \\ \text{SALES} \\ \text{RESPONSE} \end{matrix} = \frac{\text{Net Sales This Year} + \text{Net Sales Last Year}}{\text{Solicitations This Year} + \text{Solicitations Last Year}}$$

(acronymic equation)

$$\text{AVERSALESRESP} = (\text{NETSALES} + \text{NETSALESLASTYEAR}) / (\text{SOLIC} + \text{SOLICLASTYEAR})$$

(symbolic equation)

$$\text{R88} = (\text{S16} + \text{S16LY}) / (\text{S37} + \text{S37LY})$$

89 CUSTOMER SATISFACTION RATIO

Definition: Net sales divided by gross sales, multiplied by 100 to provide a percentage.

When customers return merchandise, the refund or credit transactions are recorded in the returns and allowances account. Because net sales represent the difference between gross sales and this account, the ratio of net to gross is an indicator of ultimate order fulfillment.

Customers return goods because they are defective, damaged in transit, not as advertised, not as ordered, oversold, no longer needed, or out of sheer pusillanimity. It matters little whether the error or reason for the return is centered with the company or the customer. The point is only that for whatever reason, the original transaction "failed."

Hundreds of return transactions may be involved each year for even a small business, so regardless of the reasons for the returns, the ratio is an objective measure of relative transaction success. *Relative* is an important word here, because selling policies and returned-goods policies vary widely from firm to firm. Also, for each customer electing to make a return, many others equally dissatisfied may remain silent.

It's not difficult to reduce a high rate of returns once the causes are known. Despite occasional cranks, most customers want to be satisfied. Upgrading product quality, improving what is said in advertising, and better training of salespeople are all likely to result in an increase in the value of this ratio. Another way to improve satisfaction is to spend more time with the customer. This translates to increasing the ratio of employees to customers, or (in the case of hotels, for example) the ratio of employees to space or number of rooms.

For the going business with consistent policies and no important change in product, this ratio is a good year-to-year indicator of customer satisfaction.

(verbal equation)

$$\text{CUSTOMER SATISFACTION RATIO} = 100 \text{ X } \frac{\text{Net Sales}}{\text{Gross Sales}}$$

(acronymic equation)

$$\text{CUSTSATRATIO} = 100 * \text{NETSALES} / \text{GROSSSALES}$$

(symbolic equation)

$$R89 = 100 * S16 / S15$$

90 PROPRIETARY PRODUCT RATIO

Definition: Net sales of proprietary products divided by total net sales, multiplied by 100 to provide a percentage.

Proprietary products are defined here as those perceived by the customer as difficult or impossible to obtain from another source. Patented products and unique items involving high technology come at once to mind, but this misses the point. The truth is that a proprietary product may be as mundane as a privately-branded loaf of bread, or a kit of parts to replace a radiator hose.

Proprietary products are best understood when considered from the viewpoint of the customer — not the seller. If (through any combination of price, quality, features, accessories, or labeling) the customer associates a desirable product or service with one supplier, then it qualifies as being proprietary.

Two things happen in the customer's mind. First, the characteristics of the product on an overall basis trigger a favorable response. The customer wants this item. Second, as a result of brand identification, uniqueness of packaging, or ready availability, alternate sources simply are not considered. (Even if they are, the thoughts are fleeting.) The result is a higher-than-average propensity to buy.

Businesses selling mostly proprietary products do not face the destructive competition that results when many suppliers furnish identical goods. Also, their managers enjoy more than average freedom in setting prices.

(verbal equation)

$$\textbf{PROPRIETARY PRODUCT RATIO} = 100 \text{ X } \frac{\text{Proprietary Product Sales}}{\text{Net Sales}}$$

(acronymic equation)

$$\textbf{PROPPRODRATIO} = 100 * \text{PROPPRODSALES} / \text{NETSALES}$$

(symbolic equation)

$$\textbf{R90} = 100 * S40 / S16$$

Chapter 7
Investment Ratios

In addition to the role they play as managerial tools, business ratios are deeply rooted in the needs of groups and individuals outside the company. Banks, for example, require reliable gauges of strength and liquidity on which to base their lending decisions. Investors, a second outside group, need objective tools to measure relative attractiveness of the many-available securities. The measures that interest this latter group are called investment ratios.

It can be argued that all business ratios are investment ratios. This is true because modern security analysis (in its broadest sense) means looking at anything and everything about a company that could impact its ability to meet financial obligations and provide a growing stream of earnings and dividends. Predicting the future price or dividend rate of a security is difficult at best. And so it follows that no ratio should be overlooked by an investor, however unrelated to security prices it appears.[1]

Nevertheless, a number of ratios exist that are particularly favored by the investment community — that is, brokers, analysts, portfolio managers, and individual investors. These measures examine a company's progress from a bottom-line, almost aloof perspective. On the theory that management is an art, investors are inclined to leave the managing to the artists. They have a strong propensity to look primarily at end results — that is, earnings, stock prices and dividends. Where a lender might become alarmed if debt ratios reach traditionally dangerous levels, equity investors may wait and see if earnings or dividends are affected. Unfavorable financial ratios are often tolerated if investment ratios are maintained at satisfactory levels. On the other hand, little patience is shown when investment ratios turn sour (a dividend cut, for example). A sufficient number of holders can be expected to "bail out" quickly with a consequent sudden drop in the price of the security.

This point is often overlooked by managers. Focusing on internal problems relative to product or market, they may disregard the company's owners. This attitude is usually a serious mistake, as it ignores the essential truth that capital comes only at a price. Actions taken by management that (however sensible in the long run) impact negatively on a stock's price or dividend-paying ability, often create new problems. For this reason, managers need to understand and monitor key investment ratios for their companies. Not only does this help them understand the point of view of those providing equity capital, it keeps their focus on an ultimate long-term goal for every company — maintaining a competitive investment return for owners.

Eleven measures, applicable to the performance of individual companies, are presented in this final grouping. In addition to the familiar ratios used by brokers and financial advisors to relate stock prices to earnings, book value, and sales, there are dividend ratios, business valuation ratios, and a success model.

Many other investment ratios exist which analyze popular stock market indices (such as the Dow Jones 30 Industrial Average). These ratios compare the indices to earnings, dividends, bond yields, inflation, and even the price of gold. For readers who may be interested, several are described in the Appendix.[2]

91 BOOK VALUE PER SHARE

Definition: Stockholders' equity divided by number of shares of company stock outstanding.

For the small business that cannot afford to have its shares listed on an exchange, book value per share is one time-proven indicator of relative value for the stock. Owners use it as a simple and reliable measure of progress for their company and their investment. Where new stock is sold from time to time, the ratio keeps track of any dilutive side effects of such sales.

Actual market value for the shares may be significantly greater than book if the company is profitable, growing, or in an industry attractive to investors. Market value can also be less than book if the company is in trouble, or if balance-sheet values are incapable of realization. In most circumstances, however, owners have little incentive to sell for less than book.

Variations of the statistic show market value for the company's stock if it is traded, or show a value based on some multiple of earnings common to an industry.

(verbal equation)

$$\text{BOOK VALUE PER SHARE} = \frac{\text{Stockholders' Equity}}{\text{Shares Outstanding}}$$

(acronymic equation)
BOOKSHARE = STOCKHOLDEQ / SHARE

(symbolic equation)
R91 = S14/S12

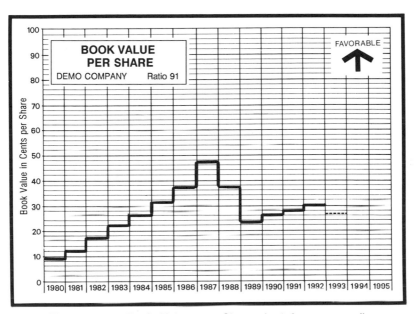

Figure 7-1. *Book Value per Share* chart for one small business — a time-proven relative indicator of value.

92 BUSINESS VALUE PREMIUM

Definition: Capitalized value of earnings less stockholders' equity, divided by stockholders' equity, multiplied by 100 to provide a percentage.

This ratio compares the value of a company's shares based on a market multiple of earnings (capitalized value) to its value based on book figures. It tells owners whether or not buyers of their company's shares are likely to pay more than book, and if so, about how much.

When the capitalized value of earnings is equal to or less than stockholders equity, earnings are probably insufficient to command much of a premium over book value. If capitalized earnings exceed book value, however, it means that the earning power of the business may warrant a higher price. The capitalized value of earnings is defined as net profit after taxes divided by a capitalization factor — the annual rate of return (expressed as a decimal) anticipated by a prudent investor. If the collective opinion of the marketplace is that a particular investment should provide an earnings return on its value equal to 15%, then that value is found by dividing net profit after taxes by .15. The factor is often arbitrarily set at twice the market interest rate prevailing for long-term bonds. Doubling the bond rate recognizes the risk inherent in equity investments. Different capitalizations may be used, of course, depending on the circumstances.

Buyers of businesses should attempt to *normalize* a company's financial statements before entering them into calculations of this type. Normalization means adjusting balance sheet and income numbers to realistic, realizable values which can be compared to similar businesses or operational plans of the new owners.[3] Remember too that estimates of value based on numbers are just that — estimates. In the end, true value is whatever a hands-off buyer and seller contractually decide it to be at time of sale.

In the equations below, capitalized value of earnings is found by dividing net profit after taxes by twice the interest rate prevailing for long-term bonds (expressed as a decimal).[4] Thus, if net profit is $100,000 and the interest rate on safe investments is 8%, the capitalized value of earnings is $625,000.

When the calculation returns a negative number, it means that the value of the business based on earnings is less (by the percentage given) than book value. In the practical world, however, negative premiums have little meaning, as most businesses have potential for being sold at figures not too far from realistic book value. The measure is undefined for companies that fail to earn a profit.

(verbal equation)

$$\text{BUSINESS VALUE PREMIUM} = 100 \times \frac{\text{Capitalized Value of Earnings} - \text{Stockholders' Equity}}{\text{Stockholders' Equity}}$$

(acronymic equation)
BUSVALPREM=
100 * (NETPROFAFTTAX / (.02 * INTERRATE) − STOCKHOLDEQ) / STOCKHOLDEQ

(symbolic equation)
R92 = 100 * (S30 / (.02 * S49) − S14) / S14

93 DIVIDEND RATE

Definition: Dividends paid (annualized) divided by number of shares outstanding.

Should a business pay dividends to its shareholders? Attitudes about this range from an emphatic "no" to an enthusiastic "yes." Opponents of dividends argue that the purpose of investing in a business in the first place is to put the money at risk in expectation of gain. Taking the money out prematurely amounts to "de-investing," and therefore makes no sense. Dividends are also opposed because in the United States they are taxed twice. Proponents say that although these things are true, dividends are the only tangible evidence of a corporation's success. Where in the normal course of business, suppliers, customers, managers and employees are regularly compensated and rewarded, shareholders may be forgotten. A positive dividend-paying policy can be a reminder to management that risk capital does not come free of cost.

The dividend rate is expressed in dollars paid annually per share. Stockholders receiving regular dividend checks use the measure to confirm that they are receiving the correct payment. The procedure is to multiply the dividend rate (adjusted for number of times per year the dividend is paid) by number of shares owned and see if it agrees with the amount received. For example, for a firm paying a "$2.00 dividend," an investor's quarterly check should be $50 if 100 shares are owned.

Dividend rates are important but provide limited information that investors can use to evaluate their holdings. They communicate only one fact — the amount of the payout. Was the payment of this dividend prudent or was it foolish? No clues are found in the number itself to answer this question. The next ratio (yield) goes further by relating the payout to the market's valuation of the underlying shares.

(verbal equation)

$$\text{DIVIDEND RATE} = \frac{\text{Dividends}}{\text{Shares Outstanding}}$$

(acronymic equation)
$$\text{DIVRATE} = \text{DIV} / \text{SHARE}$$

(symbolic equation)
$$\text{R93} = \text{S31} / \text{S12}$$

94 DIVIDEND YIELD

Definition: Dividends paid (annualized) divided by stockholders' equity, multiplied by 100 to provide a percentage.

Where the dividend rate measures payout against number of shares outstanding, dividend yield compares it to the current value of the shareholder's investment.

Investors look at dividend yield in many ways. High yields are characteristic of mature industries. When prospects for growth are minimal, investors want their reward now and market prices (which evaluate the dividend) adjust accordingly. Yields are also high when investors perceive that future payment of the dividend is uncertain. Conversely, low yields are characteristic of growing companies and industries, and businesses in which investor confidence is high.

One reason this ratio is popular with stockholders is its familiar form of presentation. That is, yields are discussed and compared just as interest rates are quoted on bank savings accounts. Most investors understand that reported *earnings* can be manipulated by management, but dividends are real. Even unsophisticated investors find meaning in a situation where a business pays out 10% of its market value each year — particularly if the bank down the street pays 6% interest on certificates of deposit. Whether the meaning found by the investor takes into account business risk or the company's ability to pay dividends at all is another question. The point is that the investors know — or think they know — what dividend yield represents.

Where the yield on a common stock is usually straightforward and easily understood, yields on mutual funds are a different matter. Thomas J. Herzfeld describes them as, " . . . a mine field strewn with complicated and conflicting data."[5] Because payouts often include capital gains and returns of capital, investors need to be cautious.

If the company's stock is quoted on an exchange, then the denominator in the equations is found by multiplying the end-of-year share price by number of shares outstanding. Otherwise, stockholders' equity (book value) is taken directly from the company's balance sheet.

(verbal equation)

$$\text{DIVIDEND YIELD} = 100 \text{ X } \frac{\text{Dividends}}{\text{Stock Price X Shares Outstanding}}$$

(acronymic equation)

$$\text{DIVYIELD} = 100 * \text{DIV} / (\text{STOCKPRICE} * \text{SHARE})$$

(symbolic equation)

$$\text{R94} = 100 * \text{S31} / (\text{S47} * \text{S12})$$

95 RETENTION RATE

Definition: Net profit after taxes less dividends paid in year, divided by net profit after taxes, multiplied by 100 to provide a percentage.

This measure tells simply what portion of the profits are left working in the business. Policies relating to the payment of dividends have more to do with pleasing shareholders than with running the company. Most managers, reasoning that they are in the best position to make money grow, will opt to pay no dividend at all. Investors, on the other hand, look to dividends as tangible proof of progress — hard evidence that their investment is paying off. Lenders also look at the dividend rate as an indicator of financial strength. A company's board of directors usually tries to balance these interests, keeping an eye on the market value of the stock.

As retention rate decreases, a company's ability to grow and achieve maximum profitability declines. The reason for this is that monies paid out often have to be replaced — by borrowing, or cutting back expansion to match available funds. Lenders look unfavorably on declining retention rates if the company's financial strength is low or waning.

A composite prepared by the Value Line Investment Survey for the year 1990 showed average retention of about 48% for 850 industrial, retail, and transportation companies.[6] Primarily because of double taxation, small businesses with few shareholders are less likely to pay dividends.

A payout rate (dividends divided by profit) is sometimes calculated. It serves the same purpose but is in inverted form. Whichever ratio Is used, the idea is the same — to monitor dividend policy relative to earnings.

This ratio is undefined when the company operates at a loss or when dividends paid exceed net profit. Dividends paid in losing years are really distributions of capital, in which case retention has no meaning.

(verbal equation)

$$\textbf{RETENTION RATE} = 100 \times \frac{\text{Net Profit After Taxes} - \text{Dividends}}{\text{Net Profit After Taxes}}$$

(acronymic equation)

$$\textbf{RTNRATE} = 100 * (\text{NETPROFAFTTAX} - \text{DIV}) / \text{NETPROFAFTTAX}$$

(symbolic equation)

$$\textbf{R95} = 100 * (S30 - S31) / S30$$

96 PRICE TO EARNINGS

Definition: Per share market price of company's stock divided by net profit after taxes per share.

What does it mean to an investor to learn that the shares of ZYX Company are selling for $30? Is that high, low, or about right? Is it time to sell, buy more, or sit tight? Some investors find answers to these questions in three ratios comparing share price to other underlying values for the company. Price to earnings (P/E) is the first of these.

When investors are optimistic about a company's prospects, they are willing to pay more for an anticipated string of future earnings. Growth and high technology stocks, for example, usually command high multiples. On the other hand, when a company's future is viewed pessimistically or the industry is uninteresting, the ratio is likely to be low. Statistics for small companies are hard to find, but average P/E ratios applicable to large firms are published weekly in financial newspapers such as Barron's.[7]

Investors do not wait to the end of the year to compute the P/E ratio. They continuously divide the stock's current price by earnings for the most recent four quarters (trailing P/E ratio). Or, they divide by the company's estimated earnings for the next four quarters (projected P/E ratio). The purpose is the same in each instance — to independently evaluate the market's judgment as to a correct price for the stock.

One way to improve understanding of the P/E ratio is to convert it to an earning-power ratio (E/P). A stock that earns $3 per share and sells for $30 thus has an earning power of 10%. This form is sometimes preferred because of its similarity to the way bank interest is quoted. Comparing the inverted ratio to prevailing interest rates is one imperfect way to evaluate the price placed on the company's shares by the market.

Another way to use this ratio is to divide it by percentage profit growth. Investors recognize that growing companies deserve higher P/E valuations. According to Peter Lynch, a P/E that's half the growth rate is very positive and one that's twice the growth rate is negative.[8]

These ratios are undefined when the company operates at a loss.

(verbal equation)

$$\textbf{PRICEEARN} = \frac{\text{Stock Price}}{\text{Net Profit After Taxes Per Share}}$$

(acronymic equation)

$$\textbf{PRICEEARN} = STOCKPRICE / (NETPROFAFTTAX / SHARE)$$

(symbolic equation)

$$\textbf{R96} = S47 / (S30 / S12)$$

97 PRICE TO BOOK

Definition: Per share market price of company's stock divided by stockholders' equity per share.

This evaluation of the company's stock price makes the comparison to book value. For small businesses, book value is often the only number owners have to tell them what their shares are worth. When the stock is traded on an exchange or in a dealers' market, quoted prices vary widely from book value, depending on the industry, its prospects, and the company's earnings record.

Although book value is an objective number (taken directly from the company's balance sheet), it does not accurately report the market value of assets less liabilities. The reason is that book values are derived historically from costs. Assets purchased years ago may be worth much more or much less than book. Policies regarding depreciation, intangible assets, and write-offs of inventory and receivables all impact directly on what is presented as book.

The ratio of market price to book value is a fairly good indicator of how investors view the future. The higher the ratio above one, the more optimistic are buyers of the shares. When the ratio equals one, it means that investors see little in the company other than its liquidation value. Ratios below one are not uncommon, even if the business is doing well. This occurs when balance sheets carry obsolete or overvalued assets (oil reserves, for example, after a drop in energy prices).

Ratios of this type depend not just on investors' views of company prospects, but on general economic conditions. When the economy is heading toward a recession, optimism declines and the ratios of stock price to book value usually decline as well.

The ratio is undefined for troubled companies with zero or negative net worth.

(verbal equation)

$$\text{PRICE TO BOOK} = \frac{\text{Stock Price}}{\text{Stockholders' Equity Per Share}}$$

(acronymic equation)
PRICEBOOK = STOCKPRICE / (STOCKHOLDEQ / SHARE)

(symbolic equation)
R97 = S47 / (S14 / S12)

98 PRICE TO SALES

Definition: Per share market price of company's stock divided by net sales per share.

Another way to evaluate the company's market price is to relate it to sales. The thinking here is that even if earnings are elusive, the realized sales base provides potential for earning a decent profit on those sales. It may take a new strategy or even a new management, but if the sales are there, the value is there!

Contrarian investors like to buy stocks with low P/S — below .75, if possible.[9] A study described in *Forbes* for the period 1980-1985 revealed that a majority of the top-performing stocks from a long list started out with P/S's below .20. Conversely, at the peak of the technology bull market some years ago, the P/S for a portfolio of stocks in a well-known technology index averaged above 4.0.[10]

One way to put a price on a business that is profitable and growing is to value it equal to its annual sales. This simplistic estimating tool has been around for a long time. Serious appraisers scoff at it, of course, and many owners would run to get in line to sell their businesses for this amount of money. Despite its shortcomings, it illustrates how price and sales are related.

(verbal equation)

$$\textbf{PRICE TO SALES} \;=\; \frac{\text{Stock Price}}{\text{Net Sales Per Share}}$$

(acronymic equation)

$$\textbf{PRICESALES} = 100 * \text{STOCKPRICE} / (\text{NETSALES} / \text{SHARE})$$

(symbolic equation)

$$\textbf{R98} = 100 * S47 / (S16 / S12)$$

99 OLYMPIC MODEL

Definition: The sum of SALES GROWTH CONSISTENCY (3) and PROFIT GROWTH CONSISTENCY (13), reduced by the absolute value of the difference between the two.

"How are we doing?" is a common question asked by business managers, owners, and outside investors. As this book attests, hundreds of ways exist to measure a company's progress or lack of it. Success for one may be failure for another, so the question really cannot be answered without defining terms and goals. But among those who ask the question are many who do not wish to take the time necessary to evaluate the objective data available to them. They want to make a quick judgment. They're looking for a back home, seat-of-the pants way to assess whether or not this year's results are consistent with a company destined for greatness.

There is no easy answer, of course. But for the reader who says, "I know, but give me an answer anyway," there is one simplistic measure that can be used to identify performance consistent with the very best companies. It arbitrarily and mercilessly equates success with consistent growth in sales and earnings. Number of years of consistent sales growth is added to number of years of consistent profit growth. If the two values are different, the score is reduced by the difference. If only one of the underlying measures is greater than zero the formula returns a score of zero, regardless of the value of the other. It is an unforgiving equation, of course, rewarding only concomitant, consistent growth of both measures. One fallback in either category (regardless of prior progress) and the score reverts to zero. For this reason, a low score does not signify poor performance. It reports only an absence of certainty that performance is the very best.

If your business scores 10 or above it deserves an award for exceptional performance.[11] Keep it up — it may become another Toys R Us or McDonald's. Scores below 10 are also very good, as they signify that both sales and earnings are growing consistently (though for a shorter length of time). A zero score? The jury is out.

The input numbers used in the equations for this measure are previously-computed ratios. The vertical lines in the verbal equation signify absolute value.

(verbal equation)

OLYMPIC MODEL =

$$\text{SALES GROWTH CONSISTENCY} + \text{PROFIT GROWTH CONSISTENCY} - \left| \text{SALES GROWTH CONSISTENCY} - \text{PROFIT GROWTH CONSISTENCY} \right|$$

(acronymic equation)

OLYMPMODEL=
SALESGROWCON+PROFGROWCON−ABS(SALESGROWCON−PROFGROWCON)

(symbolic equation)

$$R99 = R3 + R13 - ABS(R3 - R13)$$

100 BUSINESS VALUE ESTIMATE

Definition: The average of (1) tangible net worth multiplied by two, and (2) the capitalized value of net profit before taxes and interest (using twice long-term bond rates as the interest rate).

Working owners and outside investors often think about the worth of their businesses. Assuming there is no established market for the shares, one of the best ways to find the answer is to try to sell! Less drastic alternatives include paying a professional appraiser to do the job, or doing it yourself with the help of a good book on the subject.[12]

Another way to obtain an indication of value is to seek the advice of a business broker. Often for a fee, those well qualified in mergers and acquisitions can work up a detailed evaluation of the company. In addition to an estimate of value, the report may judge whether the business should or should not be sold. Evaluation reports are only a first step, and are oftentimes subjective.[13]

But what if the valuation is needed only for planning, or to communicate progress to an investor, lender, partner or spouse? If the business is promising and *solidly profitable*, an approximation of its worth can be made by averaging two values. The first is tangible stockholders' equity multiplied by two (twice book). The number is doubled because *consistently profitable* businesses are routinely valued higher than book. The second number is the capitalized value of earnings before taxes and interest. It is derived from an interest rate double that of low-risk bonds. Equity investments are expected to earn more than fixed-income investments because of their speculative character. Doubling the safe return approximates this expectation. An average of the two components provides a good starting point for valuing the business. To find the per-share valuation, divide by number of shares outstanding.

In the equations below, capitalized value of earnings before interest and taxes is found by dividing net profit before taxes and interest expense by twice the interest rate prevailing for long-term bonds (expressed as a decimal).[4] Thus, if net profit before taxes is $100,000, interest expense $20,000, and bond rates are at 8%, capitalized value of earnings before interest and taxes is $750,000.

WARNING! Appraising by formula is risky business. Any good appraiser first wants to know the purpose of the appraisal (there are many).[14] The formula above is slanted somewhat in favor of sellers.[15] Remember, true value is whatever buyer and seller (dealing at arms length) agree that it is. Also, the formula is useful only for profitable companies.

(verbal equation)

$$\text{BUSINESS VALUE ESTIMATE} = \frac{2 \times \text{Tangible Stockholders' Equity} + \dfrac{\text{Capitalized Value of Earnings Before Interest and Taxes}}{2}}{2}$$

(acronymic equation)
BUSVALEST=
(2*(STOCKHOLDEQ−INTAN)+(NETPROFBEFTAX+INTEREXP)/(.02*INTERRATE))/2

(symbolic equation)
R100=(2*(S14−S7)+(S29+S22)/(.02*S49))/2

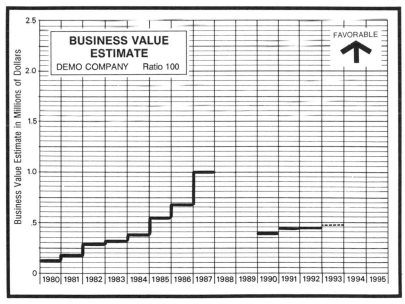

Figure 7-2. *Business Value Estimate* sample graph (for unlisted or privately held profitable companies) presents a value approximation for the shares. The estimate is undefined in those years that the firm lost money.

101 RATIO CHANGE INDICATOR

Definition: Number of ratios improved from last year reduced by number deteriorated.

This broad brush measure of change compares all appropriate ratios to their values for the previous year, providing a single number to indicate whether the business progressed or fell back. When the indicator is positive, it means that more things improved than deteriorated. When negative, it means the opposite. For a profitable, growing business, a value of zero can be viewed favorably, as it means that positive trends are intact. For a declining business, however, a zero or negative value means that things are getting worse.

Interestingly, it does not matter too much if some underlying ratios are missing when the yearly summary is prepared. The direction of yearly change tends to be the same for ratios that measure similar things. If one debt ratio has deteriorated, for example, chances are good that other debt ratios have also deteriorated. For balance, however, measures of sales, profit, capital management, expense control, marketing, and investment results should be more or less equally represented in the calculation.

This indicator can be a convenient tool for use by a board of directors in evaluating the performance of its chief executive. It may also serve as an early warning of deteriorating trends in progress or efficiency.

Care should be exercised when making the count of ratios improved and deteriorated. Some ratios signal improvement when their values increase, and others when they decline. An appendix listing of ratios includes + and − signs as suggested interpretations of improvement and decline for the ratios presented in this book.[16] But these interpretations are generalized. In certain circumstances it can be argued that the opposite direction is the favorable direction. Take the *MARKETING EXPENSE RATIO (52)* as an example. From a cost control point of view, a declining value is favorable. But if sales are not growing and more marketing is needed, an increase in the value may be favorable. For this reason, specific formulas are not provided for this indicator. Reviewers should determine for themselves which ratio changes they wish to sum, keeping in mind that it always depends on the circumstances of the company.

Notes — Chapter 7

1. Value Line Publishing Company's VALUE/SCREEN II investment analysis software, for example, provides 52 statistical facts about each of approximately 1700 actively traded companies. Of the variables in the database, only 15 have to do directly with stock price or dividends. The remaining consist of fundamental company information and classic financial ratios. *See* Bibliography, Additional Sources.

2. Appendix G.

3. Thomas P. Murphy, "What Price Independence?", *Forbes* (September 27, 1982), p. 208.

4. The acronymic and symbolic equations multiply the interest rate by .02. This is the same as doubling it and then dividing by 100 to convert the percentage to a decimal.

5. Thomas J. Herzfeld, "Open Question — Figuring Bond Fund Yields", *Barron's* (June 24, 1991), p. 38.

6. Industrial Composite, *Value Line Selection and Opinion*, (August 2, 1991), p. 747.

7. Barron's Market Laboratory, "Indexes, P/E's & Yields," *Barron's*.

8. Peter Lynch, "One Up on Wall Street," *MONEY* (January, 1989, p. 141).

9. Lawrence Minard, "The case against price/earning ratios," *Forbes* (February 13, 1984), p. 172. See also Kenneth L. Fisher, "Big Companies, Fragile Stocks," *Forbes*, (January 28, 1985), p. 126.

10. Kenneth L. Fisher, "Look Out Below," *Forbes* (March 25, 1985), p. 276.

11. Using Standard & Poor's STOCKPAK II fundamental security analysis software and a composite database of 1509 actively-traded companies, a study by the author in 1990 found that approximately half had Olympic Model scores of zero. About 44% scored above zero but below 10. Roughly 4% had scores of at least 10 but less than 20. Approximately 2% of the companies scored 20 or higher. A graph of the data and its asymptotic shape suggest that about 1% of companies maintain consistent growth in sales and earnings over very long periods of time.

12. For information on business appraisals, *See*, Shannon P. Pratt, *Valuing a Business* (Homewood, IL: Dow Jones-Irwin, 1988) *and*, Thomas J. Martin and Mark R. Gustafson, *Valuing Your Business* (New York: Holt, Rinehart and Winston, 1980).

13. Tad Leahy, "Value Judgments," *Personal Investor* (September, 1991), p. 48-53.

14. Margaret Singleton, "What's It Worth to You," *INC.* (September, 1986), p. 113-114.

15. A more conservative appraisal multiples net worth by 1.5 and capitalizes income at three times bond yields. Still another formula (more favorable to a buyer) equates the value of a small business to the sum of (1) fair market value of equipment, fixtures, and leasehold improvements, (2) inventory at seller's cost, and (3) one year's net income. Net income may need to be adjusted for owner's salary, perks, and "tax fiddles." *See*, John A. Byrne, "The Business of Businesses: How to Price a Small Business," *Forbes* (August 13, 1984), p. 112.

16. Appendix A.

Chapter 8
How to Find the Input Numbers

Newcomers to this subject may fear that considerable extra effort and staff are required to collect the information needed to calculate a large number of business ratios. This is not true. In fact, 50 input numbers are sufficient to derive all of the 101 ratios described in earlier chapters. Most of these numbers are found in the traditional balance sheet and income statement. The remainder are easily collected from other sources available to managers.

It's Easier Than You Think

How is it possible, you might ask, that only 50 pieces of information are sufficient to compute so many ratios? The answer is that the number of relationships grows geometrically as the number of information items increases. Let's assume that we are interested only in simple straight ratios (one number divided by another). The relationship possibilities for this (known as permutations) are shown in the table below:

Table 8-1
PERMUTATIONS

Number of Information Items Available	Number of Simple Relationships
2	2
3	6
4	12
5	20
10	90
25	600
50	2,450

Given 50 pieces of static information, and using only two of them at a time, it is possible to compute 2,450 ratios.[1] If year-to-year comparisons are taken into account — plus averages, trends, sums, differences, and occasional three- or four-figure computations — the number of theoretically-possible relationships (among 50 input numbers) is staggering. Most of these thousands of relationships would, of course, lack significance. The point is only to demonstrate that a very large amount of comparing power exists in a relatively small number of raw statistics.

Most of the information items needed to calculate ratios are found in financial statements provided by the company's accountants, or in income tax returns. Other important numbers (things like plant size and employee terminations) may be more difficult to obtain, but the information is usually there if you know where to look for it. The secret is to get into the habit of finding and writing down, on a regular basis, all of the figures needed to calculate the desired ratios. But remember, if some numbers simply cannot be found — no harm is done. They can be added later, or approximated if the need is timely. Even a few numbers are sufficient to start the process of ratio analysis.

As with most things in life, the language used in accounting is not always precise. Worse yet, important terms are inconsistently applied.[2] Managers unfamiliar with accounting may become frustrated when they try to find, in their own company records, the numbers used in some ratio-computing equations. Most readers know, for example, that for an incorporated business, *net worth* and *stockholders' equity* mean the same thing. But *every* reader does not know this. The widespread use of jargon can be a problem for newcomers, even those who have studied accounting at the college level.

One way to overcome this dilemma is to learn more about accounting. Confusion fades quickly as the redundant and duplicated terms are understood. The glossary to this book lists a large number of frequently used accounting words and phrases. Cross references are made between many essentially equivalent terms. It should prove helpful in matching up the line-item descriptions found in your own company records with those used in this book. Remember, one phrase is not necessarily better than another. The differences come out of tradition and style. If more help is needed, try Ralph Estes' *Dictionary of Accounting*.[3] This pocket-size A-Z reference lists hundreds of accounting terms. If all else fails, the accountant who prepares your financial statements should be willing to help out on any items that remain elusive.

Keep in mind as you collect the numbers that they tend to fall into two broad categories. Numbers in the first category describe the value or quantity of something on the last day of the accounting year. These are called *period end* numbers. Items taken from balance sheets belong in this category. Numbers in the second category are summations of transactions or events that occurred during the accounting year. These are called *period sum* numbers. Items found on the profit and loss statement fall into this category. Recognizing this difference in ratio input numbers can be helpful in understanding the meaning of a statistic, and in being sure that the numbers found are the correct ones.

The protocol suggested in this book relies on 50 specific information items. There is no magic in the number 50. It just happens to be the minimum needed to calculate the 101 ratios, measures, and models presented in the earlier chapters. Obviously, nothing precludes the collection of fewer or more. If fewer are found or used, then a lesser number of ratios will be calculated. If more are found, and the reader is able to derive the appropriate equations, then additional ratios can be calculated.

The statistics required to compute the 101 ratios come from three primary sources:

    ☐ The balance sheet (statement of financial condition)

    ☐ The profit and loss statement (income statement)

    ☐ Other internal and external sources

In the suggested protocol, 14 numbers are taken from the balance sheet, 16 from the profit and loss statement, and 20 from other sources.

Balance Sheet

The balance sheet is sometimes described as the basic accounting equation, in which assets are shown equal to liabilities plus owner equity.

$$\text{ASSETS} = \text{LIABILITIES} + \text{OWNER EQUITY}.$$

Ultimately, the effects of all transactions appear in this basic equation. It describes the financial condition of the enterprise on a specific date (usually the end of the year).

Figure 8-1 is a representative balance sheet (also known as a statement of financial position) typical in form to those used by small- and medium-size businesses. The 14 items found on the balance sheet which are most useful in the computation of business ratios are identified by circled numbers. Although the line-item descriptions may vary from one accountant's form to another, the informational content of each should be about the same.

As you review the example, you may wonder why lines that appear important (such as Total Other Assets and TOTAL LIABILITIES AND STOCKHOLDERS' EQUITY) have not been assigned numbers. The reason is that they are easily derived from entries that *have* been assigned numbers. Total Other Assets, for example, equals item (8) less the sum of items (5) and (6). TOTAL LIABILITIES AND STOCKHOLDERS' EQUITY is equal to the value of item (8). Whether one calculates ratios by hand or by computer, the goal is to record as few numbers as

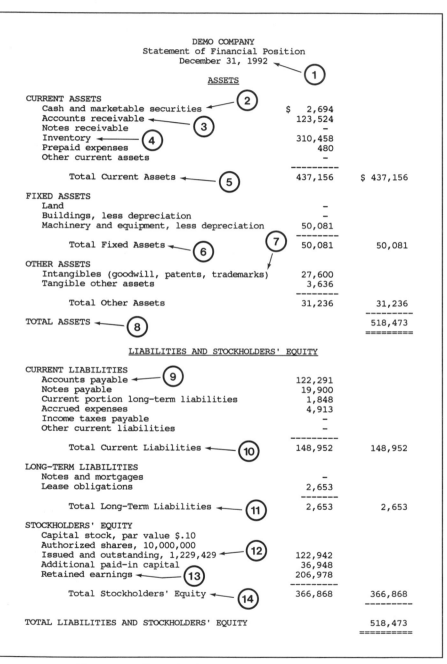

```
                        DEMO COMPANY
                 Statement of Financial Position
                      December 31, 1992   ◄──── (1)

                           ASSETS

CURRENT ASSETS                        ◄── (2)
    Cash and marketable securities ◄──         $    2,694
    Accounts receivable ◄──                       123,524
    Notes receivable        (3)                         –
    Inventory ◄──    (4)                          310,458
    Prepaid expenses                                  480
    Other current assets                               –
                                                 ---------
        Total Current Assets ◄──  (5)             437,156     $ 437,156

FIXED ASSETS
    Land                                                –
    Buildings, less depreciation                        –
    Machinery and equipment, less depreciation      50,081
                                          (7)    ---------
        Total Fixed Assets ◄──  (6)                50,081        50,081

OTHER ASSETS
    Intangibles (goodwill, patents, trademarks)     27,600
    Tangible other assets                            3,636
                                                 ---------
        Total Other Assets                          31,236        31,236
                                                               ---------
TOTAL ASSETS ◄──  (8)                                            518,473
                                                               =========

               LIABILITIES AND STOCKHOLDERS' EQUITY

CURRENT LIABILITIES        (9)
    Accounts payable ◄──                           122,291
    Notes payable                                   19,900
    Current portion long-term liabilities            1,848
    Accrued expenses                                 4,913
    Income taxes payable                                 –
    Other current liabilities                           –
                                                 ---------
        Total Current Liabilities ◄── (10)         148,952       148,952

LONG-TERM LIABILITIES
    Notes and mortgages                                 –
    Lease obligations                               2,653
                                                 ---------
        Total Long-Term Liabilities ◄── (11)        2,653         2,653

STOCKHOLDERS' EQUITY
    Capital stock, par value $.10
    Authorized shares, 10,000,000
    Issued and outstanding, 1,229,429 ◄── (12)    122,942
    Additional paid-in capital                      36,948
    Retained earnings ◄──  (13)                    206,978
                                                 ---------
        Total Stockholders' Equity ◄── (14)        366,868       366,868
                                                               ---------
TOTAL LIABILITIES AND STOCKHOLDERS' EQUITY                      518,473
                                                               =========
```

Figure 8-1. Example of a small-business balance sheet.

possible — only those needed to compute the ratios. The equations presented in this book utilize this technique wherever possible in order to simplify the task of original data collection.

Profit and Loss Statement

The net profit earned by a business enterprise is found by deducting expenses from revenues.

$$\text{PROFIT} = \text{REVENUES} - \text{EXPENSES}.$$

Revenues result from the sale of goods or the providing of services. Expenses include all the costs of producing those revenues. Where the balance sheet reflects the financial condition of the enterprise on a specific date, the profit and loss statement tells what happened over a period of time (usually one year).

Figure 8-2 is a representative profit and loss statement (also known as a *statement of earnings and retained earnings*, or an *income statement*). It is typical in form to those of most businesses. The 16 information items found on the profit and loss statement which are most useful in computing ratios are, as before, identified by circled numbers. Don't forget, some important input numbers can be calculated from the others rather than taken out on their own. PROVISION FOR TAXES, for example, is easily found by subtracting Item (30) from item (29), and there is no need to record it separately. This saves time in the collection of data without changing the results in any way.

In this example, eight varieties of operating expense — items (19) through (26) — are singled out as being the most important. For a majority of companies, these categories constitute more than 95% of total expenses. A ninth "wild card" expense category is shown as input item (27). It is there to accommodate the recording of any expense uniquely important to a particular manager or business activity. In the *Figure 8-2* example, this line item is freight out.

Income statements prepared by accountants sometimes consolidate all line items of operating expense and report only a total. A breakdown is usually provided on a separate sheet, which may or may not be included in the material available to reviewers. Insiders, of course, should encounter no difficulty in obtaining the breakdown. If the information is not available for line items (19) through (27), it is impossible to calculate the individual expense ratios. It does not prevent the computation of most other important ratios, however.

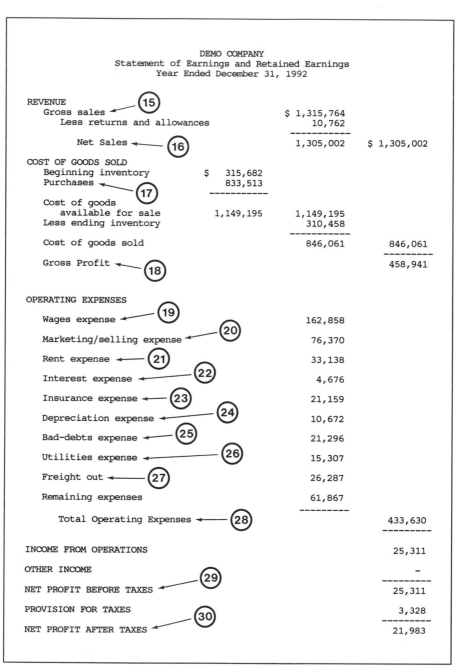

DEMO COMPANY
Statement of Earnings and Retained Earnings
Year Ended December 31, 1992

REVENUE
Gross sales ← ⑮
Less returns and allowances

$ 1,315,764
10,762

Net Sales ← ⑯

1,305,002 $ 1,305,002

COST OF GOODS SOLD
Beginning inventory $ 315,682
Purchases ← ⑰   833,513

Cost of goods
  available for sale   1,149,195   1,149,195
Less ending inventory   310,458

Cost of goods sold   846,061   846,061

Gross Profit ← ⑱   458,941

OPERATING EXPENSES
Wages expense ← ⑲   162,858
Marketing/selling expense ← ⑳   76,370
Rent expense ← ㉑   33,138
Interest expense ← ㉒   4,676
Insurance expense ← ㉓   21,159
Depreciation expense ← ㉔   10,672
Bad-debts expense ← ㉕   21,296
Utilities expense ← ㉖   15,307
Freight out ← ㉗   26,287
Remaining expenses   61,867

Total Operating Expenses ← ㉘   433,630

INCOME FROM OPERATIONS   25,311
OTHER INCOME   -

NET PROFIT BEFORE TAXES ← ㉙   25,311
PROVISION FOR TAXES   3,328
                            ㉚   ----------
NET PROFIT AFTER TAXES ←   21,983

Figure 8-2. Example small-business profit and loss statement.

Other Sources

In traditional ratio analysis, very few additional information sources are used. But as explained earlier, there are many advantages to looking beyond the two traditional financial statements for useful input numbers. In fact, it is when non-financial statistics unique to specific businesses are utilized that ratio analysis is most powerful.

What are these other input numbers? In my work I have identified 20 which have proven particularly useful. They are, of course, not the only possibilities. A manager involved in strategic planning for a business will find it worthwhile to monitor all relationships important to that business. And this may require collection of different or additional input statistics.

Finding input numbers on the balance sheet and profit and loss statement is fairly easy, once the problem of accounting jargon is overcome. The non-traditional input numbers, on the other hand, may be more difficult to collect simply because they are unfamiliar. Defining these numbers is very important if data collected over time is to be consistent in meaning. It is suggested that if managers decide to create their own ratios and base them on raw data not usually collected, they take the time and trouble to record exact definitions of terms. This allows those who follow to maintain the data collection process in a consistent manner. The 20 recommended additional input numbers (not found in the balance sheet or profit and loss statement) are:

DIVIDENDS (31). Dollar value of dividends paid to stockholders in the accounting year.

LONG-TERM DEBT MATURITIES (32). Annual dollar value of principal payments required to service long-term debt in the current year. Accountants sometimes show this number as a component of current liabilities.

TRANSACTIONS (33). Number of transactions or orders filled in the accounting year. (It doesn't matter which is used as long as it is applied consistently. The best numbers are those evidenced by invoices or sales tickets.)

PRESIDENT'S COMPENSATION (34). Gross annual wages and other compensation paid to the company's president, chief operating officer, or general manager. (Choose the individual primarily responsible for getting results.) Total executive compensation is sometimes used.

OWNERS' COMPENSATION (35). Payments to shareholders above and beyond dividends. Include consulting fees, director fees, perquisites, and wages paid to major stockholders. (For closely-held companies.)

EMPLOYEE TERMINATIONS (36). Number of employees who left the company for any reason during the year.

SOLICITATIONS (37). For mail-marketing firms, number of catalogs or flyers distributed in the accounting year. (Other businesses can use number of sales calls or total circulation of space advertising.)

SOLICITATIONS TO CUSTOMERS (38). Same as (37), but limited to solicitations directed to existing customers.

CREDIT SALES (39). The difference between total net sales and net cash sales in the accounting year.

PROPRIETARY PRODUCT SALES (40). Net sales in the accounting year of products and services that are available only from your business, or are perceived by customers as being available only from your business.

BUDGETED NET SALES (41). Dollar value of management's plan or projection for the year's net sales.

BUDGETED TOTAL EXPENSES (42). Dollar value of management's plan or projection for the year's total expenses.

BUDGETED NET PROFIT (43). Dollar value of management's plan or projection for the year's net profit. Either before-tax or after-tax profit may be used, if consistently applied.

BACK ORDERS (44). The selling price of orders received and on the books, but not yet shipped or billed at the end of the accounting year.

CUSTOMERS (45). Number of customers on the books at year end. (Differences in lines of business may require different definitions. A mail-order firm might use the number of names on its customer mailing list. A wholesale company might use its list of active accounts.)

EMPLOYEES (46). Average number of workers on the payroll over the course of the year, in full-time equivalents. The usual way to find this average is to sum the year-opening and year-closing numbers and divide by two. (If, due to seasonal factors, year-end numbers are not representative, then appropriate adjustments should be made. But be consistent!)

STOCK PRICE (47). Only for companies with shares listed on an exchange or traded in an open market — the year-end closing price in dollars per share.

FLOOR SPACE (48). Number of square feet of plant and office space utilized by the business. (If major changes occur during the accounting year, use the average of the opening and closing numbers.)

INTEREST RATE (49). Yield at year end (in percentage points) on an index of best-grade long-term corporate bonds. (*Barrons, Moodys, Investors Daily* and *The Wall Street Journal* regularly publish bond yields. Choose any available number, but be consistent from year to year.)

PRICE INDEX (50). Year-end value for any broad-ranging measure of prices such as the Consumer Price Index. Because this government statistic is not available until several months after the end of the accounting year, the latest-available number is used. It can be recorded as "preliminary," and updated later if significant changes occur. Consistency is more important than getting the latest figure. CPI information is available from the Bureau of Labor Statistics[4] or business publications such as *Barron's*.[5]

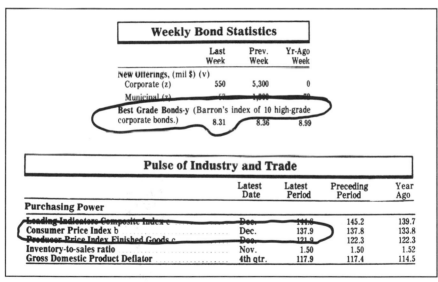

Weekly Bond Statistics

	Last Week	Prev. Week	Yr-Ago Week
New Offerings, (mil $) (v)			
Corporate (z)	550	5,300	0
Municipal (z)	63	1,900	58
Best Grade Bonds-y (Barron's index of 10 high-grade corporate bonds.)	8.31	8.36	8.99

Pulse of Industry and Trade

	Latest Date	Latest Period	Preceding Period	Year Ago
Purchasing Power				
Leading Indicators Composite Index c	Dec.	144.8	145.2	139.7
Consumer Price Index b	Dec.	137.9	137.8	133.8
Producer Price Index Finished Goods c	Dec.	121.9	122.3	122.3
Inventory-to-sales ratio	Nov.	1.50	1.50	1.52
Gross Domestic Product Deflator	4th qtr.	117.9	117.4	114.5

Figure 8-3. Bond yields and CPI information are found in *Barron's* Market Laboratory, available on most newsstands. Reprinted by permission of Barron's, © 1992 Dow Jones & Company, Inc. All Rights Reserved Worldwide.

It's worth repeating that the list of other-source statistics is only representative. Nothing prevents the collection of additional data that a manager believes are useful for computing ratios. Also, if some of the numbers suggested above are not available, no harm is done. It just means that certain ratios cannot be calculated at the present time.

Recording the Numbers

The newcomer to ratio analysis is tempted to jump right in and start calculating ratios. There is nothing wrong with this, of course, but it is not the recommended approach. Instead, the initial effort should be directed to building a historical record of the selected input numbers — before any ratios are computed. The reason for this is that some of the best information that comes from ratio analysis is the result of comparing current numbers to past numbers for the same company. This is what the calculation of averages and trends is all about. This year's ratio, in any particular category, may have little meaning if it cannot be compared to the past, or projected into the future.

How far back should one go? The usefulness of ratio information declines with age, so there is usually little point in collecting data more than 10 or 12 years old. On the other hand, because comparison with the recent past is such an important part of ratio analysis, it is a mistake to start with fewer than five years of data if the information is available.

Accurate input of statistics is facilitated if the data are first gathered and written down by hand. It doesn't matter very much how this is done. Some managers use accountant pads with a sufficient number of columns to match the data. Letter-size double entry ledger forms accommodate up to 80 information items on one side of a sheet. *Figure 8-4* illustrates the use of this form, available at most office supply stores.[6] If you wish to record data for more than a single year on one form, fold-out varieties are available accommodating 12 years of information (40 different statistics per sheet). Note the use of acronymic names to identify what is recorded. This is optional, of course. Some will prefer to use identification numbers alone, or another shorthand method.

An alternate approach uses a specially-prepared form to record one year's data. The bare form is typed once to match a company's selected input numbers, and then reproduced on a copy machine as needed. Some dedicated business-ratio software produces input forms automatically without typing. *Figure 8-5* is an example.

The reader will note occasional use of the expression N/A on the input worksheet examples. This signifies "not available" or "not applicable." But its importance is greater than might first be believed. There are times when a statistic has a value of zero (0) and times when the information simply is not available. Correct calculation of some ratios may require knowing which is the case. For that reason, it is recommend that a convention be adopted wherein N/A signifies a lack of information and 0 (zero) a true value of nil. The zero should be entered on an input sheet only when it represents a "hard zero" — that is, a factual quantity (not a lack of information). For example, the statistic indicating number of employees terminated in the year might be zero employees (0), or the information might not be available (N/A). This difference could be important when entering numbers into a computer database, or when data are later reviewed and interpreted by others.

DEMO COMPANY

NO.	NAME	VALUE	NO.	NAME	VALUE
1	YEAR	1992	26	UTILEXP	15,307
2	CASH	2,694	27	DESIGEXP	26,287
3	ACCREC	123,524	28	TOTEXP	433,630
4	INVEN	310,458	29	NETPROFBEFTAX	25,311
5	CURRASSET	437,156	30	NETPROFAFTTAX	21,983
6	FIXEDASSET	50,081	31	DIV	0
7	INTAN	27,600	32	DEBTMAT	2304
8	TOTASSET	518,473	33	TRANS	10,095
9	ACCPAY	122,291	34	PRESCOMP	43,287
10	CURRLIAB	148,952	35	OWNCOMP	8,000
11	LONGTERMLIAB	2,653	36	EMPTRMN	3.5
12	SHARE	1,229,424	37	SOLIC	8,200
13	RTDEARN	206,978	38	SOLICCUST	2,100
14	STOCKHOLDEQ	366,868	39	CREDSALES	768,236
15	GROSSSALES	1,315,764	40	PROPPRODSALES	72,011
16	NETSALES	1,305,002	41	BUDGNETSALES	1,400,000
17	PURCH	833,513	42.	BUDGTOTEXP	468,199
18	GROSSPROF	458,941	43	BUDGNETPROF	62,708
19	WAGEEXP	162,858	44	BACKORD	20,034
20	MARKEXP	76,370	45	CUST	39,512
21	RENTEXP	33,138	46	EMP	9.9
22	INTEREXP	4,676	47	STOCKPRICE	N/A
23	INSUREXP	21,159	48	SPACE	5,875
24	DEPREXP	10,672	49	INTERRATE	N/A
25	BADDEBTEXP	21,296	50	PRICEINDEX	N/A

PREPARED BY: Denise Flores

DATE: 3/9/93

Figure 8-4. Form for hand-recording input data.

```
DEMO COMPANY                    1991                STAT WORKSHEET

                NAME OF STAT              NO.           VALUE
         ------------------------------   ----      ----------------
         YEAR                        #     1              1991
         CASH                              2             2,755
         ACCOUNTS RECEIVABLE               3           117,982
         INVENTORY                         4           315,682
         CURRENT ASSETS                    5           438,566
         FIXED ASSETS                      6            45,085
         INTANGIBLES                       7            28,759
         TOTAL ASSETS                      8           512,410
         ACCOUNTS PAYABLE                  9           134,614
         CURRENT LIABILITIES              10           169,125
         LONG-TERM LIABILITIES            11                 0
         SHARES OUTSTANDING          #    12         1,223,674
         RETAINED EARNINGS                13           184,995
         STOCKHOLDERS' EQUITY             14           343,285
         GROSS SALES                      15         1,292,401
         NET SALES                        16         1,274,738
         PURCHASES                        17           856,771
         GROSS PROFIT                     18           495,316
         WAGES EXPENSE                    19           155,317
         MARKETING/SELLING EXPENSE        20           143,161
         RENT EXPENSE                     21            26,877
         INTEREST EXPENSE                 22             2,908
         INSURANCE EXPENSE                23            15,540
         DEPRECIATION EXPENSE             24            13,903
         BAD DEBTS EXPENSE                25             4,593
         UTILITIES EXPENSE                26            16,117
         DESIGNATED EXPENSE ITEM          27            32,844
         TOTAL EXPENSES                   28           465,584
         NET PROFIT BEFORE TAX            29            29,732
         NET PROFIT AFTER TAX             30            25,925
         DIVIDENDS                        31                 0
         LONG-TERM DEBT MATURITIES        32             5,163
         TRANSACTIONS                #    33            11,401
         PRESIDENT'S COMPENSATION         34            40,079
         OWNERS' COMPENSATION             35             8,000
         EMPLOYEE TERMINATIONS            36                 2
         SOLICITATIONS (TOTAL)       #    37           206,200
         SOLICITATIONS (CUSTOMERS)   #    38            85,200
         CREDIT SALES                     39           735,017
         PROPRIETARY PRODUCT SALES        40            46,575
         BUDGET NET SALES                 41         1,310,000
         BUDGET TOTAL EXPENSES            42           578,483
         BUDGET NET PROFIT AFTERTAX       43            23,517
         BACK ORDERS                      44             7,095
         CUSTOMERS                   #    45            39,738
         EMPLOYEES (AVERAGE)              46               7.9
         STOCK PRICE                      47               N/A
         FLOOR SPACE                 #    48             5,575
         INTEREST RATE               %    49               8.3
         PRICE INDEX                      50             137.9


    #=NUMBER.   %=PERCENT.   OTHER STATS IN DOLLARS.     STATS 2-14 ARE YEAR-END
    VALUES FROM BALANCE SHEET.   15-30 ARE FROM P & L STATEMENT.   15-43 ARE
    YEARLY TOTALS.   44-45 AND 47-50 ARE YEAR-END VALUES.   46 IS AN AVERAGE.
```

Figure 8-5. Computer-generated data input form.

Most accounting numbers are recorded as positive values, even when they represent negative things like liabilities. This comes out of the traditions of accounting, where classification of an item as a debit or credit determines on which side of the ledger it appears. On a balance sheet, for example, there is no such thing as negative cash. The logical equivalent to negative cash is current liability. This would be shown as a positive value on the liabilities side of the report. Therefore, when entering numbers on an input form or into a computer database, the general rule is to enter only positive values. Unfortunately, there are a few necessary exceptions. Accountants *do* acknowledge (and so record) negative values for a few *bipolar* statistics. These normally positive items hold their traditional positions in accounting records but *may* have negative signs. These exceptions (to the list of 50 protocol items suggested in this book) are retained earnings (13), stockholders' equity (14), gross profit (18), net profit before taxes (20), net profit after taxes (30), and budgeted net profit (43). For these, values may be either positive or negative. Although additional exceptions are conceivable in unusual circumstances, they are unlikely.

Variations

The protocol that derives 101 ratios from 50 input numbers was developed for small- to medium-sized American businesses organized as profit-making corporations. With care, it may also be applied to foreign corporations and unincorporated businesses.

If the company uses a medium of exchange other than the dollar, then values are recorded (and appropriate ratios calculated) in terms of that alternate unit. For example, if net sales (statistic 16) is recorded in German marks, then a ratio such as *SALES PER EMPLOYEE (8)* is understood to express marks per employee. Similarly, where the metric system is in use, floor space (statistic 48) is recorded in square meters. A ratio relating sales to space is understood to express marks per square meter. The keys to using alternate units of measure are (1) be consistent, and (2) label worksheets, reports, and graphs appropriately.

Sole proprietorships may use the protocol by following a few simple rules, and by recognizing that not all of the 101 ratios can be calculated. The first rule is to separate that which is the business from that which is personal. Second, before recording any statistics or attempting to calculate ratios, prepare an "if incorporated" financial statement applicable to the enterprise. Such a statement is a rework of the one provided by your accountant or used on your tax return, changed into the form shown in *Figures 8-1* and *8-2*. The rework adjusts for differences in how profits are calculated for proprietorships, and allows for imputing (estimating) those personal expenses which should rightly be included in ratio calculations.

Compensation of owners is one of the tricky areas. Tax collectors take the position that proprietorships cannot, from an accounting and taxation point of view, pay wages to the proprietor. The reward for a proprietor's service is profit. The "if incorporated" statement, therefore, should have added to wages and total operating expenses a sum which fairly represents the market value of the owner's services. (Such adjustments require equal, offsetting deductions in net profit.) Similarly, if you run your business from your home, you should add to rent expense and total expenses an imputed fair rental value for the home space used. These adjustments increase expenses and therefore decrease profits, but permit calculation of ratios and measures which are comparable to incorporated businesses. Each expense item on the original financial statement should be reviewed and questioned in terms of economic reality. The questions to ask are, "If my business *were* incorporated, would this or that number on the statement be different, or would other significant numbers appear on the report?"

For a typical unincorporated business, the following exceptions or adjustments usually lead to correct calculation of most applicable ratios.

> **SHARES OUTSTANDING** (12). (Not applicable)
>
> **RETAINED EARNINGS** (13). (Not applicable)
>
> **STOCKHOLDERS' EQUITY** (14). Use the net worth of the unincorporated business (business assets less business liabilities).
>
> **WAGES EXPENSE** (19). Add fair value of work done by owners.
>
> **RENT EXPENSE** (21). Add fair rental value of residential space used for business purposes.
>
> **TOTAL EXPENSES** (28). Add amounts increased in (19) and (21).
>
> **NET PROFIT AFTER TAXES** (30). Use net profit before taxes reduced by changes above and your personal marginal income-tax rate.
>
> **DIVIDENDS** (31). Use any draws not already included in wages expense.
>
> **PRESIDENT'S COMPENSATION** (34). Use imputed compensation for the most significant working owner.
>
> **OWNERS' COMPENSATION** (35). (Not applicable)
>
> **STOCK PRICE** (47). (Not applicable)

If difficulty is encountered in creating an "if incorporated" statement, chances are good that the accountant who prepared the financial statement can help in making the adjustments. And don't be surprised if some of the ratios computed are disappointing or appear out of line. Many entrepreneurs organized as sole proprietorships mix their personal and business affairs to such an extent that they simply do not know (perhaps do not want to know) how their businesses are really doing. That is one advantage of the incorporation form of business organization. It tends to report profits and other measures of performance uniformly.

Now that the input numbers have been collected and recorded, the next step is to calculate the ratios themselves. This is the subject of Chapter 9.

Notes — Chapter 8

1. For a simple computer program to calculate permutations, see Lon Poole, Mary Borchers, and Karl Koessel, *Some Common Basic Programs* (Berkeley, CA: Osborne/McGraw-Hill, Inc., 1981), p. 115-116.

2. *Forbes*, "Obfuscation, Inc.," The Numbers Game, *Forbes* (February 15, 1977), p. 78-79.

3. Ralph W. Estes, *Dictionary of Accounting* (Cambridge, MA: MIT Press, 1985). See also Joel G. Siegel and Jae K. Shim, *Dictionary of Accounting Terms* (Hauppauge, NY: Barron's Educational Series, 1987).

4   Bureau of Labor Statistics, *Summary of CPI News Release* (Washington, DC: U.S. Department of Labor).

5. Barron's Market Laboratory, Pulse of Industry and Trade, "Purchasing Power," *Barron's*.

6. Wilson-Jones double-entry ledger, form G7200 or equal. *See* Bibliography, Additional Sources.

Chapter 9
How to Calculate the Ratios

Earlier chapters describe 101 ratios meeting a variety of business needs. If the necessary input numbers have been collected and recorded, the next step is to calculate the ratios. In a modern office, this is likely to be done on a computer — but not always. In some companies, important key ratios are measured as often as every day using nothing more sophisticated than a pocket calculator. How managers and financial officers compute ratios varies widely. Some use sophisticated spreadsheet programs (entering equations and titles as needed to match the needs of an entire corporation, division, or department). Others prefer menu-driven stand-alone programs with equations already in place. A few will write their own software from scratch, using languages such as BASIC, FORTRAN, PASCAL or C.

This largely technical chapter touches on all of these possibilities. It's purpose is to explain some of the theory involved in this kind of number crunching, and to point out advantages and disadvantages of each of the methods.

Deciding Which Ratios to Monitor

Executives who have held their jobs for some time usually recognize their own managerial weaknesses. Also, they are likely to know where their firm is troubled or financially vulnerable, and which activities or departments require close control. This knowledge and experience points to the need to compile certain ratios and measures. In addition, lenders and investors may request periodic monitoring and reporting on specific relationships. A banker might insist that a minimum liquidity ratio be maintained, and a significant investor may demand a certain annual rate of growth in revenues. Out of all of this comes the basic list of necessary or "favorite" ratios for the firm in question. The list is unique to one company, having originated in day-to-day needs evolved over time.

There is no relationship between size of a firm and the number of ratios requiring review. A large company may traditionally monitor a small number of ratios, where a small company might find it helpful to examine many. Or the opposite might be true. In depends entirely on managerial style and the needs of the business.

Once a basic list is compiled, the individual in charge of ratio analysis is advised to briefly review all of the measures described in this book. If ratios are found with potential to reveal useful information (perhaps previously unknown or overlooked), they should be added to the basic list. It is true that many more ratios are available for consideration than are likely to be required or effectively used by most businesses. That is why, before the days of computers, experts cautioned against compiling more than a few significant ratios. They reasoned that the amount of time a manager could devote to mathematical analysis of the company's activities was limited. But now that computers are universally available, there is no reason to avoid the study of a large number of ratios. Selection can be made in the reviewing process.

If the reader elects to create ratios not described in this book — measures deemed important to a particular firm or line of business — some precautions are offered. First, beware of *pseudo* ratios. A pseudo ratio is one derived from statistics that cannot logically be compared. For example, the ratio of stockholders' equity to inventory probably expresses no relationship useful to a manager. Logical relationships signify some degree of causative interdependence. The ratio of income taxes to profits, on the other hand, is logical because income taxes are a function of profits (taxes rise when profits rise). The ratio of rent expense to sales is also logical because the creation and processing of sales can only be accomplished if space is available (and paid for) to carry out such activities.

A second precaution is to derive unique or custom ratios only when they compare statistics that are significant to the firm and are under at least partial control of the manager. The measure of employee income taxes withheld to employee wages is logical, but lacks significance because the ratio cannot legally be changed through managerial action.

Finding and Applying the Ratio Formulas

Most books that discuss business ratios use accounting terminology to identify the variables. Verbal instructions explain what operations are performed. *TURNOVER OF ASSETS (64)*, for example, is described as being equal to net sales divided by total assets, or:

$$\textbf{TURNOVER OF ASSETS} \ = \ \frac{\text{Net Sales}}{\text{Total Assets}}$$

Verbal equations are ideal for explaining ratios in books and the classroom. The input variables are familiar accounting words and phrases. In most cases they are easily recognized and the algebraic operations are obvious.

Serious study of business ratios, however, requires the careful preparation of worksheets and reports. A ratio with a very long name (such as *RETURN ON PRESIDENT'S COMPENSATION*) may not fit in the title column of a ledger. This leads to a need for abbreviation. As a general rule, visual recognition and understanding decline as the name becomes shorter. The tradeoff, therefore, is between economy of space (in ledgers and reports) and understandability. Also, if a computer program is written to make the calculations, variable names should be chosen that are legal for the language used. Long phrases (particularly if they include blank spaces) may not qualify. One solution to this problem is to use acronymic variable names for ratios and input numbers. They are relatively short, understandable in most situations, and readable by a computer.

The three equation types presented in this book are functionally equivalent, with each having its own set of advantages and disadvantages. One form should not be considered better than another — it is just a question of application. Different forms are provided not to confuse, but to accommodate existing preferences for method of computation and presentation.

Now, let's compute a ratio using this representative acronymic equation (from *Chapter 2*) to determine *OPERATING MARGIN (11)*:

OPERMARG=100∗(NETPROFBEFTAX+INTEREXP+DEPREXP)/NETSALES

Four input numbers are required to make the computation. Assume, for example:

Net profit before taxes	37,540
Interest expense	8,059
Depreciation expense	14,440
Net sales	1,186,000

Keeping in mind that the asterisk(∗) means multiply and the slash (/) divide:

OPERATING MARGIN = 100 ∗ (37540 + 8059 + 14440) / 1186000
= 100 ∗ 60039 / 1186000
= 100 ∗ .0506
= 5.06 %.

Ratios like this are easily calculated on a scrap of paper or desk calculator. *Understanding the Formulas* in *Chapter 1* provides more information on variable names, other algebraic operators, order of execution of calculations, and so forth.

Year __1991__

DEMO COMPANY
RATIO CALCULATION WORKSHEET

Ratio Name ___RETURN ON RISK___ Ratio No. __24__

Definition ___NET PROFIT AFTER TAXES DIVIDED BY LAST___
YEAR'S TANGIBLE STOCKHOLDERS' EQUITY, MULTIPLIED
BY 100 TO PROVIDE A PERCENTAGE, THE RESULT
REDUCED BY THE INTEREST RATE PREVAILING
FOR LONG-TERM CORPORATE BONDS.

Equation

$$R24 = 100 * S30 \Big/ (S14LY - S7LY) - S49$$

$$\left[\begin{array}{l} \text{WHERE:} \quad S30 \ = 25925 \\ \quad\quad\quad S14LY = 287360 \\ \quad\quad\quad S7LY = 29909 \\ \quad\quad\quad S49 \ = \ 8.30 \end{array} \right]$$

Calculations

$$R24 = 100 * 25925 \Big/ (287360 - 29909) - 8.30$$

$$= \quad\quad 10.07 \quad\quad\quad\quad - 8.30$$

$$= \quad\quad\quad 1.77$$

Calculated Ratio Value ___1.77___

Notes and Comments
BELOW PLAN !

Prepared by ___Denise Flores___ Date __4/9/92__

Figure 9-1. Calculation worksheet for a single ratio.

Some of the equations are more complicated, involving nested operations. Here, the propensity for error is fairly high when calculations are made on demand and without following a consistent protocol. In this situation it is recommended that worksheets be used to record the formulas and input numbers. This allows checking by others, and establishes a calculation history to be passed along to the next individual assigned to this work in the future.

Such a worksheet (for one ratio) is shown as *Figure 9-1*. There is room for all necessary information, including each step in the calculation process. At one time or another, all of us have heard a teacher say, "Show your work!" Particularly in mathematics and the sciences, we were admonished to do this for good reason. Recording all the steps is a time-honored procedure for minimizing error and facilitating checking. If an error is later discovered or suspected, the worksheet discloses exactly where it originated. Although most ratios are figured at the end of the accounting year, many are calculated as often as daily. Even year-end reports are frequently revised. For these reasons, worksheets should show preparation dates (and "as of" dates if the data are constantly changing). No, it isn't necessary to use an entire sheet of paper for each ratio. Enterprising reviewers find ways to shorten the process using available accounting forms. But remember, if the ratio is worth computing in the first place and the job is done by hand, accuracy and the ability to track errors is what counts — not the amount of paper consumed.

When computing a ratio, the result is only as meaningful as the least precise input number. If a company's net profit is $233,785 and (on average) 12 employees worked during the year, it is inappropriate to conclude that *PROFIT PER EMPLOYEE (26)* is $19,482.08. Of course, that is the number a computer or calculator displays. But because the divisor (12 employees) is known to only two significant figures, the ratio is properly *presented* with that degree of precision — $19,000.

In the same vein, rules of common sense apply to the search for *accuracy*. Accountants and engineers are trained to place great importance on the thoroughness and exactness of computations and reports. Managers, on the other hand, have a continuing need to make decisions and get things done. In many business situations, meaningful estimates in hand now may be more valuable than highly accurate data available "soon."

Keep in mind also the meaning of *greater than* and *less than*. In modern mathematics, these expressions refer to relative positions on a number line ranging from an infinitely large negative value on the left to an infinitely large positive value on the right. *Greater than* means more to the right and *less than* means more to the left. The absolute magnitudes of the numbers are significant in making these comparisons only if their signs are the same. Thus $+0.005$ is greater than $-356,454$. If a computer is used, this is the way it can be expected to interpret its instructions.

Calculating Averages

Business ratio analysis consists primarily in comparing one statistic for an accounting period to a different statistic of the same period (profits to working capital, or expenses to sales). Another way to analyze a business statistic is to create and then examine a *time series* or *set* for that same statistic. A time series is a record of values that prevailed in the past at periodic points in time right up to the present. From a mathematical point of view it doesn't matter whether the statistic is a raw number or a previously-computed ratio, nor does it matter what time base is used (daily, weekly, monthly, yearly).

There are a number of ways to examine a time series. In business, the most frequently-used methods are averaging and creating trendlines. Whichever method or combination of methods in used, the goal is to extract information from the series that is not readily apparent in its latest value. If this year's return on sales is 6.7%, for example, a cautious manager may wish to know to what extent this figure is *representative* of the company's performance. Is the number a one-year anomaly, or can it generally be relied upon in budgeting and planning for future periods?

Table 9-1 is an example of a time series of the type that might be encountered in a business situation. Values exist for 13 periods. The numbers might represent net profit (in millions), return on assets, or annual percentage growth in sales — it doesn't matter. All that matters for purposes of analysis is that the periods be equally spaced and the values represent the same thing in each period.

Table 9-1
EXAMPLE TIME SERIES

Time	Value
1992	4.4
1991	6.9
1990	7.0
1989	−19.8
1988	−11.3
1987	20.5
1986	20.0
1985	19.3
1984	19.4
1983	22.6
1982	36.4
1981	30.6
1980	54.7

An *average* (sometimes called a measure of central tendency) is a single value that summarizes or represents the general significance of a set of unequal values. Because, from period to period, the individual numbers in a series may be subject to wide swings in value, it is risky to base decisions on only the most recent number. Consider also that business reports are issued monthly, quarterly, or yearly primarily because of tradition and tax law. These calendar reporting periods may be unrelated to marketing strategies, product life cycles, or economic events. For all of these reasons, it is a good idea to periodically compute an average of any important ratio or statistic maintained as a series. Averages have the ability to smooth out period-to-period variations, and are commonly relied upon in business to tell the greater truth. Mathematicians work with many kinds of averages (modes, medians, arithmetic means, geometric means, harmonic means, quadratic means and so forth). Each has inherent advantages and disadvantages depending on application.[1] *Table 9-2* illustrates the computation of several averages using the 13 data values from *Table 9-1*.

The *arithmetic mean* of a set of numbers is found by dividing the sum of the individual values in the set by the number of numbers in the set. In a set of N numbers of values $X^1, X^2, X^3 \ldots X^N$, the mathematical notation for the arithmetic mean $(\overline{X})$ is :

$$\overline{X} = \frac{X^1 + X^2 + X^3 + \ldots X^N}{N}$$

This is the simplest, most commonly-used average. It lends itself well to "back of envelope" calculations. Just add up the values in the series and divide by the number of values.[2]

Although this simple mean is sometimes a good representation of a series, it has two disadvantages when used in business. First, it assigns the same importance to old information as it does to new. This may be undesirable when applied to an annual series, particularly if long-term trends have skewed the data or if important changes have taken place in products, markets, or management. Another disadvantage to the simple mean is that if any anomalies exist (one extremely large value in one period, for example), the resulting average may be grossly non-representative.

One way to deal with these problems is to exclude older values before computing the average. Stock market analysts do exactly this when they compile *moving* or *range-limited* averages encompassing 20 days, 200 days, a year, or even five years.[3] How many data points are retained depends on what is measured and what theory or rationale makes it logical. A company's earnings growth, for example, is frequently reported as a five-year moving average.

Table 9-2
AVERAGING METHODS

Simple Arithmetic Mean				Range-Limited Arithmetic Mean			
Year	Data Value	Weighting Factor	Product	Year	Data Value	Weighting Factor	Product
1992	4.4	1.00	4.4	1992	4.4	1.00	4.4
1991	6.9	1.00	6.9	1991	6.9	1.00	6.9
1990	7.0	1.00	7.0	1990	7.0	1.00	7.0
1989	−19.8	1.00	−19.8	1989	−19.8	1.00	−19.8
1988	−11.3	1.00	−11.3	1988	−11.3	1.00	−11.3
1987	20.5	1.00	20.5	1987	20.5	1.00	20.5
1986	20.0	1.00	20.0	1986	20.0	1.00	20.0
1985	19.3	1.00	19.3	1985	19.3	0	0
1984	19.4	1.00	19.4	1984	19.4	0	0
1983	22.6	1.00	22.6	1983	22.6	0	0
1982	36.4	1.00	36.4	1982	36.4	0	0
1981	30.6	1.00	30.6	1981	30.6	0	0
1980	54.7	1.00	54.7	1980	54.7	0	0
Sum:			210.7	Sum:			27.7
Divisor: 13		**AVERAGE: 16.2**		Divisor: 7		**AVERAGE: 4.0**	
Weighted Arithmetic Mean (Linear — 10 Periods)				Weighted Arithmetic Mean (Exponential — 80% Multiplier)			
Year	Data Value	Weighting Factor	Product	Year	Data Value	Weighting Factor	Product
1992	4.4	1.00	4.4	1992	4.4	1.00	4.4
1991	6.9	.90	6.2	1991	6.9	.80	5.2
1990	7.0	.80	5.6	1990	7.0	.64	4.5
1989	−19.8	.70	−13.9	1989	−19.8	.51	−10.1
1988	−11.3	.60	−6.8	1988	−11.3	.41	−4.6
1987	20.5	.50	10.3	1987	20.5	.33	6.8
1986	20.0	.40	8.0	1986	20.0	.26	5.2
1985	19.3	.30	5.8	1985	19.3	.21	4.1
1984	19.4	.20	3.9	1984	19.4	.17	3.3
1983	22.6	.10	2.3	1983	22.6	.13	2.9
1982	36.4	0	0	1982	36.4	.11	4.0
1981	30.6	0	0	1981	30.6	.09	2.8
1980	54.7	0	0	1980	54.7	.07	3.8
Sums:		5.50	25.8	Sums:		4.73	32.3
Divisor: 5.5		**AVERAGE: 4.7**		Divisor: 4.73		**AVERAGE: 6.8**	

Anomalies are sometimes excluded if the result is an average more representative of the data. When many data points exist, some averaging systems routinely throw out the highest and lowest values in the series. Exclusion of data in computing an average is a theoretically-acceptable practice, but should be undertaken with great care. If exclusions are made, it is important to note the fact on worksheets and reports.

A still better way to discount the significance of older information is to weight the information according to its recency:

$$\overline{X} = \frac{X^1 * W^1 + X^2 * W^2 + X^3 * W^3 + \ldots X^N * W^N}{W^1 + W^2 + W^3 + \ldots W^N}$$

Here, the data values X^1, X^2, X^3 . . . X^N are multiplied by weighting factors W^1, W^2, W^3 . . . W^N. The most recent value X^1 is weighted 100% (multiplied by one). Older values are multiplied by progressively smaller factors selected to match the particular business situation. There are many ways to select the weighting factors. One straightforward method multiplies each data value by a linearly-declining factor based on a certain number of periods. A business might, for example, decide to weight its data over a 10-year period. This year's information is weighted 100%, the previous year's 90%, the year prior to that 80%, and so forth. When the progression reaches zero, it means that data for that period (and any earlier periods) are discarded. The result is a 10-period linearly-weighted arithmetic mean. Note that this kind of weighting does not require any particular number of data points to make the computation. If only two values are available and 10-year weighting is desired, the first weighting factor is 1.0 and the second 0.9. Incidentally, a shortcut formula for the divisor in this averaging equation is $(N+1)/2$, where N is the number of periods included in the averaging computation.

Some analysts are reluctant to entirely discard older data. Instead of linear weighting, they devalue the information with time according to an exponential curve. In this approach no data are ignored. Older values are simply downweighted (according to their age) to the point of insignificance. Using an 80% multiplier, for example, this year's information is valued at 100%, the previous year's 80% (1.00 X .80), the next prior year 64% (.80 X .80), and so forth. This progression never reaches zero. As long as data values exist, they are multiplied by the appropriate factor and included in the averaging sum. The set can include as few values as one (in which case the average is equal to that value), or an infinite number of values. A shortcut computer formula for the divisor in *this* averaging equation is $(1-M \char`\^ N)/(1-M)$, where M is the multiplier (always less than one) expressed as a decimal (such as 0.80) and N the number of data values included in the series.

The median is another useful average. It is defined as the middle value of the series after it is arranged in ascending or descending order.

(If there happen to be an even number of data values, the median is the arithmetic mean of the two middle values.) Although the median is not often used in the study of business ratios, there is one very good reason to make the computation. If the mean and median differ materially, the analyst should take this as an indication that anomalies or biases probably exist in the data. It is a warning that the computed average should not be relied upon until the reason for the disparity is determined. Mean-to-median comparing is a good first step to judging whether or not a computed average is representative.

The four averages derived in *Table 9-2* originate in a real-life business situation — *RETURN ON ASSETS (20)* for an electrical supply company. This particular series was selected to illustrate averaging because the long-term downtrend in the ratio (from 54.7 in 1980 to 4.4 in 1992) was certain to result in significant differences in the averaging types. Here are the results:

Table 9-3
VARIATIONS IN RESULTING AVERAGES

Type of Average	Value
Simple Arithmetic Mean	16.2
Range-Limited Arithmetic Mean (7 years)	4.0
Linearly Weighted Mean (10 Years)	4.7
Exponentially Weighted Mean (80% Multiplier)	6.8
Median	19.4

One should not conclude from the obvious disparity that averages are useless. Better conclusions to make are that disparities stimulate the analyst to find out why they exist, and that averaging methods need to be selected to match the business situation. Each averaging method assigns more or less significance to older values. Each method assigns more or less significance to anomalies. The best average is one that includes (and weights) those data with greatest likelihood of representing near-term results. Stable, slow-growing businesses may benefit from including more older information in their computations. Changing or fast-growing businesses may not.

If only one average is to be computed for an annual business ratio series, I believe the best choice is the arithmetic mean, exponentially weighted using a percentage factor selected by the analyst. *Table 9-4* illustrates the effective downweighting that occurs for aged data as a function of the weighting percentage. The values in the table are rounded to the nearest tenth of a percent. Values less than 0.1 exist in all cases but are not shown.

Table 9-4
EXPONENTIAL WEIGHTING FACTORS

Selected Multiplier	Resulting Percentage Weights Assigned to Data Values Depending on Their Age (0 to 25 years)								
%	0	1	3	5	7	10	15	20	25
100	100	100	100	100	100	100	100	100	100
95	100	95	86	77	70	60	46	36	28
90	100	90	73	59	48	35	21	12	7
85	100	85	61	44	32	20	9	4	2
80	100	80	51	33	21	11	4	1	0
75	100	75	42	24	13	6	1	0	0
70	100	70	34	17	8	3	0	0	0
65	100	65	27	12	5	1	0	0	0
60	100	60	22	8	3	1	0	0	0
55	100	55	17	5	2	0	0	0	0
50	100	50	13	3	1	0	0	0	0

How is this table used? The analyst reviews the list of resulting weights row by row until a set is found that provides approximately the desired devaluation of the data with age. That is, based on known changes in the business, product lines, markets, and management, how much weight is to be given to data that are 3 years old, 5 years old, 10 years old? This is a subjective, managerial judgment. When the desired row is selected, the percentage weighting factor is read in the left-hand column. Remember, the goal of averaging is to find numbers that are representative of the periodically-changing values and meaningful to the business as it exists today.

Calculating and Projecting Trends

The trend of a set of data points is defined as its prevailing inclination or tendency. It is measured by best-fitting a mathematically-defined "curve" to the values using a technique called regression. This curve is then taken to be representative of the data, and from it hypothetical trendline values can be predicted for any desired point in time. The significance of this is that, as in averaging, the trendline smooths out variations in the period-to-period values. If, using the trendline, an estimate of the latest value in the series is made, the result is usually a number different from the *actual* latest value. But because this estimated value is influenced by *all* of the numbers in the set, it is considered representative of the set. The latest actual value may not be. From a managerial point of view, the trend-predicted representative value is very often more reliable for planning and decision making than the latest value.

As with averages, there are many kinds of regression (linear, geometric, exponential, and so forth). The simplest form (most suitable for analyzing general business problems) is called *linear regression* and uses the method of least squares to fit a straight line to the data points.[4] The slope of this line is taken to be representative of the series. For certain types of data, an exponential curve provides a better fit than does a straight line. A chart of net sales, for example, may have an upward bias resulting from company growth and/or inflation. When this is the case, exponential regression typically provides a more representative trendline. Trendlines are easily derived on a computer using simple algorithms.[5]

Managers are interested in trends because of a belief that they are likely indicators of what will happen in the future. This idea is deeply rooted in our thinking — that a clearly identified trend is more likely to continue than not. Trends and averages are also important to investors, particularly those who rely on so-called technical indicators. If it is true that a trend is more likely than not to continue, then it is no surprise that so many investors look to trend analysis to help them decide when to buy and sell. One way investors use trendlines is to compare the current price of a stock or commodity to a moving average of prices. If the trend of prices is positive and the current price falls below the moving average, the event is called a *crossover*. This signifies that things have changed and prices may be headed lower. Conversely, if the trend is negative and the current price rises above the moving average, the signal is that prices may be heading higher. If the average or trend itself changes direction it is called a *reversal* and is believed to be a very important signal. From a study of prices for the Dow Jones Industrial Average since 1900, Martin J. Pring concludes, " . . . with rare exception — whenever the slope of the Dow's 12-month moving average changed direction, it indicated that a very important move was underway."[6]

Great controversy exists over the significance of trends and their ability to predict the future. Common sense and human experience suggest that ignoring trends is folly. Every year the national debt of the United States increases. The trend by any measure is up. Betting that it will be lower next year is a bet few would take. Mark Hulbert says, "Academic research has shown that although the length of trends is random, trends do exist, and any consistent trend-following system will eventually profit from them."[7]

But trees don't grow to the sky. And despite wide acceptance of the importance of trends, many academic works deny their ability to predict the future. David Dreman cites a number of studies attesting to the essentially random movement of stock, bond, and commodity prices.[8] He concludes, " . . . the studies demonstrated that future price movements cannot be predicted from past changes." And, "Without exception, the findings indicated randomness in price . . ." Although these inquiries related to investing and the prices of investment vehicles (not to ratios), the differences of opinion are unsettling.

My contribution to this debate is to suggest that when human behavior is involved, trends deserve respect. Human behavior is not random. It is influenced significantly by habit and deeply-entrenched cultural biases. Translated into economic decisions and the resulting business numbers, it is logical to believe that well-defined trends are more likely than not to continue on course. But even if trend analysis is scientifically disproved of predictive value, the suggestion of predictive capability makes managers think about what the trends are telling them. Thinking results in change and action. In his book *Theory and Problems of Statistics*, Professor Murray R. Spiegel sums it up well when he says: "Coupled with an investigator's common sense, experience, ingenuity, and good judgment, mathematical [time series] analysis has proved valuable both in long-range and short-range forecasting."[9]

Using a Computer

By now it is probably apparent that if many ratios are calculated on a regular basis, the job is made easier and less prone to error if done on a computer. This section briefly discusses the kinds of software used in ratio analysis — spreadsheets, stand-alone menu-driven programs, and custom programs written by or for the analyst.

Let's start with these custom programs. Why would anyone write ratio software from scratch? The answer is that standardized solutions do not always meet the needs of unique businesses. When special problems require special answers, creative solutions are indicated. Regardless of the availability and obvious advantages of commercial software, interest in customized programs is not likely to disappear.

This is not a book about computer programming, so no attempt is made to provide general instruction in that specialty. Comment is limited to a few aspects related to ratio analysis, using the BASIC language as an example. Programmers working with other languages will find different solutions to many of the same problems.

How variable names are handled in a computer program is fundamental to its design. Modern versions of BASIC, for example, allow descriptive variable names comprised of as many as 40 characters. The names may include letters, numbers, and the decimal point, but not blank spaces or certain other words and symbols. Additional rules preclude *starting* the name with a number, or a keyboard symbol that might otherwise be acceptable (check the manual). In BASIC, the numbered line of code to calculate the value of a familiar ratio *could* be written:

```
700 RETURNONEMPLOYEECOMPENSATION=100*NETPROFITAFTERTAXES/WAGESEXPENSE
```

A variation of the above uses the decimal point to separate key words.

Using such a technique, the ratio title might be written:

RETURN.ON.EMPLOYEE.COMPENSATION

This improves readability. In some languages (not BASIC), the under-score character is used to achieve the same result.[10]

Although fully spelled-out variable names leave little doubt as to what is being computed, the approach is cumbersome and sometimes impractical. Another way is to use abbreviated names:

700 **RETEMPCOMP**=100∗NETPROFAFTTAX/WAGEEXP

In this shorthand form the variables are still recognized. This is an important advantage during program development, when more than one programmer is involved, or if user modification of programs is anticipated.

Programmers working with many similar equations may not wish to select names that visually communicate the identity of each variable. Instead (to minimize the amount of computer code), they will use shorter symbolic names:

700 **R21**=100∗S29/S19

Translating line 700, *RETURN ON EMPLOYEE COMPENSATION (21)* is equal to 100 times input statistic 29 (net profit after taxes) divided by input statistic 19 (wages expense). This form of equation (modified as explained later in this chapter) is also used in spreadsheet programs.

A variation of the symbolic variable name encloses the identification numbers in parentheses:

700 **R(21)**=100∗S(29)/S(19)

When this is the case, the computer recognizes the variables as being *dimensioned*. Early in such a program a dimension statement defines arrays by telling the computer how much memory space it needs to reserve for each group of variables (such as **R** or S). A BASIC program dimension statement (line 100) might look like this:

100 DIM R(100), S(50)

The advantage in using dimensioned variables is that algorithms can be devised that perform a large number of computations with a minimum number of program steps. This is accomplished by means of FOR-NEXT statements or DO LOOPS, depending on the language. The result is much shorter programs that run faster.

Anticipating the input of anomalies is a task that needs to be faced by all computer programmers. It is particularly significant in business ratio analysis. Most ratio equations involve division of one input number by another. What if one of the numbers is unavailable and the computer attempts to divide by zero — or both input numbers are negative and the calculation returns an illogical positive value? What if the algorithm requires comparison to last year's ratio and the number does not exist? What if a computed ratio number is so large that it cannot fit in the space allocated for it in a report. Good software (whatever its type) anticipates and overcomes most of these practical problems.

The next several pages describe a few simple business ratio programs written in BASIC. Such programs are available from a number of sources. Leon A. Wortman's, *Business Problem Solving with the IBM PC & XT* includes useful business information as well as a program listing to derive 24 common ratios.[11] Another book, *Executive Planning with BASIC* by X. T. Bui, includes a code listing which computes 10 ratios.[12] This latter program has a few extra features. It allows input of more than one year's data and also prepares simple graphs of the ratios. These are desirable enhancements. Anyone starting out to create a business ratio program might wish to acquire both of these books to see how two different authors approached the same problems. Style varies greatly among programmers.

As a further aid to self-programmers using BASIC, three sample programs are included in this book. RATIOS1.BAS (*Figure 9-2*) computes 10 common ratios and is designed around acronymic variable names. RATIOS2.BAS (*Figure 9-3*) Is functionally identical except that it is written with symbolic variable names. Running either program produces the report shown in *Figure 9-5*. These programs are easily modified and expanded to meet particular needs.

AVTREND.BAS, the third program, analyzes a keyboard-entered time series to show highest value entered, lowest value entered, arithmetic mean, exponentially-weighted arithmetic mean (with changeable weighting factor), and median. It also determines a trendline for a changeable range of the data points (using linear or exponential regression), and indicates the slope of this line in data units and as a periodic percentage change. Lastly, it provides a representative value for the latest period and also predicts the next value in the series (next month or next year) assuming the trend continues.

Although similarly short, this program is more sophisticated than the two ratio programs. It uses dimensioned symbolic variable names, mostly having one or two characters. The exponential multiplier (for averaging), the trendline range, and the type of regression (linear or exponential) may be changed in program line 140. Program notes in the appendix lead interested students or managers through some of its complexities.[13] *Figure 9-4* is a program listing in BASIC. *Figure 9-6* shows a sample report using the data in *Table 9-1*.

```
100 REM - "RATIOS1.BAS" COMPUTES 10 COMMON RATIOS
110 REM - THIS VERSION USES ACRONYMIC VARIABLE NAMES
120 '
130 REM             *****INPUT HEADING DATA*****
140 CLS: INPUT"YOUR COMPANY NAME"; COMPANY$
150 INPUT"YEAR OF DATA"; YEAR$
160 CLS: PRINT TAB(INT((78-(LEN(COMPANY$)))/2));COMPANY$
170 PRINT: PRINT TAB(25);"BUSINESS RATIOS REPORT "+YEAR$: PRINT
180 '
190 REM   *****INPUT STATISTICS FROM FINANCIAL STATEMENT*****
200 INPUT "INVENTORY"; INVEN
210 INPUT "CURRENT ASSETS"; CURRASSET
220 INPUT "INTANGIBLES"; INTAN
230 INPUT "TOTAL ASSETS"; TOTASSET
240 INPUT "CURRENT LIABILITIES"; CURRLIAB
250 INPUT "STOCKHOLDERS' EQUITY"; STOCKHOLDEQ
260 INPUT "NET SALES"; NETSALES
270 INPUT "GROSS PROFIT"; GROSSPROF
280 INPUT "NET PROFIT AFTER TAXES"; NETPROFAFTTAX
290 '
300 REM           *****COMPUTE BUSINESS RATIOS*****
310 LET GROSSMARGFACT=100*GROSSPROF/NETSALES
320 LET RETSALES=100*NETPROFAFTTAX/NETSALES
330 LET RETASSET=100*NETPROFAFTTAX/(TOTASSET-INTAN)
340 LET RETWORKCAP=100*NETPROFAFTTAX/(CURRASSET-CURRLIAB)
350 LET CURRRATIO=CURRASSET/CURRLIAB
360 LET QUICKRATIO=(CURRASSET-INVEN)/CURRLIAB
370 LET TURNWORKCAP=NETSALES/(CURRASSET-CURRLIAB)
380 LET EQRATIO=100*STOCKHOLDEQ/(TOTASSET-INTAN-CURRLIAB)
390 LET TURNASSET=NETSALES/TOTASSET
400 LET INVENDAYSALES=INVEN/(NETSALES/365)
410 '
420 REM               *****PRINT REPORT*****
430 PRINT: PRINT "GROSS MARGIN FACTOR=";
440 PRINT TAB(29) USING "#####.#%"; GROSSMARGFACT;
450 PRINT TAB(45); "RETURN ON SALES=";
460 PRINT TAB(71) USING "#####.#%"; RETSALES
470 PRINT "RETURN ON ASSETS=";
480 PRINT TAB(29) USING "#####.#%"; RETASSET;
490 PRINT TAB(45); "RETURN ON WORKING CAPITAL=";
500 PRINT TAB(71) USING "#####.#%"; RETWORKCAP
510 PRINT "CURRENT RATIO=";
520 PRINT TAB(29) USING "#####.#"; CURRRATIO;
530 PRINT TAB(45); "QUICK RATIO=";
540 PRINT TAB(71) USING "#####.#"; QUICKRATIO
550 PRINT "TURNOVER OF WORKING CAPITAL=";
560 PRINT TAB(29) USING "#####.#"; TURNWORKCAP;
570 PRINT TAB(45); "EQUITY RATIO=";
580 PRINT TAB(71) USING "#####.#%"; EQRATIO
590 PRINT "TURNOVER OF ASSETS=";
600 PRINT TAB(29) USING "#####.#"; TURNASSET;
610 PRINT TAB(45); "INVENTORY IN DAYS SALES=";
620 PRINT TAB(71) USING "#####"; INVENDAYSALES
630 PRINT: PRINT "HAVE A NICE DAY !"
640 '
650 END
```

Figure 9-2. Sample BASIC program (using acronymic variable names) computes 10 common ratios.

```
100 REM - "RATIOS2.BAS" COMPUTES 10 COMMON RATIOS
110 REM - THIS VERSION USES SYMBOLIC VARIABLE NAMES
120 '
130 REM                    *****INPUT HEADING DATA*****
140 CLS: INPUT"YOUR COMPANY NAME"; COMPANY$
150 INPUT"YEAR OF DATA"; YEAR$
160 CLS: PRINT TAB(INT((78-(LEN(COMPANY$)))/2));COMPANY$
170 PRINT: PRINT TAB(25);"BUSINESS RATIOS REPORT "+YEAR$: PRINT
180 '
190 REM   *****INPUT STATISTICS FROM FINANCIAL STATEMENT*****
200 INPUT "INVENTORY"; S4
210 INPUT "CURRENT ASSETS"; S5
220 INPUT "INTANGIBLES"; S7
230 INPUT "TOTAL ASSETS"; S8
240 INPUT "CURRENT LIABILITIES"; S10
250 INPUT "STOCKHOLDERS' EQUITY"; S14
260 INPUT "NET SALES"; S16
270 INPUT "GROSS PROFIT"; S18
280 INPUT "NET PROFIT AFTER TAXES"; S30
290 '
300 REM                  *****COMPUTE BUSINESS RATIOS*****
310 LET R9=100*S18/S16
320 LET R17=100*S30/S16
330 LET R20=100*S30/(S8-S7)
340 LET R21=100*S30/(S5-S10)
350 LET R30=S5/S10
360 LET R31=(S5-S4)/S10
370 LET R35=S16/(S5-S10)
380 LET R38=100*S14/(S8-S7-S10)
390 LET R64=S16/S8
400 LET R70=S4/(S16/365)
410 '
420 REM                    *****PRINT REPORT*****
430 PRINT: PRINT "GROSS MARGIN FACTOR=";
440 PRINT TAB(29) USING "#####.#%"; R9;
450 PRINT TAB(45); "RETURN ON SALES=";
460 PRINT TAB(71) USING "#####.#%"; R17
470 PRINT "RETURN ON ASSETS=";
480 PRINT TAB(29) USING "#####.#%"; R20;
490 PRINT TAB(45); "RETURN ON WORKING CAPITAL=";
500 PRINT TAB(71) USING "#####.#%"; R21
510 PRINT "CURRENT RATIO=";
520 PRINT TAB(29) USING "#####.#"; R30;
530 PRINT TAB(45); "QUICK RATIO=";
540 PRINT TAB(71) USING "#####.#"; R31
550 PRINT "TURNOVER OF WORKING CAPITAL=";
560 PRINT TAB(29) USING "#####.#"; R35;
570 PRINT TAB(45); "EQUITY RATIO=";
580 PRINT TAB(71) USING "#####.#%"; R38
590 PRINT "TURNOVER OF ASSETS=";
600 PRINT TAB(29) USING "#####.#"; R64;
610 PRINT TAB(45); "INVENTORY IN DAYS SALES=";
620 PRINT TAB(71) USING "#####"; R70
630 PRINT: PRINT "HAVE A NICE DAY !"
640 '
650 END
```

Figure 9-3. The same program using symbolic variable names.

```
100 REM - PROGRAM NAME "AVTREND.BAS" BY SHELDON GATES
110 REM - COMPUTES AVERAGES AND TRENDLINES
120 REM - YOU MAY MODIFY VARIABLES 'MF', 'TR', AND 'RT' IN STMT 140
130 REM - MF=WEIGHTING FACTOR / TR=TRENDLINE RANGE / RT=REGRESSION TYPE
140 MF=.8: TR=5: RT=0: REM - SEE PROGRAM NOTES
150 '
160 REM        *****INPUT HEADING DATA AND VALUES FOR EACH PERIOD*****
170 CLS: INPUT"DESCRIPTION OF STATISTIC"; S$
180 INPUT"HOW MANY PERIODS"; P: IF P=1 THEN ER=1
190 INPUT"FIRST PERIOD REFERENCE NUMBER (SUCH AS '1' OR '1990')"; FP
200 PRINT: DIM S(P), A(P)
210 FOR L=1 TO P
220 PRINT"VALUE OF STATISTIC FOR"; FP+L-1;: INPUT S(L): A(L)=S(L)
230 NEXT L: PRINT"PRESS ENTER TO VIEW REPORT";: INPUT X
240 '
250 REM           *****FIND HIGH/LOW AND COMPUTE AVERAGES*****
260 HI=S(1): LO=S(1)
270 FOR L=P TO 1 STEP -1: IF S(L)<LO THEN LO=S(L)
280 IF S(L)>HI THEN HI=S(L)
290 A3=A3+S(L): A4=A4+S(L)*MF^A5: A6=A6+MF^A5: A5=A5+1
300 FOR M=P-L TO 1 STEP -1
310 A1=A(M): A2=A(M+1): IF A1<A2 THEN 330
320 A(M)=A2: A(M+1)=A1
330 NEXT M
340 NEXT L
350 AM=A3/P: WM=A4/A6 : MD=A(INT(P/2)+1): IF LO=<0 AND RT=1 THEN ER=2
360 IF P/2=INT(P/2) THEN MD=(A(INT(P/2))+A(INT(P/2)+1))/2
370 '
380 REM              *****COMPUTE AND ANALYZE TRENDLINE*****
390 RT$="LINEAR": IF TR>P THEN TR=P
400 FOR L=1 TO TR: IF ER=2 THEN 520
410 A(L)=S(P-TR+L): IF RT=1 THEN A(L)=LOG(A(L)): RT$="EXPONENTIAL"
420 T1=T1+L: T2=T2+A(L): T3=T3+L^2: T4=T4+A(L)^2: T5=T5+L*A(L)
430 NEXT L
440 SL=(TR*T5-T1*T2)/(TR*T3-T1^2): T6=(T2-SL*T1)/TR
450 T1=SL*(T5-T1*T2/TR): T4=T4-T2^2/TR: T2=T4-T1: CC=0
460 RV=T6+SL*TR: PV=T6+SL*(TR+1): IF T4<>0 THEN CC=100*SQR(T1/T4)
470 IF RT=1 THEN RV=EXP(T6)*EXP(SL*TR): PV=EXP(T6)*EXP(SL*(TR+1))
480 SL$="FLAT": IF SGN(SL)=1 THEN SL$="RISING"
490 IF SGN(SL)=-1 THEN SL$="FALLING"
500 '
510 REM                  *****PRINT REPORT*****
520 CLS: PRINT TAB(INT((79-LEN(S$))/2)); S$
530 PRINT: PRINT TAB(INT((79-2*LEN(STR$(FP))-2)/2)); FP; "-"; FP+P-1
540 PRINT: PRINT"NUMBER OF PERIODS= ";: PRINT TAB(46); P
550 PRINT"HIGHEST AND LOWEST VALUES="; TAB(46); HI; TAB(62); LO
560 PRINT"LAST VALUE ("; FP+P-1;")"; TAB(46); S(P)
570 PRINT: PRINT"AVERAGES:"
580 PRINT"   ARITHMETIC MEAN="; TAB(46); AM
590 PRINT"   EXPONENTIALLY-WEIGHTED"
600 PRINT"      ARITHMETIC MEAN (FACTOR";MF;")="; TAB(46); WM
610 PRINT"   MEDIAN="; TAB(46); MD: PRINT: IF ER>0 THEN 700
620 PRINT RT$+" TRENDLINE (RANGE";TR;"PERIODS):"
630 PRINT"   REPRESENTATIVE VALUE FOR"; FP+P-1; "="; TAB(46); RV
640 PRINT"   PROJECTED VALUE FOR"; FP+P; "="; TAB(46); PV
650 IF RT=0 THEN PRINT"   PERIODIC SLOPE (DATA UNITS)="; TAB(46); SL;
660 IF RT=0 THEN PRINT TAB(62); SL$
670 PRINT"   PERIODIC SLOPE (%)="; TAB(46); 100*(PV-RV)/ABS(RV)
680 IF CC<>0 THEN PRINT"   CORRELATION COEFFICIENT (%)="; TAB(46);CC
690 '
700 IF ER>0 THEN PRINT: PRINT"ERROR"; ER; "- SEE PROGRAM NOTES"
710 PRINT: PRINT"THANKS FOR USING AVTREND.BAS !"
900 END
```

Figure 9-4. Program listing for AVTREND.BAS.

```
                              DEMO COMPANY

                       BUSINESS RATIO REPORT 1992

      INVENTORY? 310458
      CURRENT ASSETS? 437156
      INTANGIBLES? 27600
      TOTAL ASSETS? 518473
      CURRENT LIABILITIES? 148952
      STOCKHOLDERS' EQUITY? 366868
      NET SALES? 1305002
      GROSS PROFIT? 458941
      NET PROFIT AFTER TAXES? 21983

      GROSS MARGIN FACTOR=         35.2%    RETURN ON SALES=                1.7%
      RETURN ON ASSETS=            4.5%     RETURN ON WORKING CAPITAL=      7.6%
      CURRENT RATIO=               2.9      QUICK RATIO=                    0.9
      TURNOVER OF WORKING CAPITAL= 4.5      EQUITY RATIO=                 107.3%
      TURNOVER OF ASSETS=          2.5      INVENTORY IN DAYS SALES=        87

      HAVE A NICE DAY!
      Ok
```

Figure 9-5. Sample report — RATIOS1.BAS and RATIOS2.BAS.

```
                          RETURN ON ASSETS

                            1980 - 1992

      NUMBER OF PERIODS=                  13
      HIGHEST AND LOWEST VALUES=          54.7              -19.8
      LAST VALUE ( 1992 )                 4.4

      AVERAGES:
          ARITHMETIC MEAN=                16.20769
          EXPONENTIALLY-WEIGHTED
            ARITHMETIC MEAN (FACTOR .8 )=  6.820086
          MEDIAN=                         19.4

      LINEAR TRENDLINE (RANGE 5 PERIODS):
          REPRESENTATIVE VALUE FOR 1992 =  9.059999
          PROJECTED VALUE FOR 1993 =      14.87
          PERIODIC SLOPE (DATA UNITS)=     5.81             RISING
          PERIODIC SLOPE (%)=             64.12805
          CORRELATION COEFFICIENT (%)=    74.82418

      THANKS FOR USING AVTREND.BAS !
      Ok
```

Figure 9-6. Program report produced by AVTREND.BAS.

The Wortman programs, Bui programs, and the three programs introduced in this book are only an introduction to the what and how of using a computer to write customized business-ratio software. Keep in mind that they are only simple demonstration programs, written to explain some of the techniques of one specific type of computer programming. As far as I know they are not represented by their creators to be more than that. To keep listings short and understandable, enhanced features have intentionally been omitted. More sophisticated software would be expected to include:

- ❑ Ability to build a database of statistics covering many years
- ❑ Ability to record this database on a floppy or hard disk
- ❑ Ability to edit the database
- ❑ Ability to print reports showing what is in the database
- ❑ Ability to compute a large number of ratios
- ❑ Ability to print multi-year ratio reports
- ❑ Ability to calculate weighted averages
- ❑ Ability to identify trends and predict next year's ratio
- ❑ Ability to handle errors (such as "divide by zero")
- ❑ Ability to produce simple graphs
- ❑ Ability to print forms for hand-recording of input data
- ❑ Ability to write reports to files for subsequent editing by a word processing program

Stand-alone software with all or many of the features above can be acquired from sources listed in the Appendix. The principal advantage to using one of these programs is that algorithms for computing the ratios are in place when the program is purchased. Ratio reports are printed out almost as quickly as historical data are keyed into the database. The inexpensive ratio-computing program PC-RATIOS is an example.[14] More information on these programs (and a few sample reports) is provided in Chapter 10.

Because computer technology (and software in particular) changes so rapidly, the reader is advised to find out what is available at the time serious ratio analysis is undertaken. As interest in this subject grows, more and perhaps better products are likely to appear.

Another type of software particularly well-suited to computing and presenting business ratios is the so-called electronic or visual spreadsheet. The screen and report layouts of these programs are modeled after the multi-column ledgers traditionally used by accountants. To understand these programs, one should first review the mechanical ledgers from which they evolve. In such worksheets (often large in size), fine printed lines delineate the columns and intersecting rows. The spaces where intersection occurs are called boxes. Numbers are written by hand in the boxes to signify values appropriate to the column and row titles. In an expense ledger, for example, each column is reserved for a specific month and each row for a particular category of expense. Row 17 might be used for rent expense and column 3 for values applicable to February. Thus the box created by the intersection of row 17 and column 3 shows rent expense for February.

The principal disadvantage to mechanical spreadsheets is that whenever any number in any box is changed, all related totals need to be changed manually. Even with the aid of a calculator this is time-consuming, and there is high propensity for error. In electronic spread-sheets, on the other hand, computation is automatic (assuming the proper formulas are in place). Editing a number in one box instanta-neously changes related numbers in other boxes.

In these electronic spreadsheets, formulas (which may include constants and/or function codes) are contained in *cells* located in another electronic dimension behind the appropriate box. If the operator wants to know how a computed number is derived, the cursor is moved to its box and the formula commanded to appear on the screen. Cell formulas are often long and complex. Notes and even small essays are sometimes attached to cells to explain where numbers or formulas originate, and may be called up to the screen when needed. Spreadsheets can be altered by the operator, printed out, saved to disk, and loaded again for further revision. Spreadsheets thus serve as databases, calculators, and report and graph generators. They have remarkable power. At the time this is written, programs are available that accomodate up to 256 columns and 16,384 rows. By the time this is read, the numbers likely will have increased again.

Figure 9-7 illustrates a very simple business ratio spreadsheet report. The example computes the same measures as RATIOS1.BAS and RATIOS2.BAS, but includes three years of data. The first column is reserved for titles. Adjacent columns (one for each year) show the input statistics and computed ratios. The last column displays average values for each row. The titles, cell formulas, and input statistics are entered by the operator through the computer keyboard. Values in the ratio rows are computed and displayed automatically by the program using the formulas hidden in the cells behind each ratio box. Many more columns and rows may be utilized than shown on the example (more years, more input statistics, and more ratios). Additional columns may also added to show trends and make projections.

If a spreadsheet of the type described is prepared with formulas and titles in place (but no input statistics), and then saved to computer disk as a file, it is called a *template*. It functions in much the same way as a stand-alone program written in BASIC or FORTRAN. Within the spread-

```
                        DEMO COMPANY

            BUSINESS RATIOS REPORT - 1992

                        1990        1991        1992      AVERAGE

INPUT STATISTICS:
  INVENTORY            238,332     315,682     310,458     288,157
  CURRENT ASSETS       323,152     438,566     437,156     399,625
  INTANGIBLES           29,909      28,759      27,600      28,756
  TOTAL ASSETS         404,229     512,410     518,473     478,371
  CURRENT LIABILITIES  111,001     169,125     148,952     143,026
  STOCKHOLDERS' EQUITY 287,360     343,285     366,868     332,504
  NET SALES          1,186,578   1,274,738   1,305,002   1,255,439
  GROSS PROFIT         512,017     495,316     458,941     488,758
  NET PROFIT AFTER TAXES 31,592     25,925      21,983      26,500

RATIOS:
  GROSS MARGIN FACTOR       43.2%       38.9%       35.2%       38.9%
  RETURN ON WORKING CAPITAL 14.9%        9.6%        7.6%       10.3%
  EQUITY RATIO             109.1%      109.1%      107.3%      108.5%
  TURNOVER OF WORKING CAPITAL 5.6%       4.7%        4.5%        4.9%
  INVENTORY IN DAYS SALES     73          90          87          84
  RETURN ON SALES           2.7%        2.0%        1.7%        2.1%
  RETURN ON ASSETS          8.4%        5.4%        4.5%        5.9%
  CURRENT RATIO             2.9         2.6         2.9         2.8
  QUICK RATIO                .8          .7          .9          .8
  TURNOVER OF ASSETS        2.9         2.5         2.5         2.6


Have a nice day!
```

Figure 9-7. Simple business ratio spreadsheet report.

sheet environment, the operator first "loads" the template. This places labels and formulas into their desired positions. The next step is to key input numbers (taken from the company's financial statements and other business records) into the appropriate cells on the screen. After a few seconds, the ratio values appear as if by magic.

It should be noted that formulas contained in spreadsheet cells use yet another method for identifying variables. It is called the location method, because that is how the computer is instructed to select the numbers on which to operate. For example, the formula for *GROSS MARGIN FACTOR (8)* for 1992 is:

$$100*D24/D23.$$

This means that the value of the ratio is equal to 100 times the number found in the box located at the intersection of column D and row 24, divided by the number found in the box located at the intersection of column D and row 23. The spreadsheet *screen display* identifies each column by a letter of the alphabet and each row by a number. These location aids do not appear on the printed report, however.

Spreadsheet programs provide the user with many algebraic operators and function commands for use in formulas. In order to derive the average value of *GROSS MARGIN FACTOR (9)* for the years 1990-1992, for example, this code (it varies with the software) might be specified for box E28:

AVERAGE(B28:D28).

During calculation, when the spreadsheet program reaches box E28, it computes the arithmetic mean of the three numbers appearing in boxes B28, C28, and D28. User guides for spreadsheet software list scores of additional algebraic operators and function commands. All are based on the location method of variable identification.

In applying the protocol of this book (50 input numbers and 101 ratioo) to spreadsheels, a minimum of 151 rows are required (more if descriptions and appearance-enhancing titles are provided). The number of columns needed depends on how many years of data are studied on one sheet, and whether or not columns are provided for averages, trends, and projections. Incidentally, when the number of rows or columns exceeds the capability of the line printer, the spreadsheet software automatically breaks up the report. After printing, the pieces are reassembled. Recent releases of most programs include utilities or built-in features for printing reports in a landscape format, often eliminating the need for reassembly.

Modern spreadsheet programs are extremely powerful. They combine many of the important features of database, calculation, and word processing software. Important in ratio analysis is their ability to prepare and print graphs in a wide variety of formats.

The next chapter talks more about graphing and the importance of presentation.

Notes — Chapter 9

1. Murray R. Spiegel, *Theory and Problems of Statistics* (New York: McGraw-Hill, 1990), p. 58-86. See also Robert S. Witte, *Statistics* (New York: CBS College Publishing, 1985), p. 37-47.

2. Some analysts do not include the latest value in a time-series average. They argue that the purpose for computing the average is to find a representative past value to compare to the current or latest value, and thus the latest "compared to" value is not rightly included in the average.

3. For a discussion of a 12-month moving average, see Martin J. Pring, "Divining the Dow," *Investment Vision* (January/February, 1990), p. 20-26.

4. For an explanation of the least squares method see William Mendenhall and Robert J. Beaver, *Introduction to Probability and Statistics* (Boston: PWS-Kent Publishing, 1991), p. 398-401.

5. Lon Poole, Mary Borchers, and Karl Koessel, *Some Common Basic Programs* (Berkeley, CA: Osborne/McGraw-Hill, 1981), p. 145-146.

6. Pring, p. 22.

7. Mark Hulbert, "Whipsaw!", *Forbes* (May 14, 1990), p. 164.

8. David Dreman, *The New Contrarian Investment Strategy* (New York: Random House, 1982), p. 33-34.

9. Spiegel, p. 403.

10. Example: **PROPRIETARY_PRODUCT_RATIO**

11. Leon A. Wortman, *Business Problem Solving with the IBM PC & XT* (Bowie, MD: Brady, 1983), p. 190.

12. X. T. Bui, *Executive Planning with BASIC* (Berkeley, CA: Sybex, 1982), p. 129.

13. Program notes for AVTREND.BAS:

Variables

A( )	Time-based input statistic (modified during execution)
A1-A6	Internal variables used in computing averages
AM	Arithmetic mean
CC	Correlation coefficient
ER	Error code
FP	First period identification number
HI	Highest value input statistic
L	For-Next counter
LO	Lowest value input statistic
M	For-Next counter
MD	Median
MF	Exponential multiplying factor (default 0.8 - line 140)
PV	Projected value for future period
RT	Regression type (0=linear, 1=exponential)
RT$	Regression type description
RV	Representative value of statistic at last period
S$	Statistic description
S( )	Time-based input statistic
SL	Periodic slope
SL$	Slope characteristic (rising, flat, falling)
T1-T6	Internal variables used to compute trendline
TR	Trendline range (default 5 periods - line 140)
WM	Exponentially-weighted arithmetic mean

Error Messages

0	No errors
1	Insufficient number of data values (minimum 2)
2	Unacceptable data values - zero or negative numbers not allowed in exponential regression

Other Program Notes

1	Correlation coefficient undefined if slope=0.
2	Periodic slope (%) is rate of change between representative value (at last period) and projected value.
3	Periodic slope undefined in exponential regression.
4	Multiplying factor, trendline range, and regression type may be modified in statement 140
5	Default trendline range of 5 periods is suggested for annual business data. For monthly or other data different values are appropriate.

14. PC-RATIOS is available from McLane BookSales. *See* Bibliography, Additional Sources.

Chapter 10
How to Present the Ratios

In small companies, it is common for owners or managers to compute and analyze their own ratios. Larger firms, on the other hand, may assign the task to financial officers or staff members. Sometimes these individuals lack authority to act on what the ratios tell them. This means that if executives or general managers are to give thoughtful consideration to the information, it must be presented to them clearly and concisely. Even in small companies where ratio records are maintained informally, there is a need for neatness and consistency.

Ratio reports range in complexity from simple interoffice memos (calling attention to significant changes or trends) to notebooks presenting graphs of hundreds of ratios. Getting the busy executive's attention may itself be difficult, so it is important that the form of presentation match the actual needs and style of the decision maker. Whatever their form or complexity, ratio reports should include:

- ☐ Company name
- ☐ Period-ending date of report
- ☐ Ratio description
- ☐ Calculated value for the ratio, including the measurement unit
- ☐ Name of the individual who prepared the report.

More extensive reports may show:

- ☐ Ratio identification number, if a protocol is used
- ☐ Values for the ratio in prior years
- ☐ Averages and projections for the ratio
- ☐ Industry standard values for the ratio
- ☐ Indication of the ratio's trend — up, down, no change
- ☐ Commentary from preparer, including recommendations.

Decision makers sometimes want to know how the ratios were calculated, and may request formulas and underlying statistics. Obviously, this background material should be made available to any person charged with responsibility for acting on it. But as a general rule, the presentation of distracting information should be avoided. If a ratio is not understood, the background numbers can then be provided.

There is no way to know in advance which piece of ratio information is likely to be important in a given business situation. Although this problem can be partially solved by calculating and presenting a large number of ratios, it is still possible that important relationships will be overlooked. This is a universal information-handling problem. Most of us are deluged daily with many more facts and figures than we can assimilate. Working through this dilemma can be difficult. It is, of course, one of the important things managers are paid to do — that is, obtain and review information relevant to the business decisions being made. It follows from this that although scores of business ratios can (and perhaps should) be calculated at a staff or clerical level, it is the responsibility of the key manager to decide which of these to analyze in depth.

Ratio information is usually presented in one of two forms — numerical or graphic. Numerical presentations are the logical outgrowth of the collection and calculation process, and are perhaps best when large quantities of information are involved. Graphs, on the other hand, are easiest to read and understand.

Numerical Presentations

The simplest and perhaps most attention-getting form of numerical presentation is the interoffice memo (*Figure 10-1*). Not only does discussion of a single ratio give it a priority position in the thinking process, communicating it in the form of a memo suggests that action is required. Supporting data or recommendations may be included or attached to the memo.

Spreadsheets, whether prepared by hand or on a computer, are well suited to showing larger quantities of ratio information. *Figure 10-2* is an example of the first page of a hand-prepared report which accommodates up to six years of data. As the form provides 40 lines per page, three pages are required to list all 101 ratios described in this book. Larger forms are also available (11 X 17 inches) which accommodate 14 years of data and fold down to 8-1/2 X 11 inches.[1] Both forms fit nicely into standard three-ring binders. Each year, after the ratios are computed, their values are entered on the form in the appropriate column. When one set of sheets is filled (6 years), a new set is started for the seventh year, and so on. Note the optional use of acronymic ratio names to conserve form space.

DEMO COMPANY
INTEROFFICE MEMO

TO: Bill Jackson, President

FROM: Elmore McPherson, Marketing Manager

DATE: January 11, 1993

SUBJECT: Sales Growth

You've told me many times that ours is a growth company, and it is my job (using innovative and aggressive marketing programs) to be sure that adequate growth takes place.

Our sales growth in 1992 (just determined) was a meager 2.4%.

Although in the prior year 1991 we grew about 7.5%, over the last _five_ years we have contracted. In fact, our sales have annually declined about 11.2% on average since 1987.

In my opinion this is a direct result of cutbacks in our marketing budget which began in 1987-88. There may have been good reasons for the decisions made at that time. But now we need to _increase_ advertising, _increase_ the size of our sales staff, and gain greater understanding of the changing needs of our customers. It's the only way we will reverse this unfortunate trend.

Please let me know when we can meet to discuss this. I have some charts to show you and specific proposals to turn this situation around.

EM:jh

Figure 10-1. Example of interoffice memo single-ratio report.

If averages, trends, or other indicators are computed, it is preferable to put them on separate summary pages (because the results change each year). This is also a good place to list industry norms which might be available. Any of the techniques described in *Chapter 9* may be used to calculate whatever summaries or signals are appropriate to the company's needs. The underlying numbers required to make the summary computations are taken from the ratio spreadsheets. One or more sets of sheets may be involved in computing averages and trends, depending on the number of years of data required for the calculations. *Figure 10-3* is an example of the first page (only 40 ratios shown) of a summary report to accompany *Figure 10-2*. In this example, calculation of a 7-year linear weighted average also required data from 1986.

Exactly the same results are obtained (and much faster) using an electronic spreadsheet. Here, any summary information is included in additional columns on the same sheet because values are automatically calculated and revised when data for the next year are added. Of course, this approach requires that the user have sufficient familiarity with spreadsheet software to enter the correct ratio formulas into the proper cells.

Still another way to present computer-generated ratio information is to use dedicated software which produces journal-type reports directly. The operator using this type of program simply selects the desired report option on a menu screen, presses the correct keys, and the report is prepared on the line printer. *Figures 10-4 and 10-5* show a 101-ratio report covering a selected year and two prior years. *Figure 10-6* is a by-year report for a single ratio. Both were prepared by PC-RATIOS.[2] An advantage to dedicated software is that each step in the collection, calculation, and presentation process is menu directed. There is no need to enter formulas into cells, and in case of difficulty help screens are available to answer questions.

FINANCIAL RATIOS II is a dedicated software program that computes ratios and at the same time compares them to a built-in database of industry ratios selected by Standard Industrial Classification (SIC) codes. The database can be modified or loaded with ratio data from an external source.[3] BUSINESS VALUATION+RATIOS is another program to consider. It computes business valuations (by 30 different methods) as well as five years of ratios. It also produces 35 graphs of financial statement trends.[4] Still another program, RATIO MASTER, calculates 60 key ratios with 30 built-in graphs. It computes changes from prior years and also makes comparisons to industry averages. Up to five years of data may be entered directly from the menu or imported from a spreadsheet or ASCII file using a special utility which is included.[5] As mentioned earlier, software changes rapidly. By the time this is read, new programs will probably be available.

DEMO COMPANY
RATIO REPORT

Initials	Date
Prepared By	
Approved By	

© WILSON JONES COMPANY   G7696 ColumnWrite ®   MADE IN U.S.A.

RATIO No.	NAME	1987	1988	1989	1990	1991	1992
1	SALESGROW	29.5	-26.9	-23.1	-15.8	7.4	2.4
2	AFFGROWRATE	31.4	N/A	N/A	13.7	10.1	7.0
3	SALESGROWCON	8	0	0	0	1	2
4	BUDGCMPLSALES	124.8	66.7	71.2	77.1	97.3	93.2
5	DEFLSALESGROW	24.0	-29.8	-26.5	-20.6	4.2	N/A
6	BRKEVENSALESFACT	123.2	85.6	77.3	107.9	106.4	105.8
7	REVSPACE	378.56	276.69	230.98	212.84	228.65	222.13
8	SALESEMP	105,378	84,864	98,528	147,584	161,769	131,553
9	GROSSMARGFACT	43.7	38.5	40.2	43.2	38.9	35.2
10	BRKEVENMARG	35.5	44.9	52.0	40.0	36.5	33.2
11	OPERMARG	9.6	-4.2	-9.3	5.1	3.7	3.1
12	PROFGROW	51.9	-162.1	N/A	128.8	-17.9	-15.2
13	PROFGROWCON	4	0	N/A	1	0	0
14	BUDGCMPLPROF	45.8	N/A	N/A	107.1	110.2	35.1
15	DEFLPROFGROW	45.5	N/A	N/A	N/A	-20.4	N/A
16	ADEQPROF	54.4	N/A	N/A	N/A	86.3	180.7
17	RETSALES	5.0	-4.3	-7.8	2.7	2.0	1.7
18	RETSALESBEFTAX	8.2	-6.5	-11.8	3.2	2.3	1.9
19	RETGROSSPROF	11.5	-11.1	-19.4	6.2	5.2	4.8
20	RETASSET	20.5	-11.3	-19.8	7.0	6.9	4.5
21	RETWORKCAP	45.9	-21.2	-39.7	20.6	12.2	8.2
22	RETNETWORTH	38.0	-17.9	-32.9	15.6	10.1	7.0
23	RETINVESCAP	37.1	-12.5	-24.5	18.2	10.9	7.6
24	RETRISK	28.4	-27.5	-41.8	6.6	1.8	N/A
25	RETEMPCOMP	42.9	-26.8	-46.6	21.5	16.7	13.5
26	PROFEMP	5,283	-3,617	-7,684	3,929	3,290	2,216
27	RETPRESCOMP	2.5	-1.4	-2.3	.87	.65	.51
28	RETOWNCOMP	2.5	-1.3	-2.1	2.0	3.2	2.7
29	RETSPACE	18.98	-11.79	-18.01	5.67	4.65	3.74
30	CURRRATIO	2.7	2.5	1.7	2.9	2.6	2.9
31	QUICKRATIO	.66	.97	.67	.76	.73	.85
32	CURRDEBTEQ	50.1	56.3	115.9	43.1	53.8	43.9
33	DEBTEQ	58.0	66.2	123.2	45.4	53.8	44.7
34	DEBTASSET	35.0	37.6	51.6	28.9	33.0	29.2
35	TURNWORKCAP	6.8	6.6	9.2	5.6	4.7	4.5
36	FIXEDASSETRATIO	23.1	26.9	31.7	19.9	14.3	14.8
37	FIXEDASSETMIX	13.9	15.3	13.3	12.7	8.8	9.7
38	EQRATIO	92.7	91.0	93.2	97.8	100.0	99.2
39	SUPPFINASSET	18.6	24.2	37.7	22.5	26.3	23.6
40	DEPRRATE	21.4	25.4	23.7	28.2	30.8	21.3

PAGE 1

Figure 10-2. Sample multi-year hand-prepared ratio report.

DEMO COMPANY
SUMMARY REPORT

© WILSON JONES COMPANY   G109 Columnwrite 2

RATIO NO.	NAME	MEASURE UNIT	1992 VALUE	7-YEAR LINEAR WEIGHTED AVERAGE	TREND DIRECTION	PROJECTION FOR 1993	MEDIAN INDUSTRY NORM
1	SALESGROW	%	2.4	-3.7	UP	15.5	
2	AFFGROWRATE	%	7.0	9.9	DOWN	3.5	
3	SALESGROWCON	#	2	2	UP	2	
4	BUDGCMPLSALES	%	93.2	88.3	UP	104.9	
5	DEFLSALESGROW	%	N/A	N/A			
6	BRKEVENSALESFACT	%	105.8	101.7	UP	117.5	
7	REVSPACE	$	222.13	242.7	DOWN	200.82	
8	SALESEMP	$	131,553	128,027	UP	171,845	
9	GROSSMARGFACT	%	35.2	39.4	DOWN	36.8	
10	BRKEVENMARG	%	33.2	39.5	DOWN	29.7	
11	OPERMARG	%	3.1	1.6	UP	7.9	
12	PROFGROW	%	-15.2	23.9	DOWN	-112.1	
13	PROFGROWCON	#	0	N/A			
14	BUDGCMPLPROF	%	35.1	80.1		12.1	
15	DEFLPROFGROW	%	N/A	N/A			
16	ADEQPROF	%	180.7	N/A			
17	RETSALES	%	1.7	.3	UP	5.4	3.9
18	RETSALESBEFTAX	%	1.9	-0.0	UP	7.1	
19	RETGROSSPROF	%	4.8	.6	UP	14.1	
20	RETASSET	%	4.5	2.0	UP	15.0	7.8
21	RETWORKCAP	%	8.2	5.0	UP	29.2	
22	RETNETWORTH	%	7.0	3.9	UP	24.2	17.9
23	RETINVESCAP	%	7.6	6.4	UP	22.7	
24	RETRISK	%	N/A	N/A			
25	RETEMPCOMP	%	13.5	5.7	UP	38.8	
26	PROFEMP	$	2,216	999	UP	6,419	
27	RETPRESCOMP	X	.5	.2	UP	1.7	
28	RETOWNCOMP	X	2.7	1.5	UP	5.0	
29	RETSPACE	$	3.74	.91	UP	12.97	
30	CURRRATIO	N	2.9	2.6	UP	3.1	2.8
31	QUICKRATIO	N	.85	.78	DOWN	.74	.5
32	CURRDEBTEQ	%	43.9	59.0	DOWN	36.5	46.7
33	DEBTEQ	%	44.7	62.7	DOWN	32.9	68.3
34	DEBTASSET	%	29.2	35.0	DOWN	25.5	
35	TURNWORKCAP	X	4.5	5.9	DOWN	3.5	
36	FIXEDASSETRATIO	%	14.8	20.4	DOWN	9.0	21.6
37	FIXEDASSETMIX	%	9.7	11.6	DOWN	7.2	
38	EQRATIO	%	99.2	96.5	UP	103.2	
39	SUPPFINASSET	%	23.6	25.8	DOWN	23.0	
40	DEPRRATE	%	21.3	25.0	DOWN	25.6	

PAGE 1

Figure 10-3. Sample hand-prepared summary report.

DEMO COMPANY
BUSINESS RATIO REPORT

1992

			1990	1991	1992
	< SALES RATIOS >				
1	SALES GROWTH	%	-15.8	7.4	2.4
2	AFFORDABLE GROWTH RATE	%	13.7	10.1	7.0
3	SALES GROWTH CONSISTENCY	#	0	1	2
4	BUDGET COMPLIANCE (SALES)	%	77.1	97.3	93.2
5	DEFLATED SALES GROWTH	%	-20.6	4.2	N/A
6	BREAK-EVEN SALES FACTOR	%	107.9	106.4	105.8
7	REVENUE TO SPACE	$	212.84	228.65	222.13
8	SALES PER EMPLOYEE	$	147,584	161,769	131,553
	< PROFIT RATIOS >				
9	GROSS MARGIN FACTOR	%	43.2	38.9	35.2
10	BREAK-EVEN GROSS MARGIN	%	40.0	36.5	33.2
11	OPERATING MARGIN	%	5.1	3.7	3.1
12	PROFIT GROWTH	%	128.8	-17.9	-15.2
13	PROFIT GROWTH CONSISTENCY	#	1	0	0
14	BUDGET COMPLIANCE (PROFIT)	%	107.1	110.2	35.1
15	DEFLATED PROFIT GROWTH	%	N/A	-20.4	N/A
16	ADEQUACY OF PROFITS	%	N/A	86.3	180.7
17	RETURN ON SALES	%	2.7	2.0	1.7
18	RETURN ON SALES BEFORE TAX	%	3.2	2.3	1.9
19	RETURN ON GROSS PROFIT	%	6.2	5.2	4.8
20	RETURN ON ASSETS	%	7.0	6.9	4.5
21	RETURN ON WORKING CAPITAL	%	20.6	12.2	8.2
22	RETURN ON NET WORTH	%	15.6	10.1	7.0
23	RETURN ON INVESTED CAPITAL	%	18.3	10.9	7.6
24	RETURN ON RISK	%	6.6	1.8	N/A
25	RETURN ON EMPLOYEE COMP	X	21.5	16.7	13.5
26	PROFIT PER EMPLOYEE	$	3,929	3,290	2,216
27	RETURN ON PRESIDENT'S COMP	X	0.87	0.65	0.51
28	RETURN ON OWNERS' COMP	X	2.0	3.2	2.7
29	RETURN ON SPACE	$	5.67	4.65	3.74
	< DEBT AND CAPITAL RATIOS >				
30	CURRENT RATIO	N	2.9	2.6	2.9
31	QUICK RATIO	N	0.78	0.73	0.85
32	CURRENT DEBT TO EQUITY	%	43.1	53.8	43.9
33	DEBT TO EQUITY	%	45.4	53.8	44.7
34	DEBT TO ASSETS	%	28.9	33.0	29.2
35	TURNOVER WORKING CAPITAL	X	5.6	4.7	4.5
36	FIXED ASSET RATIO	%	19.9	14.3	14.8
37	FIXED ASSETS MIX	%	12.7	8.8	9.7
38	EQUITY RATIO	%	97.8	100.0	99.2
39	SUPPLIER FINANCING -ASSETS	%	22.5	26.3	23.6
40	DEPRECIATION RATE	%	28.2	30.8	21.3
41	INVENTORY TO CURR ASSETS	%	73.8	72.0	71.0
42	TIMES INTEREST EARNED	X	5.7	11.2	6.4
43	CASH FLOW TO DEBT MATURITY	X	4.4	7.7	14.2
44	DOOMSDAY RATIO	N	0.05	0.02	0.02
45	CASH TO TOTAL LIABILITIES	%	4.5	1.6	1.8
46	CASH TO DISBURSEMENTS	%	5.5	2.5	2.6
47	CASH TO WORKING CAPITAL	%	2.5	1.0	0.9
48	Z-SCORE BANKRUPTCY MODEL	N	8.1	7.2	7.9
	< EFFICIENCY RATIOS >				
49	TOTAL EXPENSE RATIO	%	40.0	36.5	33.2
50	EXPENSES TO GROSS PROFIT	%	92.7	94.0	94.5
51	EMPLOYEE COMP RATIO	%	12.4	12.2	12.5

Figure 10-4. First page of a sample software-prepared report presenting all available ratios for a three year period.

```
52   MARKETING EXPENSE RATIO        %        13.8         11.2          5.9
53   RENT EXPENSE RATIO             %         2.3          2.1          2.5
54   INTEREST EXPENSE RATIO         %         0.68         0.23         0.36
55   INSURANCE EXPENSE RATIO        %         1.0          1.2          1.6
56   DEPRECIATION EXPENSE RATIO     %         1.2          1.1          0.8
57   BAD DEBTS EXPENSE RATIO        %         1.2          0.4          1.6
58   UTILITIES EXPENSE RATIO        %         1.1          1.3          1.2
59   DESIGNATED EXPENSE RATIO       %         2.8          2.6          2.0
60   REMAINING EXPENSE RATIO        %         3.4          4.3          4.7
61   EXPENSE GROWTH                 %       -35.2         -1.9         -6.9
62   BUDGET COMPLIANCE(EXPENSE)     %        96.7         80.5         92.6
63   RENT TO SPACE                  $         4.98         4.82         5.64
64   TURNOVER OF ASSETS             X         2.9          2.5          2.5
65   CASH SALES MIX                 %        48.3         42.3         41.1
66   COLLECTION PERIOD (DAYS)       #        47           59           59
67   PAYMENT PERIOD (DAYS)          #        49           57           54
68   EXPENSE CONTROL RATIO          %        19.4          9.3          9.2
69   INVENTORY TURNOVER             X         2.9          2.8          2.7
70   INVENTORY IN DAYS SALES        #        73           90           87
71   INCOME TAX RATE                %        15.9         12.8         13.1
72   BACK ORDER RATIO               %         9.3          6.7         18.4
73   EMPLOYEE TURNOVER              %        56.0         25.4         35.3
74   ORDERS PER EMPLOYEE            #     1,383        1,447        1,018
75   DEFLATED WAGE GROWTH           %         4.4          4.7          N/A
76   ASSETS PER EMPLOYEE            $    50,277       65,027       52,265
77   SPACE PER EMPLOYEE (SQ FT)     #       693          707          592

     < MARKETING RATIOS >
78   AVERAGE ORDER SIZE             $       106.73       111.81       129.27
79   DEFLATED AOS CHANGE            $        18.82         1.76         N/A
80   ORDER GROWTH                   %       -35.5          2.5        -11.5
81   CUSTOMER GROWTH                %         5.2          2.4         -0.6
82   SALES PER CUSTOMER             $        30.57        32.08        33.03
83   CUSTOMER SOLIC RATIO           %         3.1         41.3         25.6
84   CUSTOMER SPACE RATIO           N         7.0          7.1          6.7
85   MARKETING GROWTH               %       -39.3        -12.6        -46.7
86   AVERAGE RETURN MARKETING       X         6.0          8.0         11.8
87   AVERAGE ORDER RESPONSE         %         7.5          8.9         10.0
88   AVERAGE SALES RESPONSE         $         6.91         9.77        12.03
89   CUSTOMER SATISFAC RATIO        %        98.8         98.6         99.2
90   PROPRIETARY PRODUCT RATIO      %         0.9          3.7          5.5

     < INVESTMENT RATIOS >
91   BOOK VALUE PER SHARE           $         0.26         0.28         0.30
92   BUSINESS VALUE PREMIUM         %       -38.9        -54.6         N/A
93   DIVIDEND RATE                  $         0.00         N/A          N/A
94   DIVIDEND YIELD                 %         1.3          N/A          N/A
95   RETENTION RATE                 %        88.0        100.0        100.0
96   PRICE TO EARNINGS              N         N/A          N/A          N/A
97   PRICE TO BOOK                  N         N/A          N/A          N/A
98   PRICE TO SALES                 N         N/A          N/A          N/A
99   OLYMPIC MODEL                  #         0            0            0
100  BUSINESS VALUE ESTIMATE        $   384,272      412,721          N/A
101  RATIO CHANGE INDICATOR         #         3           -6          -25

     INTEREST RATE (YEAR END)       %         9.0          8.3          N/A
     INFLATION RATE                 %         6.1          3.1          N/A

$=DOLLARS. %=PERCENT. N=OTHER REAL NUMBER. #=INTEGER NUMBER. X=TIMES
MULTIPLIERS: K=1,000. M=1-MILLION. B=1-BILLION. N/A=NOT ENOUGH DATA.

PC-RATIOS (tm)   02-11-1993
```

Figure 10-5. Second page of a sample software-prepared report presenting all available ratios for a three-year period.

```
                              DEMO COMPANY
DEMO                       BUSINESS RATIO REPORT              1979 TO 1992

                   NO. 58  - UTILITIES EXPENSE RATIO
                              (PERCENT)

                       1979                  N/A
                       1980                  N/A
                       1981                  0.56
                       1982                  0.43
                       1983                  0.51
                       1984                  0.13
                       1985                  0.44
                       1986                  0.66
                       1987                  0.63
                       1988                  1.01
                       1989                  1.54
                       1990                  1.08
                       1991                  1.26
                       1992                  1.17

            WEIGHTED AVERAGE                 1.02              MF=.80
                   TRENDLINE                 UP               TR=5
          1993 PROJECTION                    1.23

N/A=NOT AVAILABLE.   MF=MULTIPLYING FACTOR.   TR=TRENDLINE RANGE

PC-RATIOS (tm)   02-11-1993
```

Figure 10-6.   Sample software-prepared one-ratio report.
Values are presented for all years having data available.

Graphs

For the same reason that a picture is worth a thousand words, graphs
(whether drawn by hand or computer) are generally more effective than
numbers alone in communicating business ratio information. This is true
not just because ratios for different periods can be arranged alongside
each other, but because the human eye is trained from childhood to
automatically interpret relationships expressed visually. The graphical
presentation of two numbers having values of 1.02 and .51 respectively
communicates instantly to most viewers the concept that the first has
about twice the magnitude of the second.   This is true whether the
numbers are expressed as the lengths of bars or divisions of a pie.
Arabic numbers convey the same information, but for most of us
additional mental activity is required to firmly set the relationship in mind.
The eye is also able to discern trends on a bar or line graph that might
never be seen in a column of figures.

There are many ways to express numerical information graphically.
Bar graphs, line graphs, and pie charts are all popular for showing
business information. They may be drawn by hand on graph paper or
printed out on a computer. Many examples are shown in this book.

An important advantage in using pie charts and multi-line graphs is
that a *large number* of statistics can be viewed simultaneously. In a pie
graph, for example, each measured item is visually compared to the
whole. But it is also compared to each of the other items. A combination

graph of expense ratios shows (in the clearest possible way) just where the money has been spent. Intuitive, common-sense judgments are made quickly. Numerical reports, by comparison, are often intimidating. Depending on their format, the ability to cross-compare data may be restricted.

Modern spreadsheet software produces graphs in many different formats (bars, lines, pies, columns, steps, scatters, mixes). Data are collected from any desired combination of rows and columns on the sheet. Color and three-dimensional presentations are possible. Fonts (style and size) are individually selected to optimize titles. Patterns and shading are changed at will. Presentations may be sized, rotated, and combined. Portions of pie charts may be exploded (pulled out) for emphasis. These programs are extremely versatile in accommodating different computer systems and printers, and data are readily transferred from one application to another.

Most dedicated ratio software has at least some graph-printing capability. *Figure 10-7* is an example chart of *PROFIT GROWTH (12)* prepared by PC-RATIOS. Note that the program automatically selects a range scale (−2000 to +5000%) to accommodate data for the unusual year 1980.[6] In the following graph (*Figure 10-8*), the program has been instructed to magnify the data by a factor of 10, making it possible to read values for "normal" years.

Finally, stand-alone software is available that produces graphs from electronic files, from numbers entered at the keyboard, or by capturing data directly from the computer-screen displays of other software. *Figure 10-9* is an example software-prepared bar graph of *ORDERS PER EMPLOYEE (34)*. *Figure 10-10* is a pie chart breakdown of a company's major expenses. *Figure 10-11* is a multi-line graph presenting four important return ratios on a single chart. Lastly, *Figure 10-12* is an example of a combination bar-line graph comparing sales to marketing expenditures. All of these graphs were prepared electronically (using the software package Graph-in-the-Box) by capturing data from display screens while running other programs.[7]

Although graphs allow people to grasp trends among numbers more quickly, they are generally less accurate than numerical presentations.[8] A common practice, therefore, is to append data tables to even the most elaborate charts.

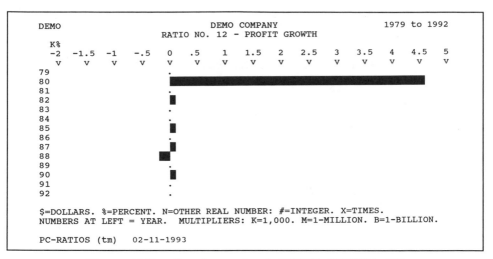

Figure 10-7. Sample graph of *PROFIT GROWTH (12)* prepared by dedicated-software. The range scale is automatically selected to accommodate the largest value.

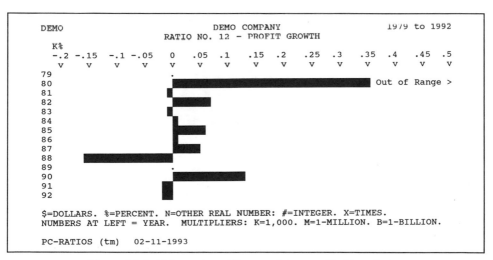

Figure 10-8. This version of the graph is magnified by a factor of 10 (using the same data) in order to read the smaller values.

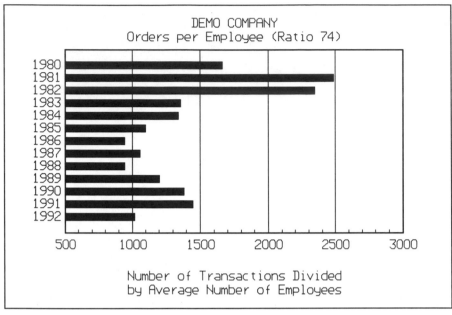

Figure 10-9. Software-prepared ratio bar graph.

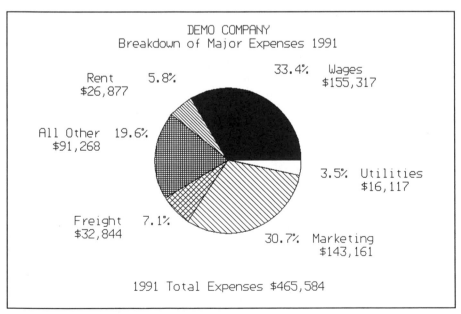

Figure 10-10. Software-prepared expense pie chart.

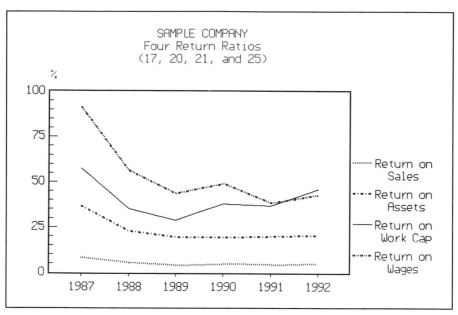

Figure 10-11. Software-prepared multi-ratio line graph.

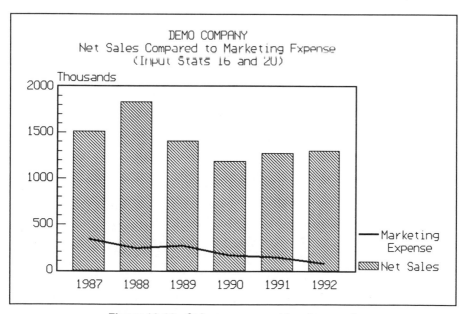

Figure 10-12. Software-prepared bar-line graph.

Standards

The process of ratio presentation may be incomplete if it fails to include historical company data or outside information relevant to the current data. These "compare to" numbers are called *standards*.

Standards are usually described as being internal or external, depending on their origin. Internal standards come from sources within the company. For example:

☐ Plans
☐ Budgets
☐ Forecasts
☐ Performance in earlier years.

A company's historical numbers resulting from different management teams, different product lines, different territories, and different store locations are all examples of internal standards. In fact, *any* historical number found in company records may be considered an internal standard if the proposed comparison is logical and useful. Some of the computer programs described earlier include features for automatic comparison to internal standards. Any report presenting data for more than one year provides an opportunity for internal-standard comparison. The three budget-compliance ratios in this book (4, 14, and 62) are internal-standard comparisons, as are the various growth ratios.

External standards originate outside the company. Sources for these standards include:

☐ Publications reporting industry norms and averages
☐ Advice found in business books and periodicals
☐ Reports from consultants
☐ Contracts
☐ Statutes and regulations.

It is human nature for managers to want to do better than (or at least as well as) their competitors and counterparts in similar businesses. That is one of the reasons why information on industry norms is so actively sought. But managers are not the only ones interested in this kind of information. Lenders compare the figures found in industry-standard publications to statements submitted by loan applicants. If the figures provided by a potential borrower appear out of line when compared to standard statement values or ratios, a closer look is suggested before the loan is made. Consultants use the information to discover anomalies and performance variances in companies under their scrutiny. Although comparisons to industry averages need to be made cautiously, they are a good first step in early identification of adverse trends or problems for a particular company.

Publishers and credit organizations develop industry standards by randomly sampling financial statements obtained from a wide variety of sources. Using sophisticated statistical techniques, they devise composite balance sheets and income statements for many different industries and lines of business. The data are sometimes broken down into sub-categories according to asset size, net sales, or number of employees. Breakdowns of this type increase the likelihood that a composite financial statement and set of ratios can be found to reasonably match the needs of a particular customer.

There are many good sources for this kind of external comparative data. One of the best known is Dun & Bradstreet's publication, *Industry Norms and Key Business Ratios, Desk Top Edition, 1990-91*. It provides common-size balance sheet and income statement account percentages plus 14 financial ratios on over 800 lines of business.[9] The ratios are organized into three categories — solvency, efficiency, and profitability. Median values are provided, as well as upper- and lower-quartile figures. The various lines of business are identified by name as well as SIC number. The reports also indicate the number of firms sampled in each category. *Figure 10-13* is an example of a Dun & Bradstreet report covering four lines of business.[10]

The Dun & Bradstreet information is also available on diskette as part of the software package Duns InSight.[11] This program allows comparison of industry data to the using firm's numbers, creation of pro forma statements, definition of custom ratios, graphing, and creation of modeled financial statements.

The Robert Morris Associates publishes 16 commonly used ratios for more than 360 lines of business. Known as *RMA Annual Statement Studies*, their reports (two pages per line of business) include 15 financial statement numbers (20 if summed values are included) with six breakdowns by company asset size and six additional breakdowns according to sales.[12] The RMA reports also provide SIC numbers and quartile breakdowns, as well as categorization according to the status of the underlying statements (unqualified, qualified, reviewed, compiled, and so forth). *Figure 10-14* is a set of sample pages from this publication for one line of business. Robert Morris Associates also publishes books on banking and credit analysis.

Another good source, available in most large libraries, is Leo Troy's *Almanac of Business and Industrial Financial Ratios*.[13] This report is broken down by industry, and further into 13 categories by size of firm. Size of firm is measured by assets, and ranges all the way from firms with no assets at all up to $250-Million. Twenty-three operating factors and ratios are provided in each category covering everything from repairs as a percentage of sales to the ratio of inventory to net income. This source also provides SIC numbers for the approximately 181 lines of business covered, and tells how many firms were sampled. An interesting feature of the Troy publication is that it provides two separate reports for each line of business. The first is for all firms — with and without income. The second includes only profitable companies. This helps overcome one criticism of standard values. That is, that failing companies skew the data and make it less useful. *Figure 10-15* is an example page showing class 5300 RETAIL TRADE - General Merchandise Stores.

Another source available in most bookstores is the Dow Jones-Irwin *Business and Investment Almanac.* It provides income statement percentages, operating ratios, and balance sheet ratios for a large number of industries.[14] This book is loaded with valuable information — things like industry surveys, SIC numbers and titles, historical price data, stock market charts and guides, investment returns, financial statement explanations, a glossary of investment and financial terms, and much more.

The U.S. Small Business Administration publishes a number of median ratios for nine broad trade categories.[15] Their figures are compiled from the statements of millions of companies. They arrange the values in five categories by number of employees (from just one to 100+). *Figure 10-16* is an example page showing median ratios of inventory to net sales for three lines of business. This source also includes business failure information and an interesting 11-page table indicating which industries are dominated by firms of small, large, and intermediate size.

In addition to the above, a large number of trade associations publish ratios for their industries. The fourth chapter of Sanzo's book lists many of these, as well as other sources which may be utilized by the manager or analyst for comparison.[16] It lists mailing addresses for more than 75 organizations publishing business ratios. Unfortunately, Sanzo's SBA book is now somewhat out of date, and many of the addresses are incorrect. But despite that, it's an excellent source of leads for the serious reviewer.

The first step in utilizing industry-standard values for a particular company is to match the firm's line of business to a category found in one of the previously-mentioned publications. Sometimes this is a straightforward process, but not always. Many businesses today cross traditional lines. Although their managers may use one "best fit" SIC for reporting purposes, the reality is that different activities are going on at the same time. When this is the case, a composite of available standard values can be devised by the manager to better match what the company does. This is justified because standard values are (to begin with) only averages of reports provided by large numbers of unique businesses.

	SIC 5199 NONDURABLE GOODS, NEC (NO BREAKDOWN) 1990 (2146 ESTAB)		SIC 5211 LUMBER & OTH BLDG MAT (NO BREAKDOWN) 1990 (1816 ESTAB)		SIC 5231 PAINT GLSS&WLPR STORS (NO BREAKDOWN) 1990 (1128 ESTAB)		SIC 5251 HARDWARE STORES (NO BREAKDOWN) 1990 (1937 ESTAB)	
	$	%	$	%	$	%	$	%
CASH	41,306	15.5	50,143	9.8	18,912	12.2	25,901	8.9
ACCOUNTS RECEIVABLE	86,610	32.5	127,164	24.9	32,708	21.1	33,467	11.5
NOTES RECEIVABLE	1,865	0.7	2,358	0.5	775	0.5	2,328	0.8
INVENTORY	62,892	23.6	193,420	37.9	57,976	37.4	155,987	53.6
OTHER CURRENT	12,792	4.8	15,661	3.1	4,805	3.1	8,440	2.9
TOTAL CURRENT	205,466	77.1	389,886	76.2	115,177	74.3	226,123	77.7
FIXED ASSETS	38,641	14.5	68,851	13.3	24,958	16.1	30,848	10.6
OTHER NON-CURRENT	22,385	8.4	53,224	10.5	14,882	9.6	34,049	11.7
TOTAL ASSETS	266,493	100.0	511,661	100.0	155,016	100.0	291,020	100.0
ACCOUNTS PAYABLE	51,167	19.2	75,225	14.8	29,763	19.2	35,795	12.3
BANK LOANS	1,332	0.5	3,070	0.6	620	0.4	873	0.3
NOTES PAYABLE	14,391	5.4	32,745	6.4	8,216	5.3	14,260	4.9
OTHER CURRENT	33,312	12.5	54,743	10.7	15,812	10.2	27,356	9.4
TOTAL CURRENT	100,201	37.6	166,293	32.5	54,411	35.1	78,284	26.9
OTHER LONG TERM	26,116	9.8	73,168	14.3	24,493	15.8	50,346	17.3
DEFERRED CREDITS	266	0.1	512	0.1	155	0.1	291	0.1
NET WORTH	139,909	52.5	271,692	53.1	75,958	49.0	162,098	55.7
TOTAL LIAB & NET WORTH	266,493	100.0	511,661	100.0	155,016	100.0	291,020	100.0
NET SALES	814,703	100.0	1,253,519	100.0	481,052	100.0	569,267	100.0
GROSS PROFIT	249,299	30.6	334,636	26.7	174,622	36.3	188,427	33.1
NET PROFIT AFTER TAX	43,179	5.3	43,608	3.0	22,609	4.7	22,201	3.9
WORKING CAPITAL	105,265	---	223,596	---	60,766	---	147,839	---

RATIOS	UQ	MED	LQ	UQ	MED	LQ	UQ	MED	LQ	UQ	MED	LQ
SOLVENCY												
QUICK RATIO (TIMES)	2.7	1.3	0.7	2.2	1.1	0.6	2.0	1.0	0.5	1.8	0.8	0.4
CURRENT RATIO (TIMES)	4.5	2.2	1.4	4.7	2.6	1.6	4.0	2.4	1.4	6.5	3.5	2.0
CURR LIAB TO NW (%)	19.4	58.5	148.8	21.4	47.6	109.8	22.0	51.2	128.8	19.3	37.8	88.1
CURR LIAB TO INV (%)	42.2	102.0	286.9	37.2	67.6	121.2	36.5	78.1	133.3	19.0	39.3	70.8
TOTAL LIAB TO NW (%)	27.5	75.8	188.2	28.5	65.5	162.7	29.4	72.1	174.6	25.7	60.0	152.6
FIXED ASSETS TO NW (%)	8.3	21.9	48.1	11.7	26.5	56.7	12.4	30.0	69.5	5.7	17.5	44.4
EFFICIENCY												
COLL PERIOD (DAYS)	20.8	36.5	55.4	21.5	33.2	47.1	15.3	24.8	36.9	9.5	17.9	28.8
SALES TO INV (TIMES)	20.0	10.1	5.1	11.0	6.8	5.1	13.4	8.0	4.5	5.6	4.3	3.5
ASSETS TO SALES (%)	16.5	8.1	50.0	28.9	28.0	51.6	23.1	32.0	45.9	36.3	48.9	69.3
SALES TO NWC (TIMES)	21.4	8.4	6.3	11.1	5.3	3.6	13.1	7.5	4.3	36.3	48.9	69.3
ACCT PAY TO SALES (%)	2.5	5.2	9.4	3.4	5.0	7.6	3.3	5.5	9.4	3.0	5.2	8.4
PROFITABILITY												
RETURN ON SALES (%)	10.2	3.8	1.1	5.1	2.9	0.5	9.1	3.8	0.9	7.0	3.6	1.1
RETURN ON ASSETS (%)	21.4	8.4	6.3	11.1	6.9	2.1	20.9	8.6	1.2	11.9	5.6	1.2
RETURN ON NW (%)	48.3	18.5		22.6	9.3		47.7	17.6	3.3	25.0	10.3	2.1

Figure 10-13. Extract from *Industry Norms and Key Business Ratios - Desk Top Edition 1990-91*. Copyright 1991. Dun & Bradstreet, Inc. All rights reserved. Reprinted with permission.

WHOLESALERS - TIRES & TUBES SIC# 5014

Current Data Sorted By Assets						Type of Statement	Comparative Historical Data	
1	4	20	13	3	1	Unqualified	31	35
	1		1		1	Qualified		3
13	14	20	3			Reviewed	42	41
7	26	10	3			Compiled	49	50
3	8	11	1			Other	25	22
46(6/30-9/30/89)			118(10/1/89-3/31/90)				6/30/85-3/31/86	6/30/86-3/31/87
0-500M	500M-2MM	2-10MM	10-50MM	50-100MM	100-250MM	NUMBER OF STATEMENTS	ALL	ALL
24	53	61	21	3	2		147	151
%	%	%	%	%	%	**ASSETS**	%	%
7.0	5.0	4.5	2.8			Cash & Equivalents	6.2	6.5
28.1	33.8	34.7	34.6			Trade Receivables - (net)	31.0	30.9
42.2	41.9	38.7	34.5			Inventory	40.4	38.0
1.8	2.3	1.0	1.7			All Other Current	1.5	1.3
79.2	83.0	78.9	73.6			Total Current	79.1	76.8
16.9	12.2	14.1	21.2			Fixed Assets (net)	15.4	16.4
.8	.4	1.0	.8			Intangibles (net)	.8	1.0
3.1	4.4	6.0	4.3			All Other Non-Current	4.8	5.9
100.0	100.0	100.0	100.0			Total	100.0	100.0
						LIABILITIES		
17.7	11.2	15.9	17.0			Notes Payable-Short Term	10.2	12.5
7.7	2.6	2.1	2.0			Cur. Mat.-L/T/D	2.8	3.4
35.2	41.9	37.5	33.8			Trade Payables	37.2	34.9
1.5	.4	.3	.2			Income Taxes Payable	.4	.6
9.2	4.2	5.9	7.5			All Other Current	6.0	6.4
71.3	60.3	61.6	60.4			Total Current	56.5	57.8
21.5	9.3	7.3	12.8			Long Term Debt	10.2	11.9
.1	.1	.2	.5			Deferred Taxes	.2	.2
.0	1.4	1.1	2.2			All Other Non-Current	1.0	1.0
7.1	28.9	29.7	24.1			Net Worth	32.1	29.1
100.0	100.0	100.0	100.0			Total Liabilities & Net Worth	100.0	100.0
						INCOME DATA		
100.0	100.0	100.0	100.0			Net Sales	100.0	100.0
31.9	25.0	22.5	25.3			Gross Profit	25.2	26.4
31.2	22.9	19.9	22.7			Operating Expenses	23.7	24.4
.7	2.0	2.7	2.5			Operating Profit	1.5	2.0
.7	.7	.4	.8			All Other Expenses (net)	.2	.5
.0	1.3	2.3	1.7			Profit Before Taxes	1.3	1.5
						RATIOS		
2.0	1.7	1.6	1.4				1.8	1.7
1.2	1.4	1.3	1.2			Current	1.4	1.3
.7	1.2	1.0	1.1				1.1	1.1
.9	.8	.8	.8				.9	.9
.5	.6	.6	.5			Quick	.6	.6
.3	.5	.4	.4				.5	.5
18 19.8	33 10.9	33 11.2	25 14.4				30 12.2	29 12.5
32 11.4	43 8.4	43 8.4	47 7.8			Sales/Receivables	40 9.1	41 8.9
47 7.8	55 6.6	53 6.9	73 5.0				55 6.6	54 6.7
41 8.8	54 6.7	47 7.8	55 6.6				53 6.9	50 7.3
76 4.8	70 5.2	64 5.7	65 5.6			Cost of Sales/Inventory	74 4.9	70 5.2
94 3.9	107 3.4	89 4.1	99 3.7				99 3.7	99 3.7
33 10.9	54 6.8	49 7.5	48 7.6				49 7.5	43 8.5
56 6.5	70 5.2	62 5.9	58 6.3			Cost of Sales/Payables	72 5.1	63 5.8
73 5.0	83 4.4	72 5.1	91 4.0				91 4.0	87 4.2
8.9	7.4	10.2	9.7				7.4	8.6
27.2	11.6	14.7	24.8			Sales/Working Capital	12.8	15.4
-16.6	22.0	73.4	95.3				32.8	38.3
3.8	4.2	4.3	4.1				5.8	5.9
(20) 1.8	(48) 2.1	(56) 1.9	(19) 2.7			EBIT/Interest	(132) 2.4	(127) 2.6
.9	.8	1.2	1.3				1.0	1.3
	6.5	3.2	7.0				5.2	3.7
	(30) 3.2	(32) 1.5	(13) 3.9			Net Profit + Depr., Dep., Amort./Cur. Mat. L/T/D	(77) 2.2	(80) 1.9
	1.2	.8	1.4				.7	.7
.4	.2	.2	.4				.2	.2
1.0	.4	.4	.7			Fixed/Worth	.4	.5
-.8	.8	1.2	2.2				.9	1.0
1.7	1.8	1.4	1.8				1.2	1.3
5.9	2.5	2.5	4.1			Debt/Worth	2.4	2.8
-6.3	4.2	5.4	9.3				5.0	5.8
79.0	24.4	31.2	38.1				25.3	29.1
(15) 12.4	(51) 11.8	(58) 10.6	15.7			% Profit Before Taxes/Tangible Net Worth	(142) 11.2	(143) 14.6
5.6	3.9	3.9	10.9				2.1	7.1
11.4	6.2	5.1	7.6				7.0	7.8
3.6	2.7	2.6	4.6			% Profit Before Taxes/Total Assets	3.2	3.8
-.4	.3	.9	2.0				.1	.9
56.4	61.3	50.3	30.7				52.6	51.4
20.1	25.4	30.2	15.1			Sales/Net Fixed Assets	23.1	22.6
12.0	15.9	13.8	9.5				12.5	10.9
4.5	3.2	3.4	3.2				3.3	3.2
3.3	2.8	2.8	2.6			Sales/Total Assets	2.7	2.6
2.4	2.4	2.4	1.9				2.2	2.2
1.1	.6	.5	.5				.6	.7
(22) 1.8	(52) 1.1	(59) .8	(20) 1.1			% Depr., Dep., Amort./Sales	(138) 1.1	(138) 1.2
3.3	1.9	1.4	1.9				1.7	1.9
	1.6	1.5					1.5	1.3
	(21) 2.0	(27) 1.9				% Officers' Comp/Sales	(44) 2.2	(56) 2.3
	2.9	3.1					3.7	3.9
21254M	192743M	808550M	1110639M	319298M	767862M	Net Sales ($)	1382628M	2004851M
6715M	68631M	277271M	405587M	178643M	299593M	Total Assets ($)	541972M	807627M

©Robert Morris Associates 1990

M = $thousand MM = $million
See Pages 1 through 15 for Explanation of Ratios and Data

Figure 10-14. Sample pages from *RMA Annual Statement Studies.*
This extensive report covers WHOLESALERS - TIRES AND TUBES.

Comparative Historical Data — **Type of Statement** — **Current Data Sorted By Sales**

6/30/87-3/31/88	6/30/88-3/31/89	6/30/89-3/31/90	Type of Statement	0-1MM	1-3MM	3-5MM	5-10MM	10-25MM	25MM & OVER
38	31	42	Unqualified	2	1	2	8	13	16
4	4	3	Qualified	1					2
39	44	50	Reviewed	8	8	10	10	12	2
44	44	46	Compiled	7	14	10	7	5	3
24	25	23	Other	2	3	5	4	7	2
				46(6/30-9/30/89)			118(10/1/89-3/31/90)		
ALL 149	ALL 148	ALL 164	**NUMBER OF STATEMENTS**	19	27	27	29	37	25
%	%	%	**ASSETS**	%	%	%	%	%	%
4.8	5.2	4.9	Cash & Equivalents	7.4	5.0	5.2	3.6	4.4	4.6
31.3	33.5	33.5	Trade Receivables - (net)	23.8	34.9	33.7	33.1	35.3	36.7
39.7	40.3	39.3	Inventory	43.7	39.6	42.1	41.6	36.9	33.4
1.0	1.3	1.7	All Other Current	1.5	2.8	2.3	.7	1.0	2.3
76.9	80.2	79.3	Total Current	76.5	82.3	83.3	79.0	77.5	77.0
16.5	14.3	15.0	Fixed Assets (net)	20.1	12.4	12.2	14.1	15.2	18.0
.7	.8	.8	Intangibles (net)	1.0	.0	.6	.8	1.3	.9
5.8	4.8	4.8	All Other Non-Current	2.4	5.2	3.8	6.1	6.0	4.1
100.0	100.0	100.0	Total	100.0	100.0	100.0	100.0	100.0	100.0
			LIABILITIES						
12.5	13.5	14.5	Notes Payable-Short Term	15.7	14.1	11.8	15.4	14.9	15.3
3.5	3.0	3.1	Cur. Mat.-L/T/D	7.5	3.7	3.1	1.9	2.0	1.8
37.1	37.8	37.5	Trade Payables	25.1	44.6	42.0	37.0	39.2	32.3
.6	.5	.5	Income Taxes Payable	1.7	.7	.2	.2	.4	.1
5.3	5.4	6.1	All Other Current	9.4	5.4	3.7	5.9	5.0	8.6
59.1	60.2	61.6	Total Current	59.3	68.6	60.7	60.3	61.6	58.1
13.3	9.3	10.8	Long Term Debt	24.0	13.5	8.0	7.5	9.1	7.4
.3	.2	.2	Deferred Taxes	.1	.0	.1	.2	.2	.7
.8	1.4	1.2	All Other Non-Current	.0	.6	2.5	1.3	.6	1.9
26.6	28.8	26.2	Net Worth	16.5	17.3	28.7	30.7	28.3	31.9
100.0	100.0	100.0	Total Liabilities & Net Worth	100.0	100.0	100.0	100.0	100.0	100.0
			INCOME DATA						
100.0	100.0	100.0	Net Sales	100.0	100.0	100.0	100.0	100.0	100.0
26.4	24.4	25.0	Gross Profit	32.9	25.8	24.9	24.2	22.3	23.3
23.8	22.1	22.8	Operating Expenses	32.0	23.8	22.6	22.0	19.5	20.5
2.5	2.2	2.3	Operating Profit	.8	2.0	2.4	2.2	2.8	2.8
.8	.0	.6	All Other Expenses (net)	.6	.6	1.0	.6	.3	.3
1.8	2.2	1.7	Profit Before Taxes	.2	1.4	1.4	1.6	2.5	2.5
			RATIOS						
1.6	1.6	1.6	Current	2.3	1.8	1.6	1.6	1.6	1.8
1.3	1.3	1.3		1.4	1.3	1.3	1.4	1.3	1.2
1.1	1.1	1.1		.8	1.1	1.2	1.1	1.0	1.1
.8	.8	.8	Quick	1.2	.8	.8	.8	.8	1.1
.6	.6	.6		.6	.6	.6	.6	.6	.6
.5	.5	.4		.2	.4	.5	.4	.4	.5
33 11.0	31 11.7	30 12.0	Sales/Receivables	18 20.0	33 11.2	33 11.0	32 11.5	29 12.6	34 10.8
42 8.6	43 8.5	43 8.4		31 11.6	41 8.8	41 8.9	41 8.9	43 8.5	47 7.7
56 6.5	57 6.4	53 6.9		55 6.6	52 7.0	55 6.6	52 7.0	56 6.5	53 6.9
57 6.4	48 7.6	48 7.6	Cost of Sales/Inventory	47 7.8	44 8.3	55 6.6	53 6.9	47 7.8	46 8.0
73 5.0	69 5.3	69 5.3		89 4.1	63 5.8	74 4.9	68 5.4	72 5.1	60 6.1
101 3.6	99 3.7	99 3.7		122 3.0	114 3.2	104 3.5	96 3.8	96 3.8	87 4.2
49 7.5	48 7.6	47 7.7	Cost of Sales/Payables	28 13.1	57 6.4	49 7.4	47 7.8	50 7.3	37 9.9
69 5.3	64 5.7	63 5.8		50 7.3	72 5.1	70 5.2	63 5.8	62 5.9	51 7.1
87 4.2	85 4.3	78 4.7		66 5.5	79 4.6	91 4.0	79 4.6	78 4.7	68 5.4
9.2	8.8	9.0	Sales/Working Capital	5.6	7.5	7.6	10.2	9.7	8.7
15.0	13.2	15.0		14.1	15.0	13.6	15.0	14.7	24.2
38.5	33.1	42.7		-32.6	50.4	22.2	50.9	NM	33.7
4.6	6.0	4.1	EBIT/Interest	6.4	5.3	2.8	3.3	3.6	4.6
(123) 2.3	(125) 2.4	(147) 2.1		(17) 2.2	(22) 2.5	(25) 2.3	(27) 1.7	(33) 1.8	(23) 3.0
1.4	1.5	1.2		1.0	.2	1.0	1.2	1.3	1.4
3.5	6.7	4.9	Net Profit + Depr., Dep., Amort./Cur. Mat. L/T/D		0.4	7.3	0.7	2.7	0.9
(86) 1.6	(76) 2.2	(87) 2.6			(15) 2.8	(15) 3.2	(14) 3.1	(22) 1.5	(15) 3.9
.7	.9	1.0			.9	1.2	.8	.7	1.1
.3	.2	.2	Fixed/Worth	.3	.2	.2	.2	.2	.3
.6	.4	.5		.6	.5	.4	.3	.5	.6
1.1	1.0	1.1		-2.3	1.0	.9	1.1	1.0	1.3
1.6	1.5	1.6	Debt/Worth	1.4	2.0	1.5	1.8	1.4	1.5
3.4	2.7	2.7		3.2	2.8	3.1	2.3	2.4	2.8
6.1	5.5	5.9		-6.8	6.7	4.5	4.3	5.8	6.2
28.9	33.5	31.6	% Profit Before Taxes/Tangible Net Worth	24.8	51.4	30.0	21.4	38.6	23.6
(144) 16.3	(140) 17.4	(150) 12.4		(13) 9.5	(23) 20.9	(26) 11.2	(27) 9.1	(36) 16.9	
7.5	5.8	5.5		5.1	10.1	1.1	3.3	6.1	9.0
7.0	8.3	7.5	% Profit Before Taxes/Total Assets	6.4	11.4	6.0	6.2	5.1	9.3
3.8	4.0	3.4		2.6	4.5	2.6	2.2	3.1	4.6
1.5	1.2	1.5		-.3	1.9	.2	.7	1.5	1.8
47.1	56.6	55.2	Sales/Net Fixed Assets	49.0	55.6	80.6	59.1	51.5	50.9
23.7	27.3	23.7		15.9	22.9	25.4	30.7	30.2	15.3
11.5	12.6	12.9		10.3	16.4	15.8	11.1	15.7	10.5
3.2	3.4	3.4	Sales/Total Assets	4.1	3.4	3.0	3.4	3.5	3.5
2.7	2.8	2.8		2.5	2.9	2.5	2.9	2.6	3.0
2.2	2.2	2.3		1.8	2.4	2.3	2.4	2.3	2.3
.7	.6	.6	% Depr., Dep., Amort./Sales	1.1	.7	.6	.5	.4	.5
(136) 1.2	(133) .9	(158) 1.1		(18) 2.1	(26) 1.4	(26) .9	(28) 1.0	(36) .8	(24) 1.1
2.0	1.7	1.8		3.4	2.4	1.8	1.3	1.4	1.9
1.4	1.4	1.5	% Officers' Comp/Sales		1.8	1.6	1.4	1.4	
(54) 2.6	(59) 2.4	(60) 2.0			(10) 2.2	(13) 1.9	(13) 2.0	(10) 1.8	
4.9	4.4	3.4			3.9	2.9	3.4	3.1	
1806120M	2114012M	3220346M	Net Sales ($)	12974M	54247M	106567M	202244M	613400M	2230914M
705068M	858322M	1234440M	Total Assets ($)	5534M	21314M	40439M	73730M	239910M	853513M

M = $thousand   MM = $million
See Pages 1 through 15 for Explanation of Ratios and Data

TABLE I: CORPORATIONS WITH AND WITHOUT NET INCOME, 1991 EDITION

5300 RETAIL TRADE:
General merchandise stores

Item Description For Accounting Period 7/87 Through 6/88	A Total	B Zero Assets	SIZE OF ASSETS IN THOUSANDS OF DOLLARS (000 OMITTED)										
			C Under 100	D 100 to 250	E 251 to 500	F 501 to 1,000	G 1,001 to 5,000	H 5,001 to 10,000	I 10,001 to 25,000	J 25,001 to 50,000	K 50,001 to 100,000	L 100,001 to 250,000	M 250,001 and over
1. Number of Enterprises	10884	714	4578	2486	1494	639	664	84	109	29	27	21	38
2. Total receipts (in millions of dollars)	230273.3	2671.1	901.1	1282.6	1825.0	1106.4	3490.0	949.9	3975.4	2137.8	3533.7	6752.2	201648.2
Selected Operating Factors in Percent of Net Sales													
3. Cost of operations	64.7	62.6	63.6	63.1	69.6	62.2	67.1	64.9	68.9	65.7	66.0	68.9	64.4
4. Compensation of officers	0.4	0.5	5.2	4.7	4.5	4.0	2.6	1.3	1.0	0.6	0.6	0.4	0.2
5. Repairs	0.5	0.9	0.5	0.5	0.5	0.6	0.5	0.5	0.5	0.4	0.6	0.4	0.5
6. Bad debts	0.5	0.1	-	-	0.1	0.1	0.3	0.3	0.6	0.1	0.2	0.2	0.6
7. Rent on business property	2.9	4.8	6.8	6.9	3.1	3.1	3.0	4.2	3.1	3.0	3.1	2.6	2.9
8. Taxes (excl Federal tax)	2.3	2.7	3.1	2.4	2.0	1.7	1.8	2.0	1.9	2.5	2.1	2.0	2.3
9. Interest	4.0	2.9	0.7	1.0	0.6	1.1	1.1	2.5	1.2	1.4	1.3	2.0	4.3
10. Deprec/Deplet/Amortiz†	2.2	2.4	2.0	1.2	1.0	1.2	1.3	2.3	1.6	1.9	1.8	2.1	2.3
11. Advertising	2.5	3.0	0.8	1.1	1.7	3.1	2.2	2.4	2.3	3.7	3.3	2.4	2.5
12. Pensions & other benef plans	1.2	0.7	0.1	0.3	0.7	1.0	0.8	0.8	0.4	0.7	0.9	0.7	1.3
13. Other expenses	21.2	22.7	17.7	16.9	15.7	21.4	19.0	23.2	19.6	20.2	20.6	19.2	21.4
14. Net profit before tax	*	*	*	1.9	1.9	0.5	0.3	*	*	*	*	*	*
Selected Financial Ratios (number of times ratio is to one)													
15. Current ratio	1.4	-	4.5	3.0	2.4	2.4	2.3	1.7	1.8	2.0	2.0	2.0	1.3
16. Quick ratio	0.8	-	1.0	0.8	0.5	0.7	0.7	0.7	0.7	0.8	0.7	0.7	0.8
17. Net sls to net wkg capital	6.5	-	6.5	6.1	7.7	5.6	5.6	6.1	7.4	6.5	5.8	6.7	6.4
18. Coverage ratio	1.9	-	1.3	4.1	3.2	3.0	2.7	0.3	2.5	3.7	3.0	1.9	1.9
19. Asset turnover	1.1	-	-	-	-	2.5	2.3	1.6	2.2	1.9	1.9	1.9	1.0
20. Total liab to net worth	2.9	2.3	2.3	2.0	1.0	1.0	1.1	2.0	1.7	1.5	1.6	2.1	3.0
Selected Financial Factors in Percentages													
21. Debt ratio	74.1	-	70.1	66.3	49.8	50.1	51.7	67.0	62.8	59.5	60.8	67.5	74.9
22. Return on assets	8.0	-	3.1	11.8	7.1	8.1	6.7	1.2	6.9	9.5	7.4	7.3	8.1
23. Return on equity	9.0	-	-	23.8	7.4	9.1	6.4	-	7.2	12.9	8.9	4.4	9.2
24. Return on net worth	31.0	-	10.3	35.0	14.1	16.3	13.8	3.7	18.5	23.5	18.9	22.6	32.1

†Depreciation largest factor

Page 244

Figure 10-15. From the book, *Almanac of Business and Industrial Financial Ratios* by Leo Troy, PhD. Copyright 1991. Used by permission of the publisher, Prentice Hall / A division of Simon & Schuster, Englewood Cliffs, N.J.

Table 8.4 Median Ratios of Inventory to Net Sales by Industry Division and Firm Size, 1976-1983 -- Continued

SIC Code	Year	Total	Employment Size of Firm					
			1-9	10-19	20-49	50-99	<100	100+
50-51	WHOLESALE TRADE							
	1976	0.1036	0.0935	0.1153	0.1223	0.1325	0.1032	0.1292
	1977	0.1098	0.0984	0.1161	0.1211	0.1257	0.1091	0.1332
	1978	0.1075	0.0934	0.1218	0.1238	0.1301	0.1069	0.1278
	1979	0.1104	0.0979	0.1179	0.1232	0.1272	0.1099	0.1280
	1980	0.1081	0.0967	0.1206	0.1193	0.1203	0.1081	0.1126
	1981	0.1088	0.0995	0.1207	0.1196	0.1158	0.1086	0.1126
	1982	0.1010	0.0863	0.1129	0.1155	0.1137	0.1007	0.1099
	1983	0.1011	0.0902	0.1092	0.1153	0.1157	0.1012	0.0972
52-59	RETAIL TRADE							
	1976	0.1837	0.2038	0.1411	0.1073	0.0592	0.1850	0.0654
	1977	0.1965	0.2187	0.1692	0.1422	0.1283	0.1983	0.1244
	1978	0.1808	0.1991	0.1516	0.1284	0.1197	0.1819	0.1099
	1979	0.1947	0.2143	0.1683	0.1419	0.1259	0.1965	0.1174
	1980	0.1971	0.2159	0.1720	0.1437	0.1263	0.1991	0.1236
	1981	0.2025	0.2235	0.1792	0.1484	0.1348	0.2045	0.1242
	1982	0.1951	0.2216	0.1711	0.1392	0.1164	0.1976	0.1059
	1983	0.2013	0.2300	0.1885	0.1556	0.1368	0.2051	0.1336
60-67	FINANCE, INSURANCE, AND REAL ESTATE							
	1976	0.0000	0.0000	0.0000	0.0000	0.0000	0.0000	0.0000
	1977	0.0000	0.0000	0.0000	0.0000	0.0000	0.0000	0.0000
	1978	0.0000	0.0000	0.0000	0.0000	0.0000	0.0000	0.0000
	1979	0.0000	0.0000	0.0000	0.0000	0.0000	0.0000	0.0000
	1980	0.0000	0.0000	0.0000	0.0000	0.0000	0.0000	0.0000
	1981	0.0000	0.0000	0.0000	0.0000	0.0000	0.0000	0.0000
	1982	0.0000	0.0000	0.0000	0.0000	0.0000	0.0000	0.0000
	1983	0.0000	0.0000	0.0000	0.0000	0.0000	0.0000	0.0000
70-89	SERVICES							
	1976	0.0129	0.0229	0.0042	0.0000	0.0040	0.0134	0.0043
	1977	0.0128	0.0225	0.0088	0.0032	0.0061	0.0131	0.0113
	1978	0.0116	0.0227	0.0016	0.0037	0.0043	0.0121	0.0093
	1979	0.0064	0.0063	0.0016	0.0000	0.0038	0.0038	0.0123
	1980	0.0058	0.0068	0.0000	0.0000	0.0041	0.0032	0.0120
	1981	0.0017	0.0000	0.0000	0.0000	0.0020	0.0000	0.0119
	1982	0.0034	0.0014	0.0000	0.0000	0.0017	0.0000	0.0102
	1983	0.0020	0.0000	0.0000	0.0000	0.0018	0.0000	0.0101

Note: Zero ratios represent very small cell samples.

Source: U.S. Small Business Administration, Office of Advocacy, Small Data Base, Financial Reference file, unpublished data, 1987.

Figure 10-16. Extract from *Handbook of Small Business Data.* Reprinted courtesy of U.S. Small Business Administration.

Assuming a satisfactory set of "compare to" values are found, they need to be communicated to key individuals and understood by all who use them. A report can be circulated, or the standard numbers might be listed in one of the columns of a summary sheet such as *Figure 10-3*. Graphs are another good way to show how the company's performance compares to averages for its industry. Additional lines or side-by-side bars are often added to existing graphs to show standard values.

The presentation of industry norm values in official company reports and graphs should be undertaken only if approved at a high level of management. This is because of the danger that individuals reading the material (inside or outside the company) may mistakenly assume that these average values have been adopted by the firm as performance targets. It's difficult enough in most situations for a management to live up to its own planning. Having to explain *why* the company numbers do or do not match those of the industry may get in the way of effectively communicating the firm's success in achieving what it has set out to do. Industry standards are good internal working tools. They reveal to managers what lenders and investors may be expecting. They alert decision makers to deteriorating trends and other dangers. Perhaps equally important, they are a constant reminder that "this company" is not the clone of a fictitious average.

The next chapter discusses the reliability of accounting data and provides some additional reasons why comparison to certain external standards should be undertaken cautiously.

Notes — Chapter 10

1. An example of the six-year form is Wilson-Jones 7206. The 14-year form is 7214. *See* Bibliography, Additional Sources.

2. PC-RATIOS is available from McLane Publications. *See* Bibliography, Additional Sources.

3. FINANCIAL RATIOS II is available from Lassen Software. *See* Bibliography, Additional Sources.

4. BUSINESS VALUATION+RATIOS is available from Innovative Professional Software. *See* Bibliography, Additional Sources.

5. RATIO MASTER is available from Intex Solutions, Inc. *See* Bibliography, Additional Sources.

6. The "K" above the range scale line means that all numbers in that line require multiplication by 1000. An "M" signifies multiplication by one million, and so forth.

7. Graph-in-the-Box is available from New England Software. *See* Bibliography, Additional Sources.

8. "Tabling the Move to Computer Graphics," *The Wall Street Journal* (January 30, 1991), p. B1.

9. Dun & Bradstreet, *Industry Norms and Key Business Ratios - Desk Top Edition 1990-91.* (Murray Hill, NJ, 1991).

10. Dun & Bradstreet, *Industry Norms and Key Business Ratios Desk Top Edition 1990-91.* Copyright 1991. Dun & Bradstreet, Inc. All rights reserved. Reprinted with permission.

11. Duns InSight is available from Dun & Bradstreet Information Services, North America. *See* Bibliography, Additional Sources.

12. Robert Morris Associates, *RMA Annual Statement Studies* (Philadelphia, PA: Robert Morris Associates, 1990).

13. Leo Troy, *Almanac of Business and Financial Ratios* (Englewood Cliffs, NJ: Prentice-Hall, 1991).

14. Sumner N. Levine, *Business and Investment Almanac* (Homewood, IL: Dow Jones-Irwin, 1983).

15. Small Business Administration, *Handbook of Small Business Data* (Washington, DC: Small Business Administration, 1988).

16. Richard Sanzo, *Ratio Analysis for Small Business*, Small Business Management Series No. 20 (Washington, DC: Small Business Administration, 1977), p. 25-38.

17. RMA cautions that the Studies be regarded only as a general guideline and not as an absolute industry norm. This is due to limited samples within categories, the categorization of companies by their primary Standard Industrial Classification (SIC) number only, and different methods of operations by companies within the same industry. For these reasons, RMA recommends that the figures be used only as general guidelines in addition to other methods of financial analysis.

Chapter 11
Conclusion

Business ratio compilation is largely a clerical process. It requires tenacity in the collection of data and accuracy in calculation. Putting ratios to profitable use is an entirely different matter. For this, experience, skill, and sometimes intuition are involved. It is a process that starts with effectively presenting the ratios and insuring they are understood. This is followed by comparing the ratios to internal and external standards. Managerial action, if any is to be taken, comes last.

Ratio Guidelines

Some readers, in reaching this chapter, may be disappointed that they have not been provided with a list or table of "right" ratio values to use as guidelines in managing their businesses. The call for such numbers is understandable. After all, why compute ratios if not to determine that they do or do not conform to some kind of limit or standard? It's tempting for an author to try to meet this need by searching through the literature to find numbers that most would agree are appropriate and reasonable for a typical business. Many such guidelines *are* mentioned in the earlier chapters of this book. But they are provided with important caveats. First, there is no such thing as a typical business. Second, managers are not paid to thoughtlessly adapt their companies to outside anecdotal guidelines.

Standards of weight and measure are based on physical laws. Business standards (whether you call them goals, guidelines, norms, or limits) are entirely different. They are dynamic — subjective and ever-changing. They invariably originate in different time periods and often under circumstances unrelated to the company using them. It is a mistake, therefore, to believe that a "good" or "healthy" limit or norm exists for each ratio. Although a skilled analyst might use these adjectives to describe average data for a line of business, such labeling is generalization. What is good for one business is not necessarily good for another. Even where average numbers provided by credit-reporting agencies are perfectly accurate and precise, they may be irrelevant to a particular business. In short, there are no right or wrong values, limits, or standards. It always depends on the industry, the particular company, the management, the business plan, the economy, and vagaries of the marketplace.

Should comparison to external guidelines and standards therefore be avoided?   Not at all.   The danger is only that an inexperienced management may substitute external generalizations for internal good judgment.   But assuming this does not happen, then it is one good way to use business ratios.   The act of comparing (to whatever norm or standard is chosen) stimulates thought and investigation.   Thought and investigation lead to discovery of ways to improve.

Managerial Action

This is not a book about management per se.   It's about *measurement*.   Business ratios are managerial tools that aid in diagnosis.   An analogy is found in the process of repairing a computer.   The technician uses an oscilloscope or voltmeter to obtain information — to discover variances inconsistent with the proper operation of the device.   Deciding *what* to do and knowing *how to do it* is a matter of training, experience, and ability.   The same is true for business ratios.   They are simply measurements — sometimes simple and static — sometimes complex and dynamic.   In either case they have a single purpose — to reveal truth to the reviewer.   Business ratio analysis is never a substitute for managerial judgment.

Taking action to correct an out-of-line ratio carries an inherent risk that the changes made will not provide the desired result — or worse, will provide some other result that is less favorable.   It is because of this dilemma that business management is viewed as an art requiring the application of skill, judgment and experience.   Harvard University's Robert N. Anthony says, "Skill in the management use of accounting information can be acquired, I believe, only through experience."[1]   He reminds us that because business organizations consist of human beings, anything they accomplish is a result of the actions of these people.   Figures only assist. Consider this example:

A company reports 3.9% *RENT EXPENSE RATIO (53)*.   In prior years the ratio averaged about 2.6%.   A middle manager is asked to look into this.   Is 3.9% too high?   If the manager is experienced, he or she already knows the answer: "It depends!"   It depends on sales.   It depends on the type and location of the business.   It depends on interest rates.   It depends on managerial strategies.   It depends on the local real estate market and the economy.   Where 3.9% could be high for one firm, it could be attractively low for another.   It depends!

The manager's job now is to collect information and ask a lot of questions.   What underlying numbers were used to compute the ratio (rent expense and net sales) for the current year as well as the years when the ratio averaged about 2.6%?   Are those numbers accurate and consistently applied?   Is the ratio higher primarily because rent expense increased or net sales declined? If a significant increase in rent expense is the cause of the ratio change, why did it increase as it did? What is the going neighborhood rental rate for similar facilities? What other properties are available now on the rental market? Should a move be considered? What is the status of the company's lease? How much would a move cost? If a significant drop in sales is the reason the ratio increased, should the focus of the inquiry be changed from rent expense to marketing, the economy, or customer satisfaction?

The point has frequently been made that the primary purpose of ratio analysis is to encourage managers to think — to find out why the numbers are what they are. Standards and guidelines provide many opportunities for comparison and thought stimulation. Asking and answering questions about significant ratios is one of the best ways to troubleshoot a failing company, or to insure the continued progress of one that is successful.

Precautions

A number of precautions should be kept in mind whenever ratios are used to make business decisions. These precautions apply not just to ratios compiled by or for the company in question, but to ratios obtained for comparison purposes from industry and credit-reporting sources.

❑ Accounting numbers are prepared under conditions of uncertainty. Important transactions may be incomplete at the end of the period. Figures provided on specific dates may obscure important seasonal changes.

❑ Unamortized or inadequately amortized assets may overstate solvency.

❑ Historical costs often have little relationship to current costs and values. Inflation is rarely taken into account.[2]

❑ Many firms operate in more than one line of business. Reports that combine activities may totally obscure trends or relationships important to the individual lines. A firm selling both at retail and wholesale, for example, may report a combined gross margin on sales that masks the likely high margin of the retail operation and low margin of the wholesale operation.

❑ Business numbers often reflect the judgment of a particular accountant, a certain accounting technique, or a traditional way of reporting for a firm or industry. Significant changes in accounting methods, one-time charges, and special events may not be revealed in time-series reports.

❑ The figures reported are sometimes grossly inaccurate. Although this usually results from record-keeping anomalies, the cause may be negligence, incompetence, or even fraud.

❏ The underlying numbers, and thus the resulting ratios, measure only the past. Interpretations that purport to predict the future are extremely risky, and should be undertaken with humility and good judgment.

❏ Ratios calculated at any point in time may obscure extreme movements which occurred during the period. Some ratios are useful only when reviewed on a monthly, weekly, or daily basis.

❏ Many popular expense ratios are functions of sales — that is, they have sales as the divisor. If, for reasons not under the control of the manager, sales decline significantly in the period (strike, economic downturn, loss of sales to a competitor), then these ratios climb — even though the direct expense may not have changed. This result of this is often an ill-advised attempt to solve the wrong problem.

❏ Ratios provided by reporting agencies and other organizations are likely to be averages, and may be out of date. Further, the difference between lower quartile and upper quartile ratio values is frequently so extreme as to suggest randomness. The range of companies studied may include near-bankrupts as well as unusual businesses following unique strategies. Information that might be valuable to an analyst (line-item expense breakdowns, for example) is often not published at all. Some of the numbers used in the computation of averages may be inaccurate — possibly false. Bringing a company's performance into line with averages is oftentimes an inappropriate strategy.

❏ A company's important structural features (product line, management ability and personality, labor relations, foreign-domestic allocation, acquisitions and divestures, pending lawsuits, environmental liability) are not revealed in ratio numbers. *Full* understanding of a company and its problems requires more information than is provided by ratio analysis.

Business ratios aid in revealing financial deficiencies and adverse trends at an early date. They point the way when the direction is unclear. But because they are not substitutes for managerial skill, they cannot (by themselves) turn a failing company into a successful one. Managers, not figures, get things done. Business ratios are valuable tools available to all managers willing to use them.

Notes — Chapter 11

1. Robert N. Anthony, *Management Accounting* (Homewood, IL: Richard D. Irwin, 1960), p. x. *See also*, Robert N. Anthony, Glen A. Welsch, and James S. Reece, *Fundamentals of Management Accounting* (Homewood, IL: Dow-Jones Irwin, 1985).

2. It *is* taken into account in other countries. For an example, *see* Patrice Duggan, "The ABCs and ADRs of Mexico," *Forbes* (June 24, 1991), p. 211.

Appendix

Appendix A
List of Business Ratios

Below is a summary listing of the business ratios featured in this book. Following the number and name of each ratio is a suggested acronymic variable name, a measurement unit symbol, and a favorable-direction indicator.

(Sales Ratios - Chapter 2)

1	SALES GROWTH	**SALESGROW**	% +
2	AFFORDABLE GROWTH RATE	**AFFGROWRATE**	% +
3	SALES GROWTH CONSISTENCY	**SALESGROWCON**	# +
4	BUDGET COMPLIANCE (SALES)	**BUDGCMPLSALES**	% +
5	DEFLATED SALES GROWTH	**DEFLSALESGROW**	% +
6	BREAK-EVEN SALES FACTOR	**BRKEVENSALESFACT**	% +
7	REVENUE TO SPACE	**REVSPACE**	$ +
8	SALES PER EMPLOYEE	**SALESEMP**	$ +

(Profit Ratios - Chapter 3)

9	GROSS MARGIN FACTOR	**GROSSMARGFACT**	% +
10	BREAK-EVEN MARGIN	**BRKEVENMARG**	% −
11	OPERATING MARGIN	**OPERMARG**	% +
12	PROFIT GROWTH	**PROFGROW**	% +
13	PROFIT GROWTH CONSISTENCY	**PROFGROWCON**	# +
14	BUDGET COMPLIANCE (PROFITS)	**BUDGCMPLPROF**	% +
15	DEFLATED PROFIT GROWTH	**DEFLPROFGROW**	% +
16	ADEQUACY OF PROFITS	**ADEQPROF**	% +
17	RETURN ON SALES	**RETSALES**	% +
18	RETURN ON SALES BEFORE TAXES	**RETSALESBEFTAX**	% +
19	RETURN ON GROSS PROFIT	**RETGROSSPROF**	% +
20	RETURN ON ASSETS	**RETASSET**	% +
21	RETURN ON WORKING CAPITAL	**RETWORKCAP**	% +
22	RETURN ON NET WORTH	**RETNETWORTH**	% +
23	RETURN ON INVESTED CAPITAL	**RETINVESCAP**	% +
24	RETURN ON RISK	**RETRISK**	% +
25	RETURN ON EMPLOYEE COMPENSATION	**RETEMPCOMP**	% +
26	PROFIT PER EMPLOYEE	**PROFEMP**	$ +
27	RETURN ON PRESIDENT'S COMPENSATION	**RETPRESCOMP**	X +
28	RETURN ON OWNERS' COMPENSATION	**RETOWNCOMP**	X +
29	RETURN ON SPACE	**RETSPACE**	$ +

(Debt and Capital Ratios - Chapter 4)

30	CURRENT RATIO	**CURRRATIO**	N +
31	QUICK RATIO	**QUICKRATIO**	N +
32	CURRENT DEBT TO EQUITY	**CURRDEBTEQ**	% −
33	DEBT TO EQUITY	**DEBTEQ**	% −
34	DEBT TO ASSETS	**DEBTASSET**	% −
35	TURNOVER OF WORKING CAPITAL	**TURNWORKCAP**	X +
36	FIXED ASSET RATIO	**FIXEDASSETRATIO**	% −
37	FIXED ASSETS MIX	**FIXEDASSETMIX**	% −
38	EQUITY RATIO	**EQRATIO**	% +
39	SUPPLIER FINANCING OF ASSETS	**SUPPFINASSET**	% −
40	DEPRECIATION RATE	**DEPRRATE**	% +
41	INVENTORY TO CURRENT ASSETS	**INVENCURRASSET**	% −
42	TIMES INTEREST EARNED	**TIMESINTEREARN**	X +
43	CASH FLOW TO DEBT MATURITIES	**CASHFLOWDEBTMAT**	X +
44	DOOMSDAY RATIO	**DOOMSRATIO**	N +
45	CASH TO TOTAL LIABILITIES	**CASHTOTLIAB**	% +
46	CASH TO DISBURSEMENTS	**CASHDISB**	% +
47	CASH TO WORKING CAPITAL	**CASHWORKCAP**	% +
48	Z-SCORE BANKRUPTCY MODEL	**BANKMODEL**	N +

(Efficiency Ratios - Chapter 5)

49	TOTAL EXPENSE RATIO	**TOTEXPRATIO**	% −
50	EXPENSES TO GROSS PROFIT	**EXPGROSSPROF**	% −
51	EMPLOYEE COMPENSATION RATIO	**EMPCOMPRATIO**	% −
52	MARKETING EXPENSE RATIO	**MARKEXPRATIO**	% −
53	RENT EXPENSE RATIO	**RENTEXPRATIO**	% −
54	INTEREST EXPENSE RATIO	**INTEREXPRATIO**	% −
55	INSURANCE EXPENSE RATIO	**INSUREXPRATIO**	% −
56	DEPRECIATION EXPENSE RATIO	**DEPREXPRATIO**	% −
57	BAD DEBTS EXPENSE RATIO	**BADDEBTEXPRATIO**	% −
58	UTILITIES EXPENSE RATIO	**UTILEXPRATIO**	% −
59	DESIGNATED EXPENSE RATIO	**DESIGEXPRATIO**	% −
60	REMAINING EXPENSE RATIO	**REMEXPRATIO**	% −
61	EXPENSE GROWTH	**EXPGROW**	% +
62	BUDGET COMPLIANCE (EXPENSES)	**BUDGCMPLEXP**	% +
63	RENT TO SPACE	**RENTSPACE**	$ +
64	TURNOVER OF ASSETS	**TURNASSET**	X +
65	CASH SALES MIX	**CASHSALESMIX**	% +
66	COLLECTION PERIOD	**COLLPRD**	# −
67	PAYMENT PERIOD	**PMTPRD**	# +
68	EXPENSE CONTROL RATIO	**EXPCNTLRATIO**	% +
69	INVENTORY TURNOVER	**INVENTURN**	X +
70	INVENTORY IN DAYS SALES	**INVENDAYSALES**	# −
71	INCOME TAX RATE	**INCTAXRATE**	% −
72	BACK ORDER RATIO	**BACKORDERRATIO**	% −

73	EMPLOYEE TURNOVER	**EMPTURN**	% −
74	ORDERS PER EMPLOYEE	**ORDEREMP**	# +
75	DEFLATED WAGE GROWTH	**DEFLWAGEGROW**	% −
76	ASSETS PER EMPLOYEE	**ASSETEMP**	$ +
77	FLOOR SPACE PER EMPLOYEE	**SPACEEMP**	# −

(Marketing Ratios - Chapter 6)

78	AVERAGE ORDER SIZE	**AVERORDSIZE**	$ +
79	DEFLATED AOS CHANGE	**DEFLAVERORDSIZECH**	$ +
80	ORDER GROWTH	**ORDGROW**	% +
81	CUSTOMER GROWTH	**CUSTGROW**	% +
82	SALES PER CUSTOMER	**SALESCUST**	$ +
83	CUSTOMER SOLICITATION RATIO	**CUSTSOLICRATIO**	% +
84	CUSTOMER SPACE RATIO	**CUSTSPACERATIO**	N +
85	MARKETING GROWTH	**MARKGROW**	% +
86	AVERAGE RETURN ON MARKETING	**AVERRETMARK**	X +
87	AVERAGE ORDER RESPONSE	**AVERORDRESP**	% +
88	AVERAGE SALES RESPONSE	**AVERSALESRESP**	$ +
89	CUSTOMER SATISFACTION RATIO	**CUSTSATRATIO**	% +
90	PROPRIETARY PRODUCT RATIO	**PROPPRODRATIO**	% +

(Investment Ratios - Chapter 7)

91	BOOK VALUE PER SHARE	**BOOKSHARE**	$ +
92	BUSINESS VALUE PREMIUM	**BUSVALPREM**	% +
93	DIVIDEND RATE	**DIVRATE**	$ +
94	DIVIDEND YIELD	**DIVYIELD**	% +
95	RETENTION RATE	**RTNRATE**	% +
96	PRICE TO EARNINGS	**PRICEEARN**	N −
97	PRICE TO BOOK	**PRICEBOOK**	N −
98	PRICE TO SALES	**PRICESALES**	N −
99	OLYMPIC MODEL	**OLYMPMODEL**	# +
100	BUSINESS VALUE ESTIMATE	**BUSVALEST**	$ +
101	RATIO CHANGE INDICATOR	**RATIOCHINDIC**	# +

% = Percent
$ = Dollars
N = Any other real number
# = Integer number
X = Times
+ = Increase in value of ratio is *usually* considered favorable
− = Decrease in value of ratio is *usually* considered favorable

Appendix B
List of Input Statistics

Below is a summary listing of input statistics used to compute the business ratios featured in this book. The data are taken from the balance sheet, profit and loss statement, and other company records.[1] Following the number and name of each input statistic is a suggested acronymic variable name, a measurement-unit symbol, and a polarity indicator.[2]

(Numbers Obtained from Balance Sheet)

1	YEAR	YEAR	# +
2	CASH	CASH	$ +
3	ACCOUNTS RECEIVABLE	ACCREC	$ +
4	INVENTORY	INVEN	$ +
5	CURRENT ASSETS	CURRASSET	$ +
6	FIXED ASSETS	FIXEDASSET	$ +
7	INTANGIBLES	INTAN	$ +
8	TOTAL ASSETS	TOTASSET	$ +
9	ACCOUNTS PAYABLE	ACCPAY	$ +
10	CURRENT LIABILITIES	CURRLIAB	$ +
11	LONG-TERM LIABILITIES	LONGTERMLIAB	$ +
12	SHARES OUTSTANDING	SHARE	# +
13	RETAINED EARNINGS	RTDEARN	$ ±
14	STOCKHOLDERS' EQUITY	STOCKHOLDEQ	$ ±

(Numbers Obtained from Income Statement)

15	GROSS SALES	GROSSSALES	$ +
16	NET SALES	NETSALES	$ +
17	PURCHASES	PURCH	$ +
18	GROSS PROFIT	GROSSPROF	$ ±
19	WAGES EXPENSE	WAGEEXP	$ +
20	MARKETING/SELLING EXPENSE	MARKEXP	$ +
21	RENT EXPENSE	RENTEXP	$ +
22	INTEREST EXPENSE	INTEREXP	$ +
23	INSURANCE EXPENSE	INSUREXP	$ +
24	DEPRECIATION EXPENSE	DEPREXP	$ +
25	BAD DEBTS EXPENSE	BADDEBTEXP	$ +

26	UTILITIES EXPENSE	**UTILEXP**	$ +
27	DESIGNATED EXPENSE LINE ITEM	**DESIGEXP**	$ +
28	TOTAL EXPENSES	**TOTEXP**	$ +
29	NET PROFIT BEFORE TAXES	**NETPROFBEFTAX**	$ ±
30	NET PROFIT AFTER TAXES	**NETPROFAFTTAX**	$ ±

(Numbers Obtained from Other Internal and External Sources)

31	DIVIDENDS	**DIV**	$ +
32	LONG-TERM DEBT MATURITIES	**DEBTMAT**	$ +
33	TRANSACTIONS	**TRANS**	# +
34	PRESIDENT'S COMPENSATION	**PRESCOMP**	$ +
35	OWNERS' COMPENSATION	**OWNCOMP**	$ +
36	EMPLOYEE TERMINATIONS	**EMPTRMN**	N +
37	SOLICITATIONS	**SOLIC**	# +
38	SOLICITATIONS TO CUSTOMERS	**SOLICCUST**	# +
39	CREDIT SALES	**CREDSALES**	$ +
40	PROPRIETARY PRODUCT SALES	**PROPPRODSALES**	$ +
41	BUDGETED NET SALES	**BUDGNETSALES**	$ +
42	BUDGETED TOTAL EXPENSES	**BUDGTOTEXP**	$ +
43	BUDGETED NET PROFIT	**BUDGNETPROF**	$ ±
44	BACK ORDERS	**BACKORD**	$ +
45	CUSTOMERS	**CUST**	# +
46	EMPLOYEES (AVERAGE)	**EMP**	N +
47	STOCK PRICE	**STOCKPRICE**	$ +
48	FLOOR SPACE	**SPACE**	# +
49	INTEREST RATE	**INTERRATE**	% +
50	PRICE INDEX	**PRICEINDEX**	N +

% = Percent
$ = Dollars
N = Any other real number
# = Integer number

1. Stats 2-14, 44-45, and 47-50 are year-end figures. Stats 15-43 are annual totals. Stat 46 is a yearly average.

2. Polarity indicator: + signifies that only positive values are meaningful (applies to most input numbers). ± identifies bipolar statistics that may have positive *or* negative values.

Appendix C
Usage Table

INPUT STATISTIC		IS USED IN THE COMPUTATION OF THESE RATIOS
YEAR	1	
CASH	2	44 45 46 47
ACCREC	3	66
INVEN	4	31 41 69 70
CURRASSET	5	21 30 31 35 41 47 48
FIXEDASSET	6	36 37 40
INTAN	7	2 20 22 23 24 32 33 36 38 100
TOTASSET	8	16 20 34 37 38 39 48 64 76
ACCPAY	9	39 67
CURRLIAB	10	21 30 31 32 33 34 35 38 44 45 47 48
LONGTERMLIAB	11	23 33 34 45 48
SHARE	12	91 93 94 96 97 98
RTDEARN	13	48
STOCKHOLDEQ	14	2 22 23 24 32 33 36 38 48 91 92 97 100
GROSSSALES	15	89
NETSALES	16	1 3 4 5 7 8 9 10 11 16 17 18 35 49 51 52 53 54 55 56 57 58 59 60 64 65 68 69 70 78 79 82 86 88 89 00 90 99
PURCH	17	46 67 72
GROSSPROF	18	6 9 19 50 69
WAGEEXP	19	25 51 60 75
MARKEXP	20	52 60 85 86
RENTEXP	21	53 60 63
INTEREXP	22	11 23 42 48 54 60 100
INSUREXP	23	55 60
DEPREXP	24	11 24 43 56 60
BADDEBTEXP	25	57 60
UTILEXP	26	30 58 60
DESIGEXP	27	59 60
TOTEXP	28	6 10 46 49 50 60 61 62 68
NETPROFBEFTAX	29	11 18 42 48 71 100
NETPROFAFTTAX	30	2 12 13 14 15 16 17 19 20 21 22 23 24 25 26 27 28 29 43 71 92 95 96 99
DIV	31	2 16 28 93 94 95
DEBTMAT	32	43
TRANS	33	74 78 79 80 87
PRESCOMP	34	27
OWNCOMP	35	28
EMPTRMN	36	73
SOLIC	37	83 87 88
SOLICCUST	38	83
CREDSALES	39	65 66
PROPPRODSALES	40	90
BUDGNETSALES	41	4
BUDGTOTEXP	42	62
BUDGNETPROF	43	14
BACKORDER	44	72
CUST	45	81 82 84
EMP	46	8 26 73 74 75 76 77
STOCKPRICE	47	94 96 97 98
SPACE	48	7 29 63 77 84
INTERRATE	49	24 92 100
PRICEINDEX	50	5 15 75 79

Appendix D
Acronymic Naming of Variables

The following short words are suggested for creating acronymic variable names.[1] They are useful in computer programs, ledgers, and spreadsheets. By tagging the words together, readily-identifiable names for input statistics and ratios are devised.

The words are applicable to singular and plural usage. Words marked by asterisk (*) are used without abbreviation.

ACC	ACCOUNT	**DEFL**	DEFLATED
ADEQ	ADEQUACY	**DEPR**	DEPRECIATION
AFF	AFFORDABLE	**DESIG**	DESIGNATED
ASSET	*	**DISB**	DISBURSEMENT
AFT	AFTER	**DIV**	DIVIDEND
AVER	AVERAGE	**DOOMS**	DOOMSDAY
BACK	*	**EARN**	EARNED/EARNINGS
BAD	*	**EMP**	EMPLOYEE
BANK	BANKRUPTCY	**EQ**	EQUITY
BEF	BEFORE	**EST**	ESTIMATE
BOOK	*	**EVEN**	*
BRK	BREAK	**EXP**	EXPENSE
BUDG	BUDGET/BUDGETED		
BUS	BUSINESS	**FACT**	FACTOR
		FIN	FINANCING
CAP	CAPITAL	**FIXED**	*
CASH	*	**FLOW**	*
CH	CHANGE		
CMPL	COMPLIANCE	**GROSS**	*
CNTL	CONTROL	**GROW**	GROWTH
COLL	COLLECTION		
COMP	COMPENSATION	**HOLD**	HOLDER
CON	CONSISTENCY		
CRED	CREDIT	**INC**	INCOME
CURR	CURRENT	**INDEX**	*
CUST	CUSTOMER	**INDIC**	INDICATOR
		INSUR	INSURANCE
DAY	*	**INTAN**	INTANGIBLE
DEBT	*		

INTER	INTEREST	**RISK**	*
INVEN	INVENTORY	**RTD**	RETAINED
INVES	INVESTED	**RTN**	RETENTION
LAST	*	**SALES**	*
LIAB	LIABILITY	**SAT**	SATISFACTION
LONG	*	**SHARE**	*
		SIZE	*
MARG	MARGIN	**SOLIC**	SOLICITATION
MAT	MATURITY	**SPACE**	*
MIX	*	**STOCK**	*
MARK	MARKETING	**SUPP**	SUPPLIER
MODEL	*		
		TAX	*
NET	*	**TERM**	*
		TRMN	TERMINATION
OLYMP	OLYMPIC	**TIMES**	*
OPER	OPERATING	**TOT**	TOTAL
ORD	ORDER	**TRANS**	TRANSACTION
OWN	OWNER	**TURN**	TURNOVER
PAY	PAYABLE	**UTIL**	UTILITY
PROF	PROFIT		
PMT	PAYMENT	**VAL**	VALUE
PRD	PERIOD		
PREM	PREMIUM	**WAGE**	*
PRES	PRESIDENT	**WORK**	WORKING
PRICE	*	**WORTH**	*
PROD	PRODUCT		
PROP	PROPRIETARY	**YIELD**	*
PURCH	PURCHASE	**YEAR**	*
QUICK	*		
RATE	*		
RATIO	*		
REC	RECEIVABLE		
REM	REMAINING		
RENT	*		
RESP	RESPONSE		
RET	RETURN		
REV	REVENUE		

1. In creating the acronymic variable names shown in this book, use of the first few letters of words occasionally resulted in duplication or a lack of clarity. When this occurred, alternate abbreviations were substituted. Example: RETURN, RETAINED, and RETENTION. Prepositions such as *in*, *on*, *of*, *per*, and *to* are not included in variable names.

Appendix E
C.P.I and Interest Rate

Historical Values

Year	Consumer Price Index[1]	Best-Grade Bond Yields[2]
1970	39.8	7.53
1971	41.2	7.17
1972	42.6	7.21
1973	46.3	7.91
1974	52.0	9.21
1975	55.6	8.85
1976	58.3	7.72
1977	62.3	7.85
1978	67.9	8.81
1979	76.9	10.36
1980	86.5	11.94
1981	94.2	13.00
1982	97.8	11.24
1983	101.5	11.85
1984	105.6	11.76
1985	109.5	9.92
1986	110.8	8.53
1987	115.7	9.70
1988	120.5	9.55
1989	126.1	8.85
1990	133.8	8.99
1991	137.9	8.31

1. December value, Consumer Price Index for All Urban Consumers (unadjusted), 1982-84=100. (Source: U.S. Department of Labor, Bureau of Labor Statistics.)

2. Value for last week of December, *Barron's* Index of 10 high-grade corporate bonds. (Source: *Barron's* Market Laboratory/Bonds.)

Appendix F
Demo Company Input Data

		1988	1989	1990	1991	1992
YEAR	1	1988	1989	1990	1991	1992
CASH	2	3,747	436	5,312	2,755	2,694
ACCREC	3	129,097	100,074	79,508	117,982	123,524
INVEN	4	283,108	230,687	238,332	315,682	310,458
CURRASSET	5	464,732	387,694	323,152	438,566	437,156
FIXEDASSET	6	89,958	64,273	51,168	45,085	50,081
INTAN	7	32,200	31,050	29,909	28,759	27,600
TOTASSET	8	587,116	483,017	404,229	512,410	518,473
ACCPAY	9	142,374	182,284	90,982	134,614	122,291
CURRLIAB	10	187,964	234,617	111,001	169,125	148,952
LONGTERMLIAB	11	33,068	14,856	5,868	0	2,653
SHARE	12	997,000	997,000	1,108,000	1,223,674	1,229,424
RTDEARN	13	263,794	131,254	159,070	184,995	206,978
STOCKHOLDEQ	14	366,084	233,544	287,360	343,285	366,868
GROSSSALES	15	1,875,875	1,443,245	1,200,495	1,292,401	1,315,764
NETSALES	16	1,833,059	1,408,956	1,186,578	1,274,738	1,305,002
PURCH	17	959,854	690,215	675,700	856,771	833,513
GROSSPROF	18	704,915	566,020	512,017	495,316	458,941
WAGEEXP	19	291,857	235,818	146,880	155,317	162,858
MARKEXP	20	241,547	269,918	163,836	143,161	76,370
RENTEXP	21	23,060	27,359	27,790	26,877	33,138
INTEREXP	22	19,561	19,910	8,059	2,908	4,676
INSUREXP	23	16,299	17,036	12,076	15,540	21,159
DEPREXP	24	22,858	15,232	14,444	13,903	10,672
BADDEBTEXP	25	22,645	5,013	14,450	4,593	21,296
UTILEXP	26	18,485	21,645	12,761	16,117	15,307
DESIGEXP	27	61,708	49,015	33,251	32,844	26,287
TOTEXP	28	823,822	732,418	474,471	465,584	433,630
NETPROFBEFTAX	29	-118,907	-166,398	37,546	29,732	25,311
NETPROFAFTTAX	30	-78,127	-109,881	31,592	25,925	21,983
DIV	31	28,266	22,659	3,776	0	0
DEBTMAT	32	18,790	13,871	10,520	5,163	2,304
TRANS	33	20,368	17,232	11,118	11,401	10,095
PRESCOMP	34	55,750	47,667	36,318	40,079	43,287
OWNCOMP	35	31,266	28,659	11,776	8,000	8,000
EMPTRMN	36	27.5	19.5	4.5	2.0	3.5
SOLIC	37	220,000	330,000	45,600	206,200	8,200
SOLICCUST	38	66,000	73,800	1,400	85,200	2,100
CREDSALES	39	788,215	634,030	613,525	735,017	768,236
PROPPRODSALES	40	N/A	N/A	10,356	46,575	72,011
BUDGNETSALES	41	2,750,000	1,980,000	1,540,000	1,310,000	1,400,000
BUDGTOTEXP	42	817,800	707,629	490,654	578,483	468,199
BUDGNETPROF	43	21,122	26,659	29,501	23,517	62,708
BACKORDER	44	N/A	25,591	9,243	7,095	20,034
CUST	45	33,010	36,900	38,812	39,738	39,512
EMP	46	21.6	14.3	8.0	7.9	9.9
STOCKPRICE	47	N/A	N/A	N/A	N/A	N/A
SPACE	48	6,625	6,100	5,575	5,575	5,875
INTERRATE	49	9.6	8.9	9.0	8.3	N/A
PRICEINDEX	50	120.5	126.1	133.8	137.9	N/A

Appendix G
Stock Market Ratios

The following ratios compare popular market indices to other investment and economic parameters. They purport to show whether stock prices are relatively cheap or dear.

DIVIDEND YIELD. Stocks are a "buy" when the yield on the Dow Jones 30 Industrial Average is 6% and a "sell" when it is 3%.[1]

PRICE TO EARNINGS. A sell signal is given when the Standard & Poor's 500 price-to-trailing-earnings ratio is 18, and a buy signal when it is 12.[2]

STOCK-BOND YIELD GAP. The difference between the yield on Barron's Index of 10 Best-Grade Corporate Bonds and the dividend yield of the Dow Jones 30 Industrial Average. Near the market highs of 1987 the gap had widened to more than 7.3%—a sell-signal level higher than prevailed in 1929.[3]

P/E VS. BOND YIELDS. Downward corrections in stock prices often occur when the price-to-expected-earnings ratio for the Standard & Poor's 500 index rises to more than 15% above the price-to-coupon ratio for Moody's Aaa corporate bonds.[4]

PRICE TO BOOK VALUE. A value of two or more for the Dow Jones 30 Industrial Average is the warning signal to sell and one or less the signal to buy.[2]

GOLDEN RULE. How much does a "share" of the Dow Jones 30 Industrial Average cost in ounces of gold? Dividing by the price of gold provides the answer. One study shows that when an investor paid about two ounces to buy the average, the purchase was made at an historically opportune time.[5]

RULE OF 20. The sum of the price-to-earnings ratio of the Dow Jones 30 Industrial Average and the percentage inflation rate tends to move up and down to the number 20.[6] Sums below 16 suggest buying opportunities.[7]

RULE OF 17. The sum of the price-to-earnings ratio of the Standard & Poor's 500 Index and the percentage inflation rate hovers around 17. Values below 10-14 suggest buying opportunities. Values above 22, on the other hand, suggest selling opportunities.[8]

FAIR VALUE. An approximation of the fair value of the stock
market (as measured by the Dow Jones 30 Industrial Average) is
found by multiplying the combined earnings of the DJI 30 by a
capitalization factor. This factor is equal to 100 divided by the
sum of the inflation rate and 3% (the rate of return lenders
historically receive for the use of money absent inflation).[9] Buy or
sell signals are given whenever the actual value of the index
moves significantly away from the fair value.

If these ratios have the ability to identify buying and selling opportunities, why are they not universally relied upon by investors and money
managers? One reason is that undervalued and overvalued markets can
persist for very long periods of time, suggesting to many that the ratios
are unreliable. The longer a market remains over- or undervalued, the
greater the likelihood that prevailing price levels are perceived as "normal"
by an increasing number of individuals. Another reason is that human
nature resists the changes in thinking required to move in and out of
markets in response to signals of fundamental analysis. ("Maybe it's
different this time," or "I'll wait a little longer and see what happens," or
"If it's what most professionals are doing, it must be right.") Also, the
outstanding shares of corporations, particularly those included in popular
averages, are increasingly held by mutual funds, pension funds, and other
institutional investors. Many of these rely on buy and hold strategies.
Significant numbers of private investors buy only for the long term,
sometimes even passing securities on to future generations without
portfolio revision. This perhaps explains why stock prices are little
influenced by rational arguments about value, even when well researched.

Notes — Appendix G

1. Richard A. Donnelly, review of *Dividends Don't Lie*, by Geraldine Weiss and Janet Lowe, *Barron's* (July 10, 1989), p. 41.

2. A. Gary Shilling, "Exits and Entrances", *Forbes* (September 16, 1991), p. 154-156.

3. Edward A. Wyatt, "Stock-Bond Yield Gap", *Barron's* (July 23, 1990), p. 22.

4. Steven Ramos, quoting Richard Pucci, "What the Analysts Think", *Forbes* (March 18, 1991), p. 144.

5. Steven D. Stoller, "The Goldon Rule", *Barron's* (May 25, 1987), p. 35.

6. Steve Kichen, quoting Eric Miller, "The rule of 20," *Forbes* (June 20, 1983), p. 31.

7. As for selling opportunities, the *Forbes* 1983 article reported a 1961 record high for the sum of 22.7. In 1983 the P/E of the Dow Jones 30 Industrial Average reached 3-digit values and the calculation produced sums exceeding 120. Kichen, however, correctly reported this as a buying opportunity, because the sum worked out to a value of less than 13 after excluding companies reporting losses.

8. This variation by the author (based on 500 stocks instead of 30) overcomes the type of statistical anomaly that occurred in 1983 (when several companies in the DJI 30 Average reported unprecedented losses). It is based on monthly average trailing P/E's and CPI inflation rates measured by regression. Buying and selling opportunities are defined as the lowest and highest 10% of values found in a rank ordering of the data. The buying figure of 12 results from the use of data ranging from 1921-1991. The buying figure of 15 uses data from 1980-1991. Interestingly, the selling figure of 20, and 17 (the median figure) are about the same whether 70 or 12 (recent) years are studied.

9. *See*, Ann C. Brown, "The New Reality," *Forbes* (February 15, 1982), p. 176.

Appendix H
Misc. Tips

Debits and Credits

Type of Account	Debit Indicates	Credit Indicates
Asset	An increase	A decrease
Expense	An increase	A decrease
Liability	A decrease	An increase
Equity	A decrease	An increase
Revenue	A decrease	An increase

Greater Than and *Less Than*

A number line reveals the meaning of "greater than" and "less than."

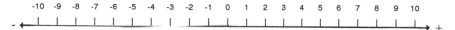

In comparing two numbers, the number on the left is *less than* the one on the right and the number on the right is *greater than* the one on the left.

Examples:

1 is greater than -6.

-1 is less than 1.

Communication for Managers

Communicating with **customers** means finding out how you can serve them, and letting them know how well you are doing it.

Communicating with **employees** means letting them know what needs to be done, finding out how well they are doing it, and offering help when needed.

Communicating with **bosses, owners**, or **boards** means finding out what they expect you to do, letting them know how well you are doing it, and asking for help when needed.

Communicating with **suppliers** means finding out how they can serve you, and letting them know how well they are doing it.

The Meaning of Management

Management means getting things done.

Good management means getting all needed things done.

Great management means getting all needed things done and making those involved feel good about it.

Solving Percentage Problems — The Three Cases

Percentage problems typically involve use of the words *of*, *is*, and *what*. Deciding whether to multiply or divide and in what order is sometimes a challenge. Three tests (performed in the order listed) lead to a correct solution.

1. **WHAT PERCENT OF** signals the first case. If the problem question includes those three words in sequence, divide by the number following *of*.

Example:	*What percent of* 300 is 600?
Answer:	200% (600/300 = 2 = 200%).
Example:	400 is *what percent of* 1600?
Answer:	25% (400/1600 = .25 = 25%).

2. **OF** signals the second case. If the first test is not met and the problem question uses the word *of* to separate the two numbers, multiply the numbers.

Example:	What is 21% *of* 384.2?
Answer:	35.1 (0.21 X 384.2 = 35.1).

3. **IS** signals the third case. If the first two tests are not met and the problem question uses the word *is* to separate the two numbers, divide by the number following *is*.

Example:	1500 *is* 5% of what?
Answer:	30,000 (1500/.05 = 30,000).

Precision — Significant Figures

The result of a mathematical operation between two numbers acquires the precision of the least precise number, and is expressed with the same number of significant figures.

Examples:

National Sales=$927,256. California Sales=10% of National Sales.

∴ California Sales=$93,000 (not $92,725.60).

Profit=$863,240. Average number of employees=101.

∴ Profit per employee=$8,550 (not $8,546.93).

Accuracy — Ranging

In addition to rounding off numbers to the appropriate degree of their precision, they should be ranged to the degree of their accuracy if the information is available.

Example:

National Sales=$927,256.   California Sales=$93,000.

Accuracy of California Sales data ± 4%.

∴ California Sales=$89,000 to $97,000, or $93,000 ± 4%.

Acknowledging the extent of inaccuracy in a report makes the report itself more accurate. Accuracy equates to truth. The meaning of the numbers is much more important than the numbers themselves.

Accuracy — Estimating

Whereas accuracy is considered essential in accounting and engineering, it is sometimes unimportant to a manager. Gaining insight into the reality of worldly matters is often accomplished as well with estimates as with exact information. Meaningful estimates in hand now may be more valuable than highly accurate numbers available in the future.

Screening and Rank Ordering

It is often necessary in business to select "one from among many." Examples that come to mind: hiring a key employee (large number of applicants), choosing a vendor (varied bids and track records), investing in a common stock (many things to look at — P/E, growth, debt, dividend, the industry). A familiar way to make a selection is by screening — that is, establishing a list of minimum requirements resulting in the rejection of "unqualified" candidates. Disadvantages to this are: (1) If the filter is set too high, no candidate qualifies. (2) If set too low, too many qualify. In either case, the frequent result is no action or a subjective decision.

Rank ordering is an alternate method of selection that a manager might consider. In rank ordering, points are assigned according to each candidate's position (high number most favorable) in each category. Advantages: (1) no candidate is discriminated against or rejected on the basis of one criterion. (2) barring ties, a "winner" is always provided. Consider the simplified example in which a small company is hiring a marketing manager. *Screening* criteria are: graduate degree in business, 7-10 years of marketing experience, impressive portfolio of successful projects in prior employment, and willingness to accept an annual salary of $58,000. Note on the following table that none of the candidates passes the basic screen.

Candidate	Education Level		Marketing Experience		Portfolio Evaluation	Asking Salary		Rank-Order Score
A	5	(Ph.D.)	3	(4 yrs.)	1	1	($95,000)	10
B	2	(B.A.)	4	(7 yrs.)	5	4	($42,000)	⑮
C	3	(M.A.)	2	(3 yrs.)	4	2	($65,000)	11
D	4	(MBA)	1	(9 mo.)	3	3	($43,000)	11
E	1	(h.s.)	5	(8 yrs.)	2	5	($29,000)	13

Candidate B earns the highest score (falling short of the screening criteria only in the matter of education). The company may, of course, elect to interview additional candidates and not make a decision at this time. Or, candidate B could be hired on a trial basis.

Any category can be overweighed. For example, if prior experience is considered particularly important, it might be double weighted. In the example above, B would remain the winner with E a close second.

Does rank ordering guarantee selection of the most qualified candidate? No. No method, including screening, does that. Although final decisions are often based a manager's instinct, rank ordering is one good way to get the process started.

Glossary

Absolute value — the value of a real or complex number not considering its sign. Example: the absolute value of -3.84 is 3.84.

Accelerated depreciation — a method of depreciation in which the cost of fixed assets is written off faster than through straight-line depreciation. Examples include *declining balance*, *sum-of-years digits*, and *unit-of-output*.

Accounts payable — amounts owed to creditors–usually suppliers of goods and services purchased for resale.

Accounts receivable — amounts due from others–usually for goods and services sold on open account.

Accrual — an earned revenue item not yet collected or an incurred expense item not yet paid.

Accuracy — the degree to which a measurement or observation is free of error.

Acid test ratio — *See*, Quick ratio.

Acronymic equation — one in which mathematical variables are expressed as acronyms or abbreviations. Example: ORDERPEREMP=TRANS — AVEREMP.

Activity ratio — a measure showing how a firm uses its resources.

Adequacy of profits — net retained profit after taxes divided by last year's total assets, divided again by the year's sales growth (expressed as a decimal), then multiplied by 100 to provide a percentage. Ratio 16.

Affordable growth rate — net retained profit after taxes divided by last year's tangible net worth, multiplied by 100 to provide a percentage. Ratio 2.

Aging schedule — a report classifying unpaid accounts receivable by date of sale–usually organized as *current, 31-60 days unpaid, 61-90 days unpaid,* and *over 90 days unpaid*. The portion of accounts in each category is an indicator of the quality of receivables.

AGR — *Abbrev.*, Affordable growth rate.

Algorithm — a set of computer program instructions intended to do a certain thing.

AOS — *Abbrev.*, Average order size.

Architectural efficiency — comparison of a plant's production to its design features and space utilization.

Arithmetic mean — *See*, Mean.

ASCII — American Standard Code for Information Interchange. *Also*, a description applied to recognizable computer characters such as letters of the alphabet.

Assets per employee — total assets divided by average number of employees. Ratio 76.

Average — a single value representing or summarizing the collective significance of a set of values.

Average daily credit sales — annual credit sales divided by 365. Variations divide by 360 (12 30-day months) or 260 (52 5-day weeks). Other variations based on quarterly or monthly credit sales divide by 91 or 30.

Average daily purchases — annual purchases divided by 365. *See*, Average daily credit sales for time variations.

Average daily sales — annual net sales divided by 365. *See*, Average daily credit sales for time variations.

Average number employees — usually found by adding opening and closing number of employees and dividing by two. Where part-time workers are employed, the figures are maintained in full-time equivalents.

Average order response — average number of orders or transactions divided by average number of solicitations, multiplied by 100 to provide a percentage. Ratio 87.

Average order size — net sales divided by number of orders/transactions. Ratio 78.

Average return on marketing — average net sales divided by average marketing expense. Ratio 86.

Average sales response — average net sales divided by average number of solicitations. Ratio 88.

Back order — an order received but not yet fulfilled.

Back order ratio — value of back orders on hand divided by average monthly sales, multiplied by 100 to provide a percentage. Ratio 72.

Backup ratio — one which is a component of another ratio.

Bad debts expense — an amount reserved or written off to reflect that portion of accounts receivable likely to prove uncollectible.

Bad debts expense ratio — bad debts expense divided by net sales, multiplied by 100 to provide a percentage. Ratio 57.

Balance sheet — the basic accounting equation or report wherein assets are shown equal to liabilities plus owner equity.

Balance sheet ratio — a financial ratio computed from numbers found in the balance sheet.

Bankruptcy — a condition in law which entitles creditors to have an estate administered for their benefit. *Also*, an inability to satisfy creditors.

BASIC — *Acronym*, Beginner's All-Purpose Symbolic Instruction Code. A computer programming language developed by John Kemeny and Thomas Kurtz at Dartmouth College, Hanover, NH.

Bipolar input number — one wherein either a positive *or* negative value is logical or permitted.

Book — a set of permanent financial records.

Book value — the value at which an asset is reported in financial statements. Original cost less depreciation.

Book value per share — stockholders' equity divided by number of shares of company stock outstanding. Ratio 91.

Bottom line — net profit after taxes. *Also*, the final result of something.

Break-even margin — total expenses divided by net sales, the result multiplied by 100 to provide a percentage. Ratio 10.

Break-even sales factor — gross profit divided by total expenses, multiplied by 100 to provide a percentage. Ratio 6.

Budget compliance (expenses) — actual total expenses divided by budgeted total expenses, multiplied by 100 to provide a percentage. Ratio 62.

Budget compliance (profits) — actual (realized) net profit after taxes divided by budgeted net profit after taxes, multiplied by 100 to provide a percentage. Ratio 14.

Budget compliance (sales) — actual (realized) net sales divided by budgeted net sales, multiplied by 100 to provide a percentage. Ratio 4.

Budgeted net profit (after taxes) — an estimate or business-plan projection for net profit in the current or a future period.

Budgeted net sales — an estimate or business-plan projection for net sales in the current or a future period.

Budgeted total expenses — an estimate or business-plan projection for total expenses in the current or a future period.

Business risk — the degree of probability that a firm will fail (or operate unprofitably) due to uncertainty of income resulting from product or market.

Business value estimate — an appraisal of business value by formula. In this book, the average of (1) tangible net worth multiplied by two, and (2) one-half the capitalized value (using long-term bond rates) of net profit before taxes and interest. Ratio 100.

Business value premium — capitalized value of earnings less stockholders' equity, divided by stockholders' equity, multiplied by 100 to provide a percentage. Ratio 92.

Buying of sales — a managerial practice whereby prices are lowered solely to attract sales, with no regard to how this may affect profitability.

C — a computer programming language.

Capital — owners' equity. *Also,* refers to long-term productive assets.

Capital ratio *or* **Capitalization ratio** — one revealing how a firm is capitalized.

Capitalized value of earnings — net profit after taxes divided by an interest rate appropriate to the degree of risk associated with those earnings.

Cash flow — gross or total cash derived from operations. Sometimes found by adding depreciation to after-tax earnings less preferred dividends.

Cash flow to debt maturities — net profit after taxes, plus depreciation expense, the sum divided by long-term debt maturities. Ratio 43.

Cash ratio — one measuring cash or cash flow.

Cash sales mix — cash sales divided by net sales, multiplied by 100 to provide a percentage. Ratio 65.

Cash to disbursements — cash divided by average monthly disbursements, multiplied by 100 to provide a percentage. Ratio 46.

Cash to total liabilities — cash divided by total liabilities, multiplied by 100 to provide a percentage. Ratio 45.

Cash to working capital — cash divided by working capital, multiplied by 100 to provide a percentage. Ratio 47.

Collection period — accounts receivable divided by average daily credit sales. Ratio 66.

Common stock ratio — *See,* Equity ratio.

Comparator — an instrument or mathematical process used to relate one measurement to another or to a standard value.

Competitive edge — refers to the business advantage one firm has over another resulting from its product, advanced technology, pricing capability, location, etc.

Consumer Price Index — a measurement of change in consumer prices determined monthly by the U.S. Bureau of Labor Statistics.

Cost of goods sold — an accounting concept to determine all costs of buying and producing finished goods sold in the accounting period. The calculation is typically made by adding beginning inventory to purchases, and then subtracting ending inventory.

Coverage ratio — one measuring availability of funds to meet obligations. *Also,* an expression of the relative magnitudes of two numbers expressed as *times.*

CPI — *See,* Consumer Price Index.

Credit — an entry on the right side of a T account.

Credit risk — the degree of probability that an account will not be paid in a satisfactory manner.

Credit sale — one not requiring immediate payment by the buyer.

Crossover — a technical indicator used by investors. A crossover occurs when the current price for a security moves below the moving average (if the trend is positive) or above the moving average (if the trend is negative).

Current asset — an asset likely to be expensed, converted into cash, exchanged, used, or sold within one operating period – usually a year.

Current assets account — a balance sheet category typically consisting of cash, marketable securities, notes and accounts receivable, inventory, and prepaid expenses.

Current debt to equity — current liabilities divided by tangible stockholders' equity, multiplied by 100 to provide a percentage. Ratio 32.

Current liability — a liability likely to be paid or satisfied within one operating period – usually a year.

Current liabilities account — a balance sheet category typically consisting of accounts payable, notes payable, taxes payable, accrued expenses, and that portion of long-term debt due within one year.

Current ratio — current assets divided by current liabilities. Ratio 30.

Custom ratio — one derived to meet the needs of a particular company.

Customer acquisition — a marketing strategy aimed at increasing the size of a company's customer base.

Customer growth — the difference between this year's number of customers and last year's number of customers, divided by last year's number of customers, multiplied by 100 to provide a percentage. Ratio 81.

Customer list — a mailing list or prospect list of firms or individuals who have purchased in the past.

Customer retention — a marketing strategy aimed at satisfying existing customers in order to maintain or increase their propensity to buy.

Customer satisfaction ratio — net sales divided by gross sales, multiplied by 100 to provide a percentage. Ratio 89.

Customer solicitation ratio — number of solicitations directed to customers divided by total number of solicitations, multiplied by 100 to provide a percentage. Ratio 83.

Customer space ratio — number of customers divided by floor space. Ratio 84.

Days sales outstanding — *See*, Collection period.

Debit — an entry on the left side of a T account.

Debt ratio — *See*, Debt to assets. *Also*, a business ratio examining or reporting on some aspect of debt. Example: Debt to equity.

Debt to assets — total liabilities divided by total assets, multiplied by 100 to provide a percentage. Ratio 34.

Debt to equity — total liabilities divided by tangible stockholders' equity, multiplied by 100 to provide a percentage. Ratio 33.

Dedicated software — a computer program designed primarily to perform one task. Examples: To maintain a mailing list, or compute business ratios.

Deflated AOS change — this year's deflated average order size reduced by last year's average order size. Ratio 79.

Deflated profit growth — the difference between this year's deflated net profit after taxes and last year's net profit after taxes, divided by last year's net profit after taxes, multiplied by 100 to provide a percentage. Ratio 15.

Deflated sales growth — the difference between this year's deflated net sales and last year's net sales, divided by last year's net sales, multiplied by 100 to provide a percentage. Ratio 5.

Deflated wage growth — the difference between this year's deflated average wage and last year's average wage, divided by last year's average wage, multiplied by 100 to provide a percentage. Ratio 75.

Deflation — a decrease in price levels which results when spending decreases relative to the supply of goods.

Deflator — a factor used by statisticians to adjust between values in different periods as they may be affected by a change in the worth of the currency.

Denominator — the number below the line in a fraction. In the case of 7/16, 16 is the denominator or divisor.

Depreciation — the periodic accounting allocation of an asset's cost (less salvage) over its useful life.

Depreciation expense ratio — depreciation expense divided by net sales, multiplied by 100 to provide a percentage. Ratio 56.

Depreciation rate — depreciation expense divided by fixed assets, multiplied by 100 to provide a percentage. Ratio 40.

Depreciation ratio — *See*, Depreciation expense ratio.

Designated expense ratio — any designated line item of expense divided by net sales, multiplied by 100 to provide a percentage. Ratio 59.

Dimension statement — specifies maximum values for variable subscripts in arrays and allocates computer memory storage accordingly.

Direct response business — one in which the seller deals directly with the buyer by mail or telephone. Characterized by an absence of go-betweens and face-to-face salespersons.

Disbursement — a payment.

Dividend — money or securities distributed to shareholders out of net corporate profits. If the company operates at a loss, the distribution is a return of capital.

Dividend policy — decisions by a company's board of directors as to whether or not dividends are to be paid and (if so), the amount to be paid.

Dividend rate — dividends paid (annualized) divided by number of shares outstanding. Ratio 93.

Dividend yield — dividends paid (annualized) divided by stockholders' equity, multiplied by 100 to provide a percentage. Ratio 94.

Division of labor — the breakdown of production tasks into components, and the assigning of each to different persons, groups, departments, machines, etc.

Doomsday ratio — cash divided by current liabilities. Ratio 44.

Double taxation — occurs when the same income is taxed twice. Example: A U.S. corporation pays income tax on earnings and its shareholders pay personal income tax on the portion of those same earnings received as dividends.

Doubling up — a pricing strategy in which selling prices are arbitrarily set at twice cost.

DSO — *Abbrev.*, Days sales outstanding. *See*, Collection period.

E/P — *Abbrev.*, Earnings to price ratio. *See also*, Price to earnings.

Earnings management — accounting practices intended to modify or control reported profits. Example: Legal reduction of income taxes through accelerated depreciation or aggressive write-off of doubtful accounts and inventory.

Efficiency ratio — a business ratio examining or reporting on skill and competency in the management of company resources.

Employee compensation ratio — wages expense divided by net sales, multiplied by 100 to provide a percentage. Ratio 51.

Employee terminations — number of employees (in full-time equivalents) who left the company for any reason during the accounting period.

Employee turnover — number of annual terminations divided by average number of employees, multiplied by 100 to provide a percentage. Ratio 73.

Equity capital — funds invested in an enterprise by shareholders, as opposed to funds furnished by lenders.

Equity ratio — tangible stockholders' equity divided by the difference between total tangible assets and current liabilities, multiplied by 100 to provide a percentage. Ratio 38.

Expense control ratio — percentage change in net sales reduced by percentage change in total expenses. Ratio 68.

Expense growth — the difference between this year's total expenses and last year's total expenses, divided by last year's total expenses, multiplied by 100 to provide a percentage. Ratio 61.

Expenses to gross profit — total expenses divided by gross profit, multiplied by 100 to provide a percentage. Ratio 50.

Exponential regression — a mathematical technique which best fits an exponential curve to a set of data points. *See*, Regression curve.

Exponential weighting factor — used in averaging. A multiplier assigned to data values in a time series, wherein the importance of older values is reduced or devalued according to age and an exponential curve.

External standard — one which originates outside the company. Example: An industry norm value for debt to equity.

Fair value — the estimated or hypothetical value of a stock or index based on a capitalization of earnings.

Financial risk — the degree of probability that a firm will fail (or operate unprofitably) due to a reliance on fixed-income obligations to pay for productive assets.

Financial strength — the degree to which financial risk is low.

Fixed asset ratio — fixed assets divided by tangible stockholders' equity, multiplied by 100 to provide a percentage. Ratio 36.

Fixed asset — tangible property used to produce goods or services and expected to be held for more than one year or one operating period.

Fixed assets mix — fixed assets divided by total assets, multiplied by 100 to provide a percentage. Ratio 37.

Fixed assets turnover — *See*, Turnover of assets.

Fixed income obligation — a security, usually a bond or note, that specifies payment of a fixed rate of interest.

Floor space — area utilized in performance of the business function.

Floor space per employee — number of square units of floor space (such as feet or meters) divided by average number of employees.

FORTRAN — a computer programming language.

Function command — a computer instruction. Example: SQR=square root.

Fuzzy logic — a path to problem solving or product design taking human nature into account, as opposed to one relying exclusively on scientific and mathematical reasoning.

Gearing — *See*, Leverage.

General ledger — a book containing all of a firm's individual ledgers.

Greater than > — the position of a value *more to the right* on a number line characterized by an infinitely large negative value on the left and an infinitely large positive value on the right.

Gross margin — revenue received from sales less cost of goods sold.

Gross margin factor — gross profit divided by net sales, multiplied by 100 to provide a percentage. Ratio 9.

Gross profit — *See*, Gross margin.

Gross profit on sales — *See*, Gross margin.

Gross profit percentage — *See*, Gross margin factor.

Gross sales — revenues received from sales operations before adjustments and deduction of sales discounts, returns and allowances.

Growth company — one characterized by faster-than-average increases in earnings and the expectation of comparable increases in market value.

Growth stock — the stock of a growth company.

High-rent location — one where, due to supply and demand factors, rents are set at above-average rates. Example: Retail shops in fashionable locations where customers have a high propensity to spend more.

Illiquid asset ratio — a variation of Fixed assets mix, ratio 37, in which intangibles are included in the numerator.

Illogical ratio — one wherein the elements lack causative interdependence.

Imputed rental cost — a reasonable or logical equivalent rent cost assigned to real property that is owned outright.

Income statement — *See*, Profit and loss statement.

Income statement ratio — a financial ratio computed from numbers found in the profit and loss statement.

Indicator — a measuring or signaling tool.

Industry norm — representative value for a ratio or other business statistic found by averaging values reported by many companies in one industry.

Inflation — an increase in price levels which results when spending increases relative to the supply of goods.

Input number or statistic — a value entered into an equation used to compute a business ratio.

Insurance expense — costs associated with protecting the company against the risks of being in business. Usually property, casualty, and liability insurance but not employee group insurance.

Insurance expense ratio — insurance expense divided by net sales, multiplied by 100 to provide a percentage. Ratio 55.

Intangible asset — a claim or resource having no physical substance. Examples: Trademarks, patents, organization costs, goodwill.

Integer — a whole number, as used in counting. Example: 216 is an integer, but 216.34 is not an integer.

Interest expense — the cost of borrowed money.

Interest expense ratio — interest expense divided by net sales, multiplied by 100 to provide a percentage. Ratio 54.

Interest rate — the sum or price paid for the use of borrowed money, expressed as a percentage.

Internal marketing — activities associated with a company's day-to-day operations intended to help in the acquisition and retention of customers. As opposed to advertising, marketing, selling, etc.

Internal standard — one which originates inside the company. Example: The amount budgeted for a particular expense in the current year.

Interstatement ratio — a financial ratio computed from numbers found in the profit and loss statement *and* the balance sheet.

Inventory — the stock of goods (finished as well as in process) owned and held by a business, usually for resale but often for internal consumption. *Also*, a detailed list of such items together with their values.

Inventory in days sales — inventory divided by average daily sales. Ratio 70.

Inventory to current assets — inventory divided by current assets, multiplied by 100 to provide a percentage. Ratio 41.

Inventory turnover — cost of goods sold divided by average inventory.

Investment ratio — a business ratio of primary interest to owners and investors. Example: Dividend rate.

Investment turnover — *See*, Turnover of assets, ratio 64.

Journal — a book of original entry. Example: Daily sales journal.

Keystone — a pricing policy wherein suppliers sell to retailers at one-half the price they sell to consumers.

Ledger — a summary book of T accounts.

Less than < — The position of a value *more to the left* on a number line characterized by an infinitely large negative value on the left and an infinitely large positive value on the right.

Leverage — the use of non-equity capital to increase return on equity.

Leverage ratio — one telling what percentage of the firm's assets are financed by borrowing. Example: Debt to equity.

Like-kind numbers — those able to be described in some common fashion and thus logically compared. Example: Dollar-value business statistics originating in the same year.

Logical ratio — one wherein the factors are characterized by causative interdependence.

Line item — a single element or entry in a financial statement or plan.

Line-item expense ratio — *See*, Designated expense ratio.

Linear regression — a mathematical technique which best fits a straight-line to a set of data. *See*, Regression curve.

Liquidation value — the amount of cash likely to be received for assets when the company is going out of business, often in forced or hurried circumstances.

Liquidity — the ability to convert assets into cash in order to meet obligations. Usually refers to current assets and current liabilities.

Liquidity ratio — *See*, Current ratio.

Logical operator — a symbol denoting a mathematical test to be performed on multiple relations. Example: **IF** A>B **THEN** C=0.

Long-term liability — a debt not expected to be paid or not due within one year.

Long-term debt maturities — the annual value of principal payments required to service long-term debt in the current year.

Macro — computer program or algorithm saved as a series of keystrokes for use in another program or algorithm.

Markdown — the amount by which a selling price is reduced. Often expressed as a percentage of the original selling price.

Market risk — the degree of probability that prices for goods, services, or securities will move in an unfavorable direction.

Marketing expense ratio — marketing/selling expense divided by net sales, multiplied by 100 to provide a percentage. Ratio 52.

Marketing growth — the difference between this year's marketing expense and last year's marketing expense, divided by last year's marketing expense, multiplied by 100 to provide a percentage. Ratio 85.

Marketing ratio — a business ratio examining or reporting on some aspect of the company's marketing activities.

Marketing/selling expense — costs associated with promoting the company and its products in the marketplace. Examples: Advertising, publicity, commissions for salespersons.

Markup — an amount added to the cost price of goods to arrive at the selling price. Usually expressed as a percentage of the cost price.

MDA — *Abbrev.*, Multiple discriminant analysis.

MD&A — *Abbrev.*, Management discussion and analysis. A section in corporate annual reports typically following the chair's letter.

Mean — a representative value (average) for a set of numbers–obtained by dividing the sum of the items by the number of items.

Measure of central tendency — *See*, Average.

Measurement unit — a description of how a thing is gauged. Example: The dollar is the measurement unit for U.S. currency.

Median — the middle number of a set of numbers arranged in order of magnitude. In the case of an even number of numbers in the set, the median is the arithmetic mean of the two numbers in the middle.

Medium of exchange — something commonly accepted in exchange for goods or services. Usually money.

Method of least squares — a statistical procedure to define the best-fitting regression line for a set of data.

Model — a system of data, premises, and conclusions expressed mathematically as a description of a thing or state of affairs.

Monetary unit — a measurement unit for money, such as yen or peso. *See*, Medium of exchange.

Money — a thing meeting three requirements: unit of account, medium of exchange, and store of value.

More than — *See*, Greater than.

Moving average — one wherein the oldest value in the set is discarded when a new value is added to the set.

Multiple discriminant analysis — a statistical technique used to classify an observation into one of several *a priori* groupings dependent upon the individual characteristics of the observation.

N/A — not available or not applicable.

Net — less something.

Net income — *See*, Net profit after taxes.

Net profit after taxes — that remaining from revenues after all costs and expenses (including income taxes) have been deducted or accrued.

Net profit before taxes — that remaining from revenues after all costs and expenses (except income taxes) have been deducted or accrued.

Net sales — gross sales reduced by returns and allowances and discounts for cash.

Net worth — the interest of the owners in a company's assets. *See*, Stockholders' equity (for a corporation).

Non-financial information — business statistics measured in non-monetary units. Example: Number of employees.

Non-integer number — a number not included in the set of whole numbers used for counting. Examples: 3.6, or 1/2.

Number line — a straight horizontal line of infinite extent upon which each point represents a real number according to its distance in a negative or positive direction from a point taken as zero.

Numerator — the number above the line in a fraction. In the case of 7/16, 7 is the numerator or dividend.

Occupancy cost — *See*, Imputed rental cost.

Olympic model — the sum of *Sales growth consistency* and *Profit growth consistency*, reduced by the absolute value of the difference between the two. Ratio 99.

Operating expense — one applicable to the normal business function, as opposed to a non-operating expense or one associated with financing the business.

Operating margin — net profit before taxes plus interest and depreciation, the result divided by net sales and multiplied by 100 to provide a percentage. Ratio 11.

Operating profit — net profit before taxes plus interest expense and depreciation.

Operator — a symbol denoting a mathematical function or operation. Example: "+" meaning to add what comes before to what comes after.

Order growth — the difference between this year's number of orders and last year's number of orders, divided by last year's number of orders, multiplied by 100 to provide a percentage. Transactions are often substituted for orders. Ratio 80.

Order of execution — referring to the correct sequence of operations that must be adhered to in mathematical equations and computer algorithms.

Orders processed per employee — number of orders (or transactions) divided by average number of employees. Ratio 74.

Overall ratio — *See*, Profitability ratio.

Owner equity — *See*, Stockholders' equity.

Owners' compensation — in addition to dividends; wages, fees, perquisites and other compensation paid to major shareholders in closely-held corporations. Example: Consulting fees paid to an owner.

PASCAL — a computer programming language.

P/B — *Abbrev.*, Price to book.

P/E — *Abbrev.*, Price to earnings.

P/S — *Abbrev.*, Price to sales.

Payment period — accounts payable divided by average daily purchases. Ratio 67.

Payout rate — dividends paid in year divided by net profit after taxes, multiplied by 100 to provide a percentage. *See also*, Retention rate.

Period end number — the value or quantity of something on the last day of the accounting period.

Period sum number — summations of transactions or events that occurred during the accounting period.

Permutation — an ordered arrangement of a given set of objects.

Plant space — *See*, Floor space.

PPI — *Abbrev.*, Producer Price Index.

Precision — the degree of refinement to which a measurement is made or an operation performed.

Premium property — *See*, High-rent location.

President's compensation — gross wages and other compensation paid to the company's president.

Prevailing inclination or tendency — *See*, Trend.

Price to book — market price of a company's stock divided by stockholders' equity per share. Ratio 97.

Price to earnings — market price of a company's stock divided by net profit after taxes per share. Ratio 96.

Price to sales — market price of a company's stock divided by net sales per share. Ratio 98.

Producer Price Index — a measurement of change in wholesale and commodity prices determined monthly by the U.S. Bureau of Labor Statistics.

Profit and loss statement — a summary report of a company's revenues, expenses, and resulting net income for the accounting period.

Profit growth — the difference between this year's net profit after taxes and last year's net profit after taxes, divided by last year's net profit after taxes, multiplied by 100 to provide a percentage. Ratio 12.

Profit growth consistency — number of consecutive years net profits after taxes have exceeded those of the prior year. Ratio 13.

Profit per employee — net profit after taxes divided by average number of employees. Ratio 26.

Profit ratio or profitability ratio — a business ratio examining or reporting on some aspect of profits. Example: Operating margin.

Proprietary product — a good or service available from only one source, or perceived as being available from only one source.

Proprietary product ratio — net sales of proprietary products divided by total net sales, multiplied by 100 to provide a percentage. Ratio 90.

Pseudo ratio — one derived from statistics which cannot logically be compared. Example: Ratio of accounts receivable to shares outstanding.

Purchases — value of merchandise (or raw material in the case of manufacturing) acquired for resale in the accounting period.

Quick assets — current assets less inventory.

Quick ratio — quick assets divided by current liabilities. Ratio 31.

Range-limited average — *See*, Moving average.

Ratchet-up expense — one easier to increase than to decrease. Example: Employee compensation.

Rate — an amount or degree of something measured against something else on a per-unit basis.

Ratio change indicator — number of ratios improved from a prior period reduced by number deteriorated. Ratio 101.

Ratio identification number — part of a business-ratio computation protocol.

Real number — any number able to be represented by a point on a number line. Values representative of physical quantities (dollars, meters, pounds) are real numbers.

Reciprocal — the value one (1) divided by a value. Example: The reciprocal of 25 is .04.

Regression curve — a mathematical model which, on the basis of sample data and using the method of least squares, is used to estimate the value of a variable A corresponding to the value of a variable B.

Remaining expense ratio — those expenses not otherwise measured by an expense ratio divided by net sales, multiplied by 100 to provide a percentage. Ratio 60.

Rent expense — the cost of leasing real property used to perform the business function.

Rent expense ratio — rent expense divided by net sales, multiplied by 100 to provide a percentage. Ratio 53.

Rent to space — rent expense divided by area of rented floor space. Ratio 63.

Repeat customer — one who buys again and again.

Representative value — a predicted or expected value for something. Example: An average.

Retained earnings — the amount of net profit accumulated and reinvested in a business and not distributed to shareholders in the form of dividends.

Retention rate — net profit after taxes less dividends paid in the period, divided by net profit after taxes, multiplied by 100 to provide a percentage. Ratio 95.

Return on employee compensation — net profit after taxes divided by employee compensation, multiplied by 100 to provide a percentage. Ratio 25.

Return on gross profit — net profit after taxes divided by gross profit, multiplied by 100 to provide a percentage. Ratio 19.

Return on invested capital — net profit after taxes plus interest expense on long-term debt, the sum divided by last year's tangible stockholders' equity plus last year's long-term liabilities, the result multiplied by 100 to provide a percentage. Ratio 23.

Return on investment — received income divided by the amount of an investment, usually expressed as a percentage.

Return on net worth — net profit after taxes divided by last year's tangible stockholders' equity, multiplied by 100 to provide a percentage. Ratio 22.

Return on owners' compensation — net profit after taxes divided by the sum of dividends and other compensation paid to owners (for closely-held companies). Ratio 28.

Return on president's compensation — net profit after taxes divided by president's compensation. Ratio 27.

Return on risk — net profit after taxes divided by last year's tangible stockholders' equity, multiplied by 100 to provide a percentage, then reduced by the interest rate prevailing for long-term corporate bonds. Ratio 24.

Return on sales — net profit after taxes divided by net sales, multiplied by 100 to provide a percentage. Ratio 17.

Return on sales before taxes — net profit before taxes divided by net sales, multiplied by 100 to provide a percentage. Ratio 18.

Return on space — net profit after taxes divided by floor space area used to perform the business function. Ratio 29.

Returns and allowances — credits and adjustments to recognize returned or unsatisfactory goods, freight damage, etc.

Revenue to space — net sales divided by floor space area used to perform the business function. Ratio 7.

Reversal — when a moving average or trend changes direction.

Reviewer — one who analyzes financial reports and information.

ROI — *Abbrev.*, Return on investment.

ROIC — *Abbrev.*, Return on invested capital.

Sales growth — the difference between this year's net sales and last year's net sales, divided by last year's net sales, then multiplied by 100 to provide a percentage. Ratio 1.

Sales growth consistency — number of consecutive years sales revenues have exceeded those of the prior year. Ratio 3.

Sales per customer — net sales divided by average number of customers. Ratio 82.

Sales per employee — net sales divided by average number of employees. Ratio 8.

Sales ratio — one examining or reporting on some aspect of sales. Example: Sales growth.

Self-insurance — a practice involving the regular set-aside of funds to cover possible losses, in lieu of the purchase of coverage from insurance underwriters.

Set — a collection of things or numbers that are of the same kind – that is, members of a clearly defined category. Example: The set of "hours in the day" includes 24 elements or members.

Shares issued and outstanding *or* **Shares outstanding** — refers to company stock actually owned by investors, as opposed to stock unissued or held by the company as treasury shares.

SIC — *Abbrev.*, Standard Industrial Classification.

Sole proprietorship — an unincorporated business owned by one person.

Solicitations — a measurement of the number of marketing overtures made to generate sales. Example: Number of catalogs mailed in the period.

Solicitations to customers — *See*, Customer solicitation ratio.

Solvency — the degree to which a firm is able to pay debt obligations as they come due.

Solvency ratio — one measuring the relationship between debt and equity.

Space — *See*, Floor space.

Spreadsheet — ledger sheet having data laid out in rows and columns. *Also*, a class of computer software.

Stand-alone software — *See*, Dedicated software.

Standard industrial classification — a system of numbers identifying different industries and lines of business.

Statement of earnings and retained earnings — *See*, Profit and loss statement.

Statement of operations — *See*, Profit and loss statement.

Stock price — per share market price of a company's stock.

Stockholders' equity — that portion of a corporation's assets owned by its stockholders.

Straight ratio — one number divided by another.

Supplier financing of assets — accounts payable divided by total assets, multiplied by 100 to provide a percentage. Ratio 39.

Symbolic equation or formula — one in which mathematical variables are expressed using symbols. Example: $R17 = 100 * S30 / S16$.

T account — a two-column form used to record debits and credits for an account.

Time offset — the comparing of statistics from one time period with those of a slightly different time period, to more realistically show cause and effect. Example: The comparing of last month's catalog mailings with this month's sales.

Time series — a set of numbers ordered in time.

Times — meaning multiplied by. *Also*, the measurement unit for a coverage ratio.

Times interest earned — net profit before taxes, plus interest expense, the sum divided by interest expense. Ratio 42.

Total assets — the sum of all claims and rights appearing on the balance sheet. Equal to the sum of total liabilities and stockholder equity.

Total expense ratio — total expenses divided by net sales, multiplied by 100 to provide a percentage. Ratio 49.

Total expenses — the sum of all individual line-items of expense.

Trend — the prevailing inclination or tendency of a set of data points.

Trendline — a mathematically defined curve which describes a trend.

Turnover — a description of total revenue.

Turnover of assets — net sales divided by total assets. Ratio 64.

Turnover of working capital — net sales divided by working capital. Ratio 35.

Turnover ratio — one measuring the extent of the reduction and subsequent replacement of something.

Undefined ratio — a measurement made meaningless or illogical by the use of illegal input numbers.

Unearned compensation — in tax accounting, income received other than from one's personal labor.

Utilities expense — cost of services required to support the physical plant. Examples: Electricity, gas, water, garbage collection.

Utilities expense ratio — utilities expense divided by net sales, multiplied by 100 to provide a percentage. Ratio 58.

Value-added tax — a tax levied at each stage of production and distribution on the difference between the value of output and the value of purchased materials or other input.

Variable — a quantity that changes.

Variable name — a word or symbol representing a changing number. Examples: $S(16)$=net sales and NETPROF=net profit.

Venture capitalist — one who invests in new businesses, usually those that are untried and risky.

Verbal equation or formula — one in which mathematical variables are expressed as words or phrases. Example:
  PAYMENT PERIOD = Accounts Payable / Average Daily Purchases.

Wages expense — employee compensation.

Weighting factor — used in averaging. A multiplier assigned to data values in a time series, whereby the importance of older values is reduced or devalued according to age.

Working capital — current assets reduced by current liabilities.

Write-off — the reduction or elimination of an account because it is uncollectible, or the reduction in an asset's book value.

Z-score bankruptcy model — the sum of four (or more) factored ratios used in the prediction of bankruptcy. *See*, Ratio 48 *and* Altman, Edward I.

Bibliography

Books and Periodicals

Albert, Kenneth J. *Straight Talk About Small Business*. New York: McGraw-Hill Book Co., 1981.

Altman, Edward I. *Corporate Financial Distress*. New York: John Wiley & Sons, 1983.

Anthony, Robert N. *Management Accounting*. Homewood, IL: Richard. D. Irwin, 1960. *See also*, Anthony, Robert N., Welsch, Glen A., and Reece, James S. *Fundamentals of Management Accounting*. Homewood, IL: Dow Jones-Irwin, 1985.

Ball, Michael. "Z-Factor: Rescue by the Numbers." *INC.* (December, 1980), p. 45-48.

Barron's Market Laboratory. *Barron's*.

Barron's. (May 25, 1987), p. 35. (July 10, 1989), p. 41. (July 23, 1990), p. 22.

Bernstein, Leopold. "Ratio, Change and Trend Analysis as an Audit Tool." *The Journal of Accountancy* (February, 1964).

Bladen, Ashby. "A Matter of Delicate Timing." *Forbes* (May 11, 1981), p. 330.

Brown, Ann C. "The New Reality." *Forbes* (February 15, 1982), p. 176.

Brown, Sister Isadore. *The Historical Development of the Use of Ratios in Financial Statement Analysis to 1933*. Washington, DC: The Catholic University of America Press, 1955.

Bui, X. T. *Executive Planning with Basic*. Berkeley, CA: SYBEX, 1982.

Bureau of Labor Statistics. *Consumer Price Index* and *Producer Price Index*. Washington, DC: U. S. Department of Labor.

Bureau of Labor Statistics. *Summary of CPI News Release*. Washington, DC: U.S. Department of Labor.

Byrne, John A. "The Business of Businesses: How to Price a Small Business." *Forbes* (August 13, 1984), p. 111-112.

Donnelly, Richard A. A review of *Dividends Don't Lie*, by Geraldine Weiss and Janet Lowe. *Barron's* (July 10, 1989), p. 41.

Downs, John, and Goodman, Jordan Elliot. *Barron's Finance and Investment Handbook*. Hauppauge, NY: Barron's Educational Series, 1990.

Dreman, David. *The New Contrarian Investment Strategy*. New York: Random House, 1982.

Duggan, Patrice. "The ABCs and ADRs of Mexico." *Forbes* (June 24, 1991), p. 211.

Dun & Bradstreet. *Industry Norms and Key Business Ratios, Desk Top Edition, 1990-91*. Murray Hill, NJ: 1991.

Estes, Ralph W. *Dictionary of Accounting*. Cambridge, MA: MIT Press, 1985.

Fisher, Kenneth L. "Look Out Below." *Forbes* (March 25, 1985). p. 276.

Fisher, Kenneth L. "Big Companies, Fragile Stocks." *Forbes* (January 28, 1985), p. 126.

Follett, Robert J. R. *How to Keep Score in Business*. Chicago: Follett Publishing Co., 1978.

Forbes. (February 15, 1977), p. 78-79. (June 20, 1983), p. 31. (March 18, 1991), p. 144.

Foster, G. *Financial Statement Analysis*. Englewood Cliffs, NJ: Prentice-Hall, 1978.

Foulke, R. A. *Practical Financial Statement Analysis*. New York: McGraw-Hill Book Co., 1968.

Garrison, Richard D. *Managerial Accounting*. Homewood, IL: Richard D. Irwin, 1991, p. 659.

Gupta, L. C. *Financial Ratios for Monitoring Corporate Sickness*. New Delhi: Oxford University Press, 1983.

Hatfield, Henry R. *Accounting: Its Principles and Problems*. Lawrence, KS: Scholars Book Co., 1971.

Herzfeld, Thomas J. "Open Question - Figuring Bond Fund Yields." *Barron's* (June 24, 1991), p. 38.

Horrigan, James O. "A Short History of Financial Ratio Analysis." *The Accounting Review*, Vol. XLIII, No. 2 (April, 1968), p. 286.

Hulbert, Mark. "Whipsaw!" *Forbes* (May 14, 1990), p. 164.

Killman, Barbara T. "More Practical Uses for Z Factor." *INC.* (February, 1981), p. 10.

King, John T. "The ABC's of Z factor." *INC.* (April 1981), p. 12.

Kichen, Steve. "The rule of 20." *Forbes* (June 20, 1983), p. 31.

Kichen, Steve, and Ramos, Steven. "Margin for Improvement." *Forbes* (June 25, 1990), p. 234.

Kyd, Charles W. "Formula for Disaster?" *INC.* (November 1985), p. 123.

Kyd, Charles W. "How Fast is Too Fast?" *INC.* (December, 1986), p. 123-126.

Leahy, Tad. "Value Judgments." *Personal Investor* (September, 1991), p. 48-53.

Levine, Sumner N. *The 1983 Dow Jones-Irwin Business and Investment Almanac*. Homewood, IL: Dow Jones-Irwin, 1983.

Longstreet, Roy W. *Viewpoints of a Commodity Trader*. New York: Frederick Fell, 1968.

Lynch, Peter. "One Up on Wall Street." *MONEY* (January, 1989), p. 141.

Martin, Thomas J. and Gustafson, Mark R. *Valuing Your Business*. New York: Holt, Rinehart and Winston, 1980.

Mendenhall, William, and Beaver, Robert J. *Introduction to Probability and Statistics*. Boston, MA: PWS-Kent Publishing Co., 1991.

Metcalf, Wendell O. *Starting and Managing a Small Business of Your Own*. Small Business Starting and Management Series Volume 1. Washington, DC: Small Business Administration, 1973.

Minard, Lawrence. "The case against price/earnings ratios." *Forbes* (February 13, 1984), p. 126.

Mueller, Gregory J. *Financial Ratios as Predictors of Bankruptcy: A Multivariate Approach*. San Diego, CA: A thesis presented to the faculty of San Diego State University, 1975.

Murphy, Thomas P. "What Price Independence?" *Forbes* (September 27, 1982), p. 208.

Murphy, Thomas P. "Commandments" *Forbes* (August 1, 1983), p. 178.

Perry, Kenneth W. *Accounting An Introduction*. New York: McGraw-Hill Book Co., 1971.

Peterson, Donald M. *Financial Ratios and Investment Results*. Lexington, MA: Lexington Books, D. C. Heath, 1974.

Platt, Harlan D. *Why Companies Fail.* Lexington, MA: D. C. Heath, 1985.

Pool, Lon; Borchers, Mary; and Koessel, Karl. *Some Common Basic Programs.* Berkeley, CA: OSBORNE/McGraw-Hill, 1981.

Pouschine, Tatiana. "Tiffany: Act II." *Forbes* (November 11, 1991), p. 70-77.

Power, Christopher. "Light in Dark Corners." *Forbes* (August 1, 1983), p. 133.

Pratt, Shannon P. *Valuing a Business.* Homewood, IL: Dow Jones-Irwin, 1988.

Pring, Martin J. "Divining the Dow." *Investment Vision* (January/February, 1990), p. 20-26.

Ramos, Steven, quoting Richard Pucci, "What the Analysts Think." *Forbes* (March 18, 1991), p. 144.

Reilly, Frank K. *Investments.* Hinsdale, IL: Dryden Press, 1982.

Robert Morris Associates. *RMA Annual Statement Studies 1990.* Philadelphia, PA: 1990.

Rukeyser, Louis. *Louis Rukeyser's Business Almanac.* New York: Simon and Schuster, 1988.

Sanzo, Richard. *Ratio Analysis for Small Business.* Small Business Management Series No. 20. Washington, DC: Small Business Administration, 1977.

Shilling, A. Gary. "Exits and entrances." *Forbes* (September 16, 1991), p. 154-156.

Siegel, Joel G., and Shim, Jae K. *Dictionary of Accounting Terms.* Hauppauge, NY: Barron's Educational Series, 1987.

Singleton, Margaret. "What's It Worth to You?" *INC.* (September, 1986), p. 113-114.

Spiegel, Murray R. *Schaum's Outline of Theory and Problems of Statistics.* New York: McGraw-Hill Book Co., 1990.

Stoller, Steven D. "The Golden Rule." *Barron's* (May 25, 1987), p. 35.

Tamari, M. *Financial Ratios, Analysis and Prediction.* London: Paul Elek Ltd., 1978.

Troy, Leo. *Almanac of Business and Industrial Financial Ratios.* Englewood Cliffs, NJ: Prentice-Hall, 1990.

Tucker, Spencer A. *Successful Managerial Control by Ratio-Analysis.* New York: McGraw-Hill Book Co., 1961.

Value Line Selection & Opinion. "Industrial Composite." *Value Line Investment Survey* (January 31, 1986), p. 354.

Wall, Alexander, and Duning, Raymond. *Ratio Analysis of Financial Statements.* New York: Harper & Bros., 1928.

Wall Street Journal. (January 30, 1991), p. B1.

Weston, J. Fred, and Brigham, Eugene F. *Essentials of Managerial Finance.* Hinsdale, IL: CBS College Publishing, 1982.

Westwick, C. A. *How to Use Management Ratios.* New York: John Wiley & Sons, 1973. *See also*, 1987 edition. Epping, Essex [U.K.]: Gower Press, Ltd.

World Book Encyclopedia. Chicago: World Book, Inc., 1987. Vol. 16.

Wortman, Leon A. *Business Problem Solving with the IBM PC & XT.* Bowie, MD: Robert J. Brady Co., 1983.

Wyatt, Edward A. "Stock-Bond Yield Gap." *Barron's* (July 23, 1990), p. 22.

Zwick, Jack. *A Handbook of Small Business Finance.* Small Business Management Series No. 15. Washington, DC: Small Business Administration, 1975.

Additional Sources

BUSINESS VALUATION+RATIOS. Innovative Professional Software, 7140 E. Heritage Place North, Englewood, CO 80111.

Duns InSight. Dun & Bradstreet Information Services, North America, One Diamond Hill Road, Murray Hill, NJ 07974.

FINANCIAL RATIOS II. Lassen Software, P.O. Box 1190, Paradise, CA 95927.

GRAPH-IN-THE-BOX. New England Software, Greenwich Office Park #3, Greenwich, CT 06831.

PC-RATIOS. McLane BookSales, P.O. Box 25556, Tempe, AZ 85285.

RATIO MASTER. Intex Solutions, Inc., 161 Highland Ave., Needham, MA 02194.

VALUE/SCREEN II. Value Line Publishing Co., 711 Third Ave., New York, NY 10017.

Wilson-Jones columnar pads. ACCO USA, Inc. 770 South ACCO Plaza, Wheeling, IL 60090-6070.

Index

Sheldon Gates is the founder and former president of *Jensen Tools*, an international supplier of high-tech tool kits. He did his undergraduate work in physics at the University of Michigan, and earned a master of science degree in business at Arizona State University. Gates served in the intelligence community in the 1950's, and later worked for *Motorola* as a radar design engineer. He is a charter member of the Phoenix Direct Marketing Club, and the author of research papers treating such diverse subjects as industrial soldering and land economics. He lives with his wife near Scottsdale, Arizona.

NOTES